Digital Culture & Society

Vol. 9, Issue 2/2023

Marcus Burkhardt, Jonathan Kropf, Carsten Ochs,
Tatjana Seitz (eds.)
**Frictions: Conflicts, Controversies
and Design Alternatives
in Digital Valuation**

[transcript]

Indexed in EBSCOhost databases

Bibliographic information published by the Deutsche Nationalbibliothek
The Deutsche Nationalbibliothek lists this publication in the Deutsche
National-bibliografie

© **2025 transcript Verlag, Bielefeld**
transcript Verlag | Hermannstraße 26 | D-33602 Bielefeld | live@transcript-verlag.de

Cover concept: Kordula Röckenhaus, Bielefeld
Typeset: Mark-Sebastian Schneider, Bielefeld
Printing: Elanders Waiblingen GmbH, Waiblingen

ISSN: 2364-2114
eISSN: 2364-2122
Print-ISBN 978-3-8376-6358-7
PDF-ISBN 978-3-8394-6358-1

Content

Introduction

Frictions. Conflicts, Controversies, and Design Alternatives in Digital Valuation

Marcus Burkhardt, Jonathan Kropf,
Carsten Ochs, Tatjana Seitz

Techno-utopian promises of innovation, prosperity, and progress through digital technologies abound in policy documents, social media conferences, keynote presentations, and reports.[1] In recent years, artificial intelligence has been at the centre of these promises. Since the launch of ChatGPT on November 30, 2022, the public image of AI has been dominated by large language models (LLMs) and their generative capacities. By now, LLMs have become multimodal, i.e. they are also capable of processing spoken language and images. The current "AI revolution", however, is just one of many revolutions in digital technologies that have taken place over the last 80 years. During this time, the face of the digital has changed again and again, and so have its socio-technical entanglements. Common to all digital computers is the decomposition of information into binary and discrete states of 0 and 1 and their open-ended programmability. These principles delineate the fundamental limits of computability. Alan Turing is credited with developing the theoretical model of the programmable computer in 1936. He conceptualised what subsequently became known as the Universal Turing Machine: a machine designed to solve a specific mathematical problem posed some decades beforehand by David Hilbert. In doing so, Turing not only formulated a theory of digital computers but also demonstrated what such machines are fundamentally incapable of doing (Turing 1937; Heintz 1993).

Within the principle limits of computability, however, a space of contingent developments and alternative designs of the digital has unfolded, full of frictions and conflicts, as the chequered history of computing shows. This history ranges from the mainframes of the early days of computing through the era of home and personal computers to networked and mobile media, platforms, cloud services, and, most recently, machine-learning-driven "artificial intelligence". It would be easy to recount these developments as a history of mere technological progress that rests on the exponential growth of processing and storage capacities as well

1   Funded by the Deutsche Forschungsgemeinschaft (DFG, German Research Foundation)—Project-ID 262513311—SFB 1187 and by the Federal Ministry for Research and Education (BMBF)—Research Project BeDeNUTZ ID 16KIS1891K.

DOI 10.14361/dcs-2023-0202

DCS | Digital Culture and Society | Vol. 9, Issue 2 | © transcript 2025

as on the increasing miniaturisation of computing devices. Yet such a perspective would fall short of acknowledging the plurality of the digital which results from the fact that computers do nothing unless they are instructed, i.e. programmed to fulfil a given task. The indeterminacy of computers goes hand in hand with the ambivalent attributions to, and valuations of the digital. On the one hand, digital technologies are primarily considered to be drivers of innovation and solutions for small and grand challenges alike. From this perspective, "the digital" appears to be problematic only because there is still too little of it: insufficient broadband infrastructure, too few digital services in public administration, too little digital transformation in and of organisations, insufficient digital learning and teaching, too few skills to make meaningful use of the potentials offered by digital technologies, etc. Consequently, policymakers, technologists, and businesspeople alike frequently call for more digitization. The capacity to accumulate, analyse and utilise data is seen as a key factor in leveraging the potentials of digital innovation, e.g. in the contexts of artificial intelligence or the restructuring of services and business models to be data-driven or data-based. Data is often hailed as the "new oil" in these fields, while critics seek to expose the drilling metaphor as a "capitalist-colonialist fantasy" that sustains "the myth of perpetual economic growth" (Taffel 2021).

On the other hand, digital technologies have increasingly becoming controversial. While digitally networked media were praised in the 1990s and 2000s for their emancipatory potential—empowering social movements and driving revolutionary social transformation towards democracy—the discourse has become more critical in recent years (Castells 1996; Zuboff 2019). Contrary to the promise of stability and seamless operation, Paul N. Edwards (2021) argues that platforms are quite the opposite: "platforms are infrastructures on fire" (322). They are full of crises, emergency responses, quick fixes, and unresolved social issues produced through technological design that favours profit over humans (e.g. data breaches, leaks, whistleblowing, fake news, monitoring, humanising, and fact-checking AI written text). The debates about filter bubbles, hate speech, fake news, bias, microtargeting, platforms, and surveillance capitalism highlight the dangers of digital technologies by pointing towards injustices, possible exclusions, and emerging power asymmetries, while also exposing the solutionism of the technology industry as an ideology (Benjamin 2019; Broussard 2019; Gray/Suri 2019; Amoore 2020; Crawford 2021; McQuillan 2022). Central concerns include the intensification of data "capture" (Agre 1994), the algorithmic operationalisation of personal data in largely opaque systems, and the extractivist economy it engenders. With the proliferation of smart devices such as smartphones, smart watches, and smart speakers as well as the ongoing push toward smart cities, humans, technologies, and environments have become entangled in increasingly complex yet seemingly frictionless infrastructures of datafication and data-based as well as machine-learned computation. This absence of friction has become a defining, yet problematic, characteristic of our present socio-technical condition. A frictionless user experience conceals the contradictions, power asymmetries, and polarisations that shape our digital cultures.

While the ideal of frictionlessness is deeply rooted in design and the development of digital technologies, there are also alternative design approaches, as Lena Teigeler and Carolin Gerlitz show in their contribution to this special issue of *Digital Culture & Society,* with reference to seamful design (Chalmers et al. 2003). Critique is thus voiced not only from the margins by technology users but also from the centre of digitisation processes. One example is the development of distributed systems for social networks and web services in the so-called "Fediverse". Cryptocurrencies based on distributed blockchain technologies go even further by propagating a digital alternative to state-backed currencies. Hence, several papers in this special issue conceive the notion of frictions as a kind of potential, i.e. as an analytical entry point. Rather than perceiving the materiality of powerful platforms like the Meta conglomerate or Twitter as a fixed condition, frictions present an opportunity to contest the dominant platform architectures and explore how these socio-technical systems could have been designed differently. Therefore, the architecture of the platform, and by extension, the digital, becomes a space where different interests are not only imposed through actionable grammars but importantly, are negotiated. For Felix Raczkowski, as well as for Oliver Ruf and Aleksandra Vujadinovic, frictions become sources of "trouble" (Star 1990) that uncover taken-for-granted rules and values as opportunities to question the design of dominant architectures. These frictions strategically introduce unconventional usage practices into structured data flows, which may become modes of contestation. Design frictions, therefore, can be understood as opportunities to examine and actively intervene in the social, technical, cultural, and political conditions that create trouble-some frictions in a wider sense.

This brief excursion through the history and present of the computer and its discourses illustrates the ambivalences and contradictions of the digital, which defies simple evaluation. This issue of *Digital Culture & Society* takes the notion of frictions as a starting point for a situated analysis of our digital present. We see frictions as sites where criticism is sparked and design alternatives are explored. Frictions also occur below the threshold of discursive attention and treatment. We contend that the material, practical, and semiotic frictions occurring in the socio-digital realm can be understood as value conflicts. This special issue aims to develop a shared vocabulary around frictions as an analytical approach to critically engaging with the digital. By bringing together research from media studies, science and technology studies (STS), and sociology, this issue begins to synthesise and systematise the structural inconsistencies that frictions expose. In this sense, the special issue is concerned with the exploration of new forms of critical positioning. The contributions explore how these conflicts and clashes are provoked by (the interfering of) processes of valuation (Dewey 1939; Heuts/Mol 2013; Mau 2019; Kropf/Laser 2019; Nicolae et al. 2019; Berli et al. 2021; Lee et al. 2022; 2024), which operate on various layers.

However, frictions do not only pervade the present digital condition. In fact, there is a long-standing tradition in the humanities and social sciences of grappling with the phenomenon of friction, particularly when we consider the notion of contradiction as a related concept. As early as 1872, Marx (2003) introduced the idea that European societies' socio-technical modernity is shaped by fundamental contradictions: the class interest of the Bourgeoisie in extracting ever more surplus value from labour is in structural conflict with the interest of the working class. Friction, in this context, seems to result from social contradictions established by humans (albeit unconsciously), and they pertain to the whole of society, with value being defined in a rather fixed way by the amount of work that goes into the crafting of goods. However, while Marx viewed these observable frictions as inherent to the nature of social structures, his descendants started to conceive of contradictions in a less rigid way. Thus, Giddens (1981) came up with the notion of "structural principles", i.e. principles that, even if structuring the whole of society in a contravening way, do not do so simply "by nature", but by successively increasing their range. For example, the contradiction between public authorities (which aim to raise taxes) and private economies (which strive to avoid them) is structural only to the extent that the resulting friction shapes society at large; it is thus the outcome of the structural principle that has come to be known as the public/private distinction, a distinction/principle that pervades any sector of society whatsoever. In contrast to Marx, however, Giddens is much more interested in the actual practices performing this distinction, and in the mechanisms enforcing its implementation. By paving the way for approaches that are ready to focus more on the actual practices on the ground that constitute contradictions, we might say that Giddens has contributed to the development of approaches that work with an even more "fluid" idea of structural principles. As an example of this is the heteronormative distinction between male and female, which is considered an ever-present principle (Löw 2001), regardless of whether one refers to this principle in relation to the "whole" of society or not.

Having said this, in cultural and social theory, frictions are increasingly being traced back less and less to large-scale models of the social. Instead of positing contradictions produced by humans (as the terminological element "diction" suggests) and structuring society-at-large based on pre-fixated values of things, we might interpret contemporary approaches as the result of a gradual shift toward: the inclusion of nonhuman actors (such as digital media); observable on-the-ground-practices (instead of assumed large-scale structures); and processes of valuation (instead of setting out from pre-conceived ideas of value and its creation). This is not to bid farewell to seemingly "universals", such as global capitalisms, but to recognise that even "Capitalism only spreads as producers, distributors, and consumers strive to universalize categories of capital, money, and commodity fetishism." (Tsing 2005: 4) Replacing the notion of contradiction with the one of friction, the latter becomes a virtual aspect (in the Deleuzian sense) of any socio-technical-media-cultural event: "friction reminds us that heterogeneous and unequal encounters can lead to new arrangements of culture and power." (ibid: 5)

Locating contemporary research in media studies, STS, and sociology within this line of reasoning, we can see how present-day investigations into the conflicts, controversies, and design in, and of, practices of digital valuation are perfectly equipped to empirically reveal a plethora of human-nonhuman frictions occurring at any scale of socio-technical reproduction. On the one hand, the digitization of valuation practices raises again multifarious—and well-known—issues media studies, STS, and sociology are bound to deal with, such as digitization itself, the role of infrastructures, power and agency, automation and judgement, and accountability among others (Lee et al. 2022); and it is certainly true that the digitisation of the valuation may have "unique implications for how social order is established, challenged, and maintained" (Lee et al. 2024: 1). Consider, for example, the novel modes of producing social inequality through digital scoring and ranking, and the repercussions this might have for the structural differentiation of society (Mau 2023; Eubanks 2018; Fourcade/Healy 2017; 2024). Moreover, when focusing more narrowly on the data-related aspects of digitisation, the "politics of data friction" (Bates 2018) come into focus: from frictions emerging at the micro-level within interdisciplinary research teams that rely on different types of data (Edwards et al. 2011), through government efforts at the meso-level to create standardised "technologies to settle 'data frictions'" (Pelizza 2016), to Zuboff's (2019) call to offer resistance to the epochal shift towards the macro-structures of surveillance capitalism. Frictions in digital valuation come in all shapes and sizes, and they involve the most variegated heterogeneity of materialities, processes, and actors.

What still unites these frictions, however, is that they concern values and value clashes—how to conceive of them? Our understanding of values and value clashes is rooted in the field of valuation studies. Values are traditionally understood as relatively stable preferences or ideas of what is desired. For example, these ideas are taken into account when choosing between alternative courses of action (and the respective means) or motivating action in the first place (Beckers 2018; Friedrichs 2020). While Max Weber (1972: 12-13) described value-oriented action as one of several types of action, Talcott Parsons assumed that all action necessarily had a normative component. Unlike Weber, Parsons also stood for the assumption that social order was dependent on a uniform value system (Parsons 1968; cf. Krüger 2022: 167-169). Valuation studies move beyond such static and objectifying concepts of value. Instead, they think of values in a dynamic, processual, and situated way: "value is no longer intrinsic to an object, and it is no longer the cause of the various forms of value attribution; rather, it becomes the result of these valuations" (Heinich 2020: 4). Therefore, one must examine the situational processes in which things, people, ideas, etc. are made valuable or invaluable (Kjellberg/ Mallard 2013). Although valuation studies are reluctant to commit themselves to specific theoretical schools or paradigms, there is an obvious influence of classical American pragmatism and recent French pragmatism Actor–network theory (ANT, Economics, and Sociology of Conventions). For a classic pragmatist, such as Dewey, values should not be understood deontologically, but as practical "judgement devices" that guide action in problematic situations. Therefore, when considering values, they must always be considered in relation to the constraints of the situation and other values that might be affected. In Dewey's processual understanding, values are the result of past problem solving and might change in the light of new situations (Dewey 1939; van de Poel/Kundina 2022). This process-oriented, located perspective on valuation not only fits very well with the above-mentioned shift from "structural principals", or contradictions, to "frictions". Moreover, it enables research to grasp the value clashes between pluralities, multiplicities, or heterarchies of value orders. It is consequently also at the core of influential approaches in valuation studies, such as the economics and sociology of conventions (see Boltanski/Thévenot 2006; Kappler et al. in this issue). Therefore, when talking about friction, a plurality of conflicting valuations can generally be expected.

In this rather basic form, valuations are components of all (human) activity. However, digitisation and valuation have a special interrelationship. First of all, valuations have become ubiquitous in the digital world. Today, almost everything and everyone is rated, ranked, or reviewed—doctors, teachers, hotels, tourist attractions, books, social media posts, or sneakers, to name only a few examples (Mau 2019; Fourcade/Healy 2024). This takes place partly on specific websites like TripAdvisor or Yelp, partly as an element of the sales (e.g. Amazon) and booking process (e.g. Airbnb), or in social interaction (e.g. Instagram). Star ratings, like buttons or written reviews, involve users in the valuation process, while user behaviour is tracked and becomes the basis for algorithmic recommendations. Human valuations and machine valuations, each following their own inscribed valuation principles, intertwine here (Reckwitz 2020). Furthermore, digitisation acts as an accelerator of value clashes: processes of datafication and platformisation often have disruptive effects in historically evolved areas of society. This leads to implicit or explicit value clashes, for example, when metric performance criteria are introduced in fields like journalism, which has traditionally committed to other logics of valuation (Petre 2021). Technological innovation is often implemented in the light of specific value orientations, e.g. to increase efficiency, but in actual use the associated promises can prove to be deceptive or prevent appropriate consideration of other values. In these cases, the notion of frictions can be used as a lens for analysing the underlying value conflicts.

Interestingly, digital technologies are often designed and promoted as tools to reduce frictions and increase efficiency. The contributions to this special issue, however, unpack the many ways in which frictions occur in their development, deployment, and usage. Christian Schulz, for example, reconstructs the frictions between the social and the economic dimensions of social media platforms. By scrutinising the genealogy of Facebook's "zeldas"—a currency-like platform feature conceptualized at Facebook in 2007 but discarded during its design phase—he portrays this process as a frictional episode of platform design. Whereas the inclusion of zeldas would have introduced a monetary dimension to the like button, it would have undermined the economy of liking that rests not on scarcity but on excess. Also focusing on platform infrastructuring, Lena Teigeler and Carolin Gerlitz analyse the interplay between seamlessness and seamfulness in the design and development of APIs (application programming interfaces), as media for the circulation of data and cooperation between platform companies and developers. Through a close analysis of a seemingly innocuous data point in the Twitter/X's API, the source metric, they shed light on the seams of valuation that underpin the dynamic, and on the controversial relationship between platforms and their environments.

Karolin Kappler, Florian Neft, and Katharina Ebner, meanwhile, refer to the Economics/Sociology of Conventions (E/SC) approach to study the frictions and value conflicts associated with the introduction of health analytics. They show how the digitisation of healthcare is creating new tensions through conflicts with existing conventions. What is framed as process optimisation, therefore, requires novel forms of coordination between the human and non-human actors involved. However, even attempts to take plural values into account may fail if the underlying paradigm, the material-symbolic order in which these attempts are made, is itself problematic. This is exemplified by Jens Hälterlein's article, which deals with different types of modelling during the COVID-19 pandemic. He examines the case of a modelling software that attempts to take into account a plurality of values, but at the same time follows a scientific ideal and thus contributes to an epistemisation of politics. In their contribution, Sebastian Koth, Anne Krüger, and Sascha Friesike analyse "ResearchHub", a platform for scientific research. The project attempts to solve some problems of conventional journal peer review by introducing market mechanisms and quantified modes of coordination. However, the authors note, frictions arise as new logics are introduced to established practice creating new problems and amplifying old ones (such as the "Matthew Effect"). The authors conclude that a digital peer review system, modelled on the principles of quantification and commodification, introduces a form of science governance that fails to resolve the problems and value conflicts known from conventional peer review

Lukas Schmitz's ethnographic account of the frictions arising from the integration of smart speakers into the habitual socio-material practices of dwelling allows us to draw similar conclusions. Although loaded with the promise of increasing efficiency in a frictionless way, smart speakers, when integrated into domestic life, generate fictions in two different, yet related ways. First, they may clash with users' "attachments", i.e. with their routines, desires, ideas, affects, and bodily habits that have been established in the past. Second, there may be multiple, and sometimes incommensurable, justifications and values users' refer to in order to legitimise smart speaker use. However, value clashes may also emerge in a more "immanent" way, i.e. affect the value that is being materially and discursively negotiated in the first place. Thus, Miriam Fahimi and Katharina Kinder-Kurlanda show how the value of transparency undergoes repeated changes when it travels through multifaceted webs of socio-material relations. Drawing on an ethnography conducted during the development of an algorithmic system, the authors trace a gradual shift in how transparency is understood within the field of credit scoring. Hence, the case study reveals that frictions may emerge not only among the actual versions of a value itself, but also within the material relations enacting differing types and versions of a value's "evolution".

For some authors, authenticity is a concept particularly rich in both values and conflicts. In his contribution, Felix Raczkowski explores the question of authenticity in relation to truth (e.g., fake news, fake profiles, fake data) from a historical perspective, highlighting it as a prominent topic within the internet community since the early 1990s. Hegemonic efforts frame authenticity through a binary logic translating social interaction into pre-formatted "grammars of action" (Agre 1994), rendering social activities into a predictable and controllable value. Building on this insight, the paper examines how authenticity has evolved at three different points in the history of web cultures. Specifically, it examines practices of resistance as conflicts over value in everyday life to understand how truth is produced by contesting dominant representations. While Raczkowski analyses the computational representation of authenticity from a historical perspective, Oliver Ruf and Aleksandra Vujadinovic examine the appification of authenticity. In their contribution, the authors compare the technical interpretation of authenticity proposed by two contemporary social media apps: Instagram and BeReal. Building on Silvio Lorusso's (2023) concept of a "commentary," the authors explore how the app BeReal's branding efforts serve as an alternative design—and, consequently, a commentary—on the representation of authenticity framed by Instagram's design choices. By creating material alternatives, these designs bring value conflicts to the surface at the level of the Graphical User Interface (GUI), allowing for the engagement, exploration, and testing of alternative design modes while facilitating a critique of dominant design solutions and their promise to be the most optimal architecture for social interaction.

To summarise the points made by the papers assembled in this volume, we may state that they illustrate how frictions pervade the digital assemblages of the present in various dimensions. They pertain to:

- *the imaginaries of technology adoption:* as frictions between the techno-promises of efficiency, on the one hand, and the laborious issues that have to be settled before some newly introduced technology can be used "smoothly", on the other hand;
- *the materialities of value construction:* as frictions between different versions of how some "identical" value is enacted in practice (such as transparency, see above);

- *the enactment of practices:* as frictions between some entrenched practice and its "attachments" (Hennion 2007), on the one hand, and the scripts and affordances (Schulz-Schaeffer 2021) of novel technologies, on the other hand;
- *the tactics of users:* as frictions between the affordances offered by technology, on the one hand and unruly and idiosyncratic usage practises, on the other hand;
- *the translation of values:* as frictions occurring when practices of valuation are translated from one scheme of valuation to another (for example, from a qualitative into a quantitative register, with loss caused by the reduction into discrete values);
- *the controversies of design:* as frictions that characterise negotiations, interpretations, and the grammars of technological agencies.

In contributing to this special issue, the authors and articles assembled in this journal have advanced the task of empirically identifying the frictions pervading our media-saturated socio-digital world. We would like to extend our gratitude to all of them for their patience and for adhering to the sometimes cumbersome, but ultimately rewarding project of repeatedly revising their analyses to eventually publish them in this journal. We would also like to thank our anonymous reviewers, who took on the burden of constructively criticizing and supporting the development of the articles published in this special issue: we are extremely thankful for your cooperation. Lastly, we would like to thank the editors for the opportunity to edit this special issue, as well as transcript for their ongoing support and patience throughout this project.

List of References

Agre, P. E. (1994): "Surveillance and Capture: Two Models of Privacy." The Information Society, 10(2), pp. 101–127. https://doi.org/10.1080/01972243.1994.99 60162

Amoore, L. (2020): Cloud Ethics. Algorithms and the Attributes of Ourselves and Others. Durham/London: Duke.

Bates, J. (2018): "The Politics of Data Friction." Journal of Documentation, 74 (2), pp. 412–29.

Beckers, T. (2018): "Werte." In: J. Kopp/A. Steinbach (eds.), Grundbegriffe der Soziologie. Wiesbaden: Springer, pp. 373-377.

Benjamin, R. (2019): Race After Technology. Abolotionist Tools for the New Jim Code. Cambridge, UK, et al.: Polity.

Boltanski, L./Thévenot, L. (2006): On Justification: Economies of Worth. Princeton University Press.

Broussard, M. (2019): Artificial Unintelligence. How Computers Misunderstand the World. Cambridge, MA/London: MIT.

Berli, O./Nicolae, S./Schäfer, H. (eds.) (2021): Bewertungskulturen. Wiesbaden: Springer VS.

Castells, M. (1996): The Rise of the Network Society. Cambridge, MA, et al.: Blackwell.

Chalmers, M./MacColl, I./Bell, M. (2003): "Seamful Design: Showing the Seams in Wearable Computing." 2003 IEE Eurowearable, pp. 11–16. https://doi.org/10.1049/ic:20030140.

Crawford, K. (2021): Atlas of AI. Power, Politics, and the Planetary Costs of Artificial Intelligence. New Haven/London: Yale University Press.

Dewey, J. (1939): "Theory of Valuation." In: International Encyclopedia of Unified Science, 2(4), pp. 1-66.

Edwards, P.N./Mayernik, M.S./Batcheller, A.L./Bowker, G.C./Borgman, C.L. (2011): "Science Friction: Data, Metadata, and Collaboration." Social Studies of Science, 41(5), pp. 667–690.

Edwards, P. N. (2021): "Platforms Are Infrastructures on Fire". In: T. S. Mullaney/B. Peters/M. Hicks/K. Philip (eds.), Your Computer Is on Fire. The MIT Press, pp. 313–36.

Eubanks, V. (2018): Automating Inequality. How High-Tech Tools Profile, Police, and Punish the Poor. New York: St. Martin's Press.

Fourcade, M./Healy, K. (2017): "Seeing Like a Market." Socio-Economic Review (2017/1), pp. 9–29.

Fourcade, M./Healy, K. (2024): The Ordinal Society. Camridge, MA/London: Harvard University Press.

Friedrichs, J. (2020): "Wert." In: D. Klimke/R. Lautmann/U. Stäheli/C. Weischer/H. Wienold (eds.), Lexikon zur Soziologie. Wiesbaden: Springer, p. 864.

Giddens, A. (1981): A Contemporary Critique of Historical Materialism. Stanford: Stanford University Press.

Gray, M.L./Suri, S. (2019): Ghost Work. How to Stop Silicon Valley from Building a New Global Underclass. Boston: Houghton Mifflin Harcourt.

Heinich, N. (2020): "A Pragmatic Redefinition of Value(s): Toward a General Model of Valuation." Theory, Culture & Society, 37(5), pp. 75-94.

Heintz, B. (1993): Herrschaft der Regel. Zur Grundlagengeschichte des Computers. Frankfurt a.M.: Campus.

Heuts, F./Mol, A. (2013): "What Is a Good Tomato? A Case of Valuing in Practice." Valuation Studies, 1(2), pp. 125–146

Hennion, A. (2007): "Those Things That Hold Us Together: Taste and Sociology." Cultural Sociology, 1(1), pp. 97–114.

Kjellberg, H./Mallard, A. (2013): "Valuation Studies? Our Collective Two Cents." Valuation Studies, 1(1), pp. 11-3.

Krüger, A.K. (2022): Soziologie des Wertens und Bewertens. Bielefeld: transcript.

Kropf, J./Laser, S. (eds.) (2019): Digitale Bewertungspraktiken. Für eine Bewertungssoziologie des Digitalen. Wiesbaden: Springer VS.

Lee, F./Mennicken, A./Reilly, J./Ziewitz, M. (2022): "Digitizing Valuation." In: Valuation Studies, 9(1), pp. 1-10.

Lee, F./Mennicken, A./Reilley, J./Ziewitz, M. (2024): "Experiences of digitized valuation." Valuation Studies, 11(1), pp. 1–8.

Löw, M. (2001): Raumsoziologie. Frankfurt a.M.: Suhrkamp.

Lorusso, S. (2023): What Design Can't Do: Essays on Design and Disillusion. First edition. Set Margins, #26. Eindhoven: Set Margins'.

Marx, K. (2003): Das Kapital. Kritik der politischen Ökonomie. Köln: Parkland.

Mau, S. (2019): The Metric Society: On the Quantification of the Social. Cambridge, UK, et al.: Polity.

Mau, S. (2023): "Digitale Scorings als Statusmarker. Eine ungleichheitssoziologische Annäherung." Berliner Journal für Soziologie, 33, pp. 255-287.

McQuillan, D. (2022): Resisting AI. An Anti-Fascist Approach to Artificial Intelligence. Bristol: Bristol University Press.

Nicolae, S./Endreß, M./Berli, O./Bischur, D. (eds.) (2019): (Be)Werten. Beiträge zur sozialen Konstruktion von Wertigkeit. Wiesbaden: Springer VS.

Parsons, T. (1968): The Structure of Social Action. A Study in Social Theory with Special Reference to a Group of Recent European Writers. New York, et al.: Free Press.

Pelizza, A. (2016): "Disciplining Change, Displacing Frictions: Two Structural Dimensions of Digital Circulation Across Land Registry Database Integration." TECNOSCIENZA: Italian Journal of Science & Technology Studies, 7(2), pp. 35–60.

Petre, C. (2021): All the News That's Fit to Click: How Metrics Are Transforming the Work of Journalists. Princeton: Princeton University Press.

Reckwitz, A. (2020): Society of Singularities. Cambridge, UK, et al.: Polity.

Star, S. L. (1990): "Power, Technology and the Phenomenology of Conventions: On Being Allergic to Onions." The Sociological Review, 38(1_suppl), pp. 26-56.

Taffel, S. (2021): "Data and Oil: Metaphor, Materiality, and Metabolic Rifts." New Media & Society, 25(5), pp. 980-998, https://doi.org/10.1177/14614448211017887.

Tsing, A.L. (2005): Friction: An Ethnography of Global Connection. Princeton, et al.: Princeton University Press.

Turing, A. M. (1937): "On Computable Numbers, with an Application to the Entscheidungsproblem." Proceedings of the London Mathematical Society (1937/1), pp. 230–265.

van de Poel, I./Kudina, O. (2022): "Understanding Technology-Induced Value Change: A Pragmatist Proposal." Philosophy & Technology, 35(2), 40, https://doi.org/10.1007/s13347-022-00520-8

Weber, M. (1972): Wirtschaft und Gesellschaft. Grundriss der verstehenden Soziologie. Tübingen: Mohr.

Zuboff, S. (2019): The Age of Surveillance Capitalism: The Fight for a Human Future at the New Frontier of Power. New York: Public Affairs.

Tracing the Seams

A Historical Exploration of X's Software Ecosystem

Lena Teigeler and Carolin Gerlitz

Abstract

Since its launch in 2006, Twitter, now called X, has invited external developers to connect to the platform by opening an application programming interface (API). Multiple developers used this opportunity to build apps, alternative Twitter clients, or custom scripts for automation, creating distinct ways of being on Twitter through so-called software "sources" which have been shown underneath each tweet. In this paper, we explore the analytical potential of the source metric for studying frictions of valuation between Twitter and its software ecosystem. By observing the usage of different sources over a historical period from 2009-2021, we explore how interoperability, facilitated through application programming interfaces, is actually enacted and negotiated by external stakeholders and platform politics. We draw on the notions of seamless- and seamfulness to describe these negotiations and offer a nuanced way of thinking about friction. We claim that in the case of Twitter's app ecosystem the attempt to create seamless data flows is opening the possibility for new types of seams to occur. As the source metric was removed both from the interface and the API as part of Twitter's relaunch as "X", we argue that the removal of the source metric flattens the heterogeneous origins/seams of platform data and reflect on the role of tracing seams in empirical platform research.

Keywords

Platform Studies, Seams, Twitter/X Ecosystem, Data Interoperability, Valuation

Introduction

On 14 November 2022, Elon Musk announced a change in the display of tweets on Twitter, now X: "We will finally stop adding what device a tweet was written on (waste of space & compute) below every tweet. Literally, no one even knows why we did that". The data point Musk was referring to, however, did not merely provide information about the devices from which people tweet. Rather, Musk referred to the so-called source metric (Gerlitz/Rieder 2018) which provides information about the software or "utility" a tweet originated from. This software can be specific to a device, such as Twitter for Android or Twitter for iPhone, but can also refer to cross-posted content from other platforms, social media management clients, games, or the web. It entails customised software, non-public scripts, or automated tweeting from Internet of Things-devices - only to name a few. Within this paper, we want to unfold the argument that this source metric and its deprecation offer an analytical entry point to explore frictions in valuation between platforms and their developer ecosystem (Helmond 2015). We develop this argument in the current debate on the APIcalypse (Bruns 2019), the increasing restrictions platforms set up for external stakeholders to access their data, most notably researchers, but also developers. These increasing restrictions are in stark contrast to the more permissive data politics of the platform in its early years: Only shortly after its launch in 2006, Twitter enabled external developers to connect to its platform by offering a so-called application programming interface (API). Through the API, external developers could gain access to (get) and produce (post) platform data within the data points defined by Twitter. These data points were largely corresponding to the data users could input via the public interface, such as tweets including mentions, handles, and hashtags, but also went beyond that, for instance by offering metadata or information on and URLs of sources. Twitter actively invited developers to explore existing and produce new data, analytics, and use cases. The opening of the Twitter API enabled the development of third-party clients such as TweetDeck or professional social media clients such as Hootsuite or Sprinklr. These clients offered alternative interfaces, ways of reading, sorting, or writing tweets. It also resulted in customised software, including automation and bot making utilities. The API was central for the platformisation of Twitter, as it allowed the platform to be "built on" (Puschmann/Burgess 2013: 4) and by doing so, become an interface for the interests of heterogeneous external stakeholders including developers, other platforms, webmasters, users and advertisers (Poell et al. 2019). APIs have been considered as enablers of innovation and ecosystem development, whilst enabling platforms to control data access, limits, and use cases (van der Vlist et al. 2022). Previous research on platforms and their development ecosystem has explored how apps are built to stretch, re-interpret, and alter the functionalities of platforms but have been closely watched and regulated by platforms themselves (Gerlitz et. al 2019). Twitter's/X' source metric offers a particular entry point to explore frictions in valuation emerging through the engagement with and regulation of platform APIs. In this paper, we want to explore how the source metric can be deployed as an empirical access point to explore frictions between platforms, user practices and external developers. We suggest that these frictions can be found when looking at the interplay between seamless and seamful circulation of platform data, bringing together HCI and platform studies discourses.

In 2009, Twitter started to show sources underneath tweets and made that data point available via the API following the introduction of OAuth authentification and a registration process for apps. Since then, Twitter was subject to lively and inventive developer activities, including apps that copied, altered, tweaked or reinterpreted its functionalities or adjusted them for objectives such as cross-posting, professional social media management, to running botnets or custom software. Twitter watched the emerging third-party ecology closely and regularly intervened and regulated in the freedoms granted - by rules, restricting access or discontinuing sources. In January 2023, as part of the rebranding of Twitter as "X", the source metric was removed from both public interfaces and APIs. Simultaneously, many existing apps lost their access and were shut down overnight, followed by a retroactive modification of the developer agreement prohibiting the service of most third-party clients (Wiggers 2023).

Previous research has shown that the source metric can function as an indicator of highly diverse use practices (Gerlitz/Rieder 2013; Robinson 2016)—as content cross-posted from Facebook or Instagram is difficult to compare with manually generated tweets on the web interface or automatic posts from games, Internet of Things-devices or bot accounts (Gerlitz/Weltevrede 2019). Different sources enable very different practices, some of which may not be desired or supported by the platform. Their heterogeneity suggests that tweets themselves are not an unproblematic, straightforwardly countable first order metric (Power 2004)—and here we treat metrics as medium-defined, countable data category—but rather a composite or second order metric which commensurates (Espeland/Stevens 1998) heterogeneous practices into a single count.

By removing sources from both the user interface and the Twitter API, the platform flattens and obscures the heterogenous origins of its data and its diverse third-party ecosystem. This decision is in line with, so we suggest, principles of seamless design (Weiser 1999) as proposed in Human Computer Interaction (HCI), which moves data flows and data boundaries into the background for the sake of ease of use. Musk may not see a reason to keep that information alive, but other Twitter users do so—for instance for meme purposes—and researchers as well: Twitter's source metric was unique, as no other platform provided such insights into the software and applications that are built on top of them.

Focusing on the question how the source metric enables us to study valuation frictions emerging in the context of the API, the paper grounds its claims on an experimental empirical exploration by unfolding a historical perspective on the most used sources between 2009-2021. In a first step, the paper links debates on seamful/-lessness from HCI with platform studies. The exploration then turns to a historical exploration of Twitter sources, drawing on a workaround of a random sample (Morstatter et al. 2014). We trace the rise and fall of sources, both Twitter native and third-party owned, and the friction their presence and popularity created. We attend to the specificity of practices unfolding from different sources and their development over time, focusing on how they are informed by seamless and seamful data circulations and work as indicators for frictions in valuation. Through this approach, the paper generates links between platform and valuation studies, as well as HCI discourses on seamful- and seamlessness.

Platforms and (the Imaginary of) Seamlessness

In order to explore the analytical potential of the source metric for studying frictions of valuation in platform contexts, we embed our empirical work in debates on seamless design, platform, and valuation studies. The discussion of seamless (and later also seamful) design originates from human computer interaction (HCI) (Weiser 1999) and its quest to enable user agency by making designed objects easy, straightforward, and non-reflexive to use. As suggested in his influential plea, Weiser argued that "a good tool is an invisible tool. By invisible, I mean that the tool does not intrude on your consciousness; you focus on the task, not the tool" (ibid: 51). Seamlessness, Weiser continues, enables user agency, as users can focus on advancing their practice rather than understanding the inner workings of the tool. A lack of transparency was not considered problematic, but enabling (Chalmers et al. 2003). However, seamlessness has also been discussed critically, including by later works of Weiser himself: making users aware of the underlying functionalities can also facilitate reflexive and agential use. Advocates of seamfulness suggest "that inaccuracies, uncertainties, and boundaries in a system can be exploited as a resource" (Inman/Ribes 2019: 6) or that design should take the messiness of the world as a central component that should not be concealed but be deployed to enable agency (Dourish/Bell 2007). Seams, it is important to note, do not equate with frictions. Rather, they introduce moments of configurability, unequal distribution of access and can introduce a level of transparency or visibility and explicate the underlying conditions of design to work (Chalmers et al. 2003)—making them amenable for interrogation but also appropriation. They point to possible gaps, boundaries, or uncertainties, which can be exploited and/or open up conflict and friction. HCI discourses on seams have been taken up by infrastructure studies, which focus on seams as moments of accountability, in which the functioning, the power structures, the diversity of access to infrastructure can be explicated. Infrastructures, Bowker and Star suggest (1999), can be contested and made accountable in the moment of breakdown. Vertesi (2014) takes this one step further and argues that infrastructures entangle seamlessness and seamfulness in specific ways: they are designed to operate seamless, but to ensure this, they may need well placed seams for configuration. Within this paper, we take the capacities of seams to render underlying technology or data infrastructures accountable as pathways to inquire into platform valuation. Twitter's decision to open up APIs to diverse developers can be understood as an investment into seamless data exchange, whilst displaying the source underneath Tweets can be read as deployment of seams that render the heterogenous origins of tweets open. As seams also refer to moments of configurability and uncertainty, API regulations such as rate limits or content restrictions can be considered as seams for developers that data must pass in order to interoperate in seamless ways. To link the discussion closer to Twitter, we situate the exploration of seams in the context of platform studies.

Platforms studies have been characterised by two key perspectives: the first focuses on the distribution of agency and power across platforms and their stakeholders. The second focuses on the technical capacity of platforms to become interoperable and be built upon by its stakeholders. Within the first strand of platform research, platforms have been theorised from a socio-political perspective focusing on how they bring together and speak to a multiplicity of stakeholders. Setting themselves up as seemingly neutral intermediaries (Gillespie 2010), platforms have been considered as material, semiotic, and communicative interfaces for different user groups that all follow their very own agenda which is partial and not neutral. Such definition as social intermediary that enables relations between groups that otherwise would not enter into relation with each other is closely linked to earlier managerial definitions of platforms (cf. Rochet/Tirole 2006; Gawer 2015; Alaimo/Kallinikos 2016) which focus on platforms' capacity to operate as two or multi-sided markets—bringing together markets that have otherwise not been connected and generating so-called network effects (Rochet/Tirole 2006). Key critical concern of these relational accounts on platforms is how agency is distributed across the actors involved, namely end users, companies, media or politics, and how their relations are being governed, regulated and explicated (Gorwa 2019). This strand of platform studies is critical regarding the agential asymmetries built into them, including infrastructures of monitoring and surveillance (Zuboff 2019). It also inquires into what we understand as data practices (Burkhardt et al. 2022), namely the specific practices which draw on, repurpose, recontextualise and (re-)evaluate data and the way these practices relate stakeholders to each other. It is here that this strand of platform research ties in with debates on valuation (Vatin 2013)—even though platform and valuation studies do not share a history of extensive mutual recognition—by asking how the different stakeholders of platforms realise the value of platform data differently and what frictions may emerge (Gerlitz 2018).

The second strand of platform literature takes the material-technical dimension of data interoperability and stakeholder connectivity as its starting point. Platforms, Bogost and Montfort (2009) argue, are characterised by technical interoperability, computational building blocks, and data exchanges. They are (technically) designed to allow external stakeholders to build and programme on top of their capacities, functionalities, or data, for instance by opening access to data and functionality via application programming interfaces (API) or offering app or software development kits (SDKs) (van der Vlist & Helmond, 2021). In this sense, computational perspectives on platforms ask how platforms accomplish interoperability or seamless data exchanges and what possible translation points, boundary infrastructures or seams are required to do so. Here, platform studies increasingly intersected with Science and Technology Studies as well as infrastructure studies (Plantin et al. 2016), exploring how platforms and their data integration features are gaining similarity to infrastructures and vice versa.

Research on platform valuation intersects the social-political and computational strands on platforms (Poell et al. 2019). Platform data are considered stable in form, but open to different interpretations and set up to operate across multiple contexts and valuation regimes (Beer 2016; Gerlitz 2018; van Dijck 2011). Each stakeholder may introduce their own valuation and interpretation of platform data/functionalities and platforms determine which they support or disable through means of API regulations and governance. While platform cross-posting and syndication is key to most social media platforms, Twitter has been the only platform explicating its diversity of sources through the source metric. It has been an indication, a trace of the platforms' multiplicity of data and valuation regimes, while most other platforms conceal the involvement of third-party apps, even though they cultivate a diverse ecosystem of connected apps (see: Gerlitz et. al 2019). For this reason, platform data have been considered as multi-valent, as having the technical capacity to speak to multi registers of valuation (Gerlitz 2018). It is here in the context of de- and re-contextualising platform data and functionality, that platform studies and valuation studies begin to intersect. Following Vatin, valuation bridges between evaluation, the assessment of value, and valorisation, the generation of value (Vatin 2013). Valuation studies are interested to explore by which practices and in which orders of worth (Boltanski & Thevenot 1991) phenomena are evaluated (Lamont 2012), how value is socially decided upon and which practices are entangled, especially quantification, ranking and calculative practices. Valuation studies have paid particular interest to conflicting forms of valuation, such as heterogeneous orders of worth. While some authors identified divergences in (e)valuation due to different orders of worth as a problem (Boltanski & Thevenot 1991), others such as Stark (2009) identified them as a source of productive frictions, especially in business settings, where heterarchies of worth and value may foster innovation. In the context of platforms, new interpretations of platform data by third parties and developers are also actively invited in and used as a source of innovation (van Dijck 2011) similar to Stark's heterarchies, but are regularly problematised by platforms themselves. Whether or not a different interpretation of valuation results in a friction or not, however, is subject to situated evaluation by platforms or their stakeholders.

Valuating platform data therefore involves both its material-technical underpinnings and infrastructures as well as heterogeneous stakeholders and their relations. In the context of social media platforms, the entanglement of multiple stakeholders requires platforms to render data exchange to a certain degree seamless in order to invite stakeholders and their data (practices) in, whilst platforms seek to remain in control over the seams. How seamful/seamless design is related to frictions in valuation is a sub-question the paper will attend to.

Tweet Sources as a Methodological Entry Point for Studying Frictions in Valuation

In this paper, we use the so-called source metric, the software from which people engage in social media platforms, as a methodological starting point to trace seamful and seamless data exchange and indicators for valuation frictions in the context of Twitter. The source data point to the heterogeneous ecosystem of third-party apps that build on top of platforms and use the interpretative flexibility (Bijker et al. 1987) of its data and functionality for their own purposes. They entail alternative clients, social media managers, cross posting from other platforms, automated scripts, and many other practices. Twitter sources have mainly been studied in the context of one-off random samples to account for average practices (Gerlitz/Rieder 2018) or case based samples (Robinson 2016) to study their role in issues. In order to deploy the source metric for the study of friction valuation, we propose opening up a historical perspective on the deployment, rise and fall, and regulation of sources. As noted above, we treat the source metric as a seam which explicates heterogeneous stakeholders and user practices in platform ecologies. Accounting for the historical popularity of software from which tweets are sent will allow us to explore which sources users engaged with and how the third-party periphery evolved over time. Therefore, we worked with random samples, to account for average use of sources on the platform of English tweets from the years 2009 until 2021. This period was selected as the source metric was available since 2009 and the sample was retrieved within the scope of a larger research project that was started in 2021. The tweets were retrieved by the end of 2022 and the retrieval was interrupted by the deprecation of Twitter's Academic API at the beginning of 2023, which is why data from 2022 is not included. Hence, this research was directly affected by the changes introduced by Musk.

For a long time, random samples of up to 1 percent of all tweets (still 4.5 million per day) could be retrieved through the Twitter streaming API. At the point of data retrieval in 2022, the main access to Twitter for research was its Academic API which only allowed data retrievals based on keywords, hashtags, or tweet/user ids. To circumvent this affordance, Luca Hammer, our scientific programmer, developed a custom script to connect to the Academic API and specified the negative query "-nobodyeverusedthatword" to retrieve all tweets not containing this word. We further specified English as the tweet language and queried for all tweets that were published within the first ten seconds of every hour of the first day of the months January, April, July, and October for each year from 2009 until 2021. We chose the limited time span of 10 seconds to not exceed the rate limit of 10 million tweets per month. The resulting data sample is therefore only representative to a limited extent, but it serves as an entry point to explore the analytical capacities of the source metric. This approach produced 13 samples which have grown larger over the first years, decreased again from 2014, and have reached their highest number in 2021. Overall, we took 11.358.299 tweets into account, which were published with the help of 60.010 different sources.

Within this sample, we further differentiated the sources in: native apps, that is Twitter apps provided for different devices and operating systems and operated by the platform itself, like Twitter for Android or the Twitter Web Client (figure 1), and non-native apps, which are apps developed and made available to users by third-party operators, and in many cases offer altered or added functionalities to the platform (figure 2). We specifically zoomed into the 10 most used sources (figure 4) and the 20 most used non-native sources (figure 5), and observed how much they were used during the observed years. We created categories according to the functionalities they offer (figure 6) and profiled the source-specific practices (figure 7 and 8). The last two steps allowed us to explore how sources deploy and eventually re-evaluate platform data and functionality in new ways compared to those suggested by the platform and whether this may introduce seamful or seamless data circulation and open up frictions in valuation. For contextual information on these apps' functionalities and their prevalence, we visited their websites and archived versions of their websites captured by the Internet Archive's Wayback Machine, entries in developer forums, tech press releases, the developer documentation of Twitter/X and external apps and archived tweets from the Wayback Machine.

The Rise and Fall of Sources

In a first step, we inquired into the overall number of different sources within our datasets. In total, we encountered 60010 distinct sources. The number of sources increased from 2009-2015 (225-11990 sources) and then declined until 2021 (7489 sources). These numbers give an indication of the highly heterogeneous data origins of Twitter data which are rendered invisible or seamless on the platform now. To further examine the rise and decline of sources we set out to explore the internal composition of sources per year further, by first looking into the distribution between Twitter owned native sources (figure 1) and third-party sources (figure 2). Native sources are designed and controlled by the platform. Non-native sources, however, have been designed by external developers which may deploy data in potentially fictitious ways. The first entail sources such as the Twitter Web Client and have been complemented by diverse device centric sources such as Twitter for Android, Twitter for iPhone, and Twitter for Blackberry but also purchased third-party sources such as TweetDeck (which continues to run under this name in the source data after its purchase in 2011). 99 percent of all sources are non-native and only 0,2-0,9 percent are native.

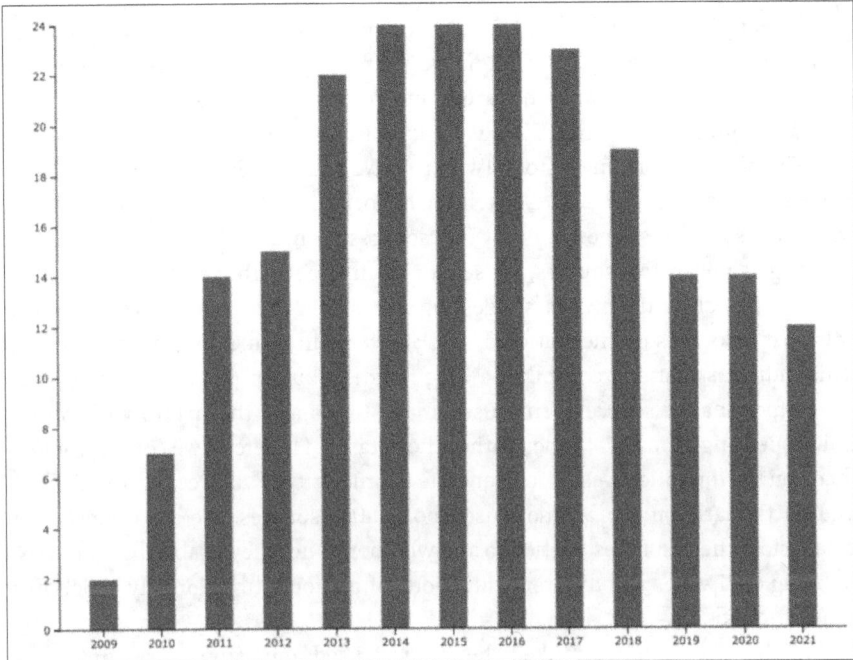

Figure 1: Number of different Twitter native sources per year.

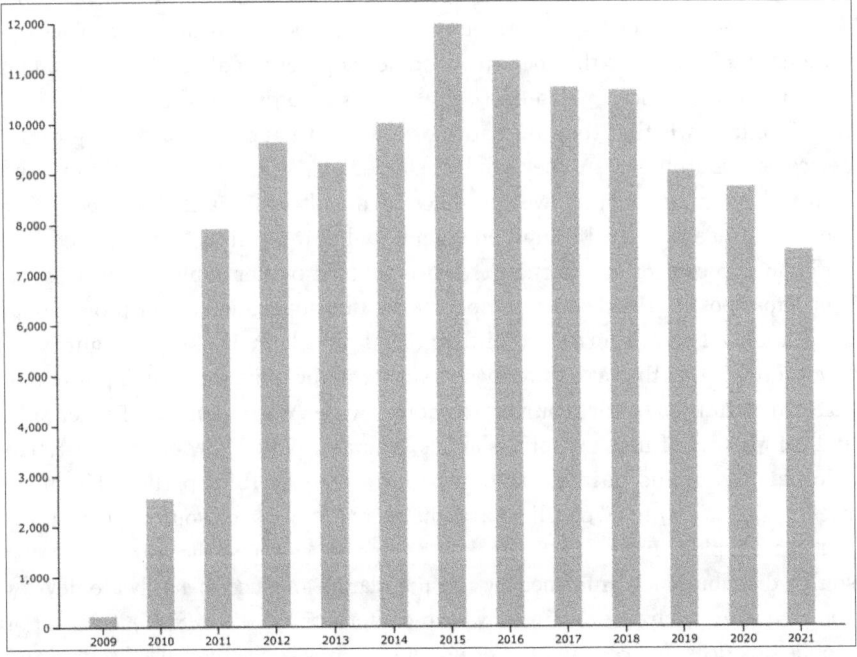

Figure 2: Number of different third-party sources per year.

A different picture unfolds if we look at the number of tweets sent and whether they come from a native or a non-native source (figure 3). We see a rise in the number of tweets per random sample up until 2015, then a dip, and then an increase from 2018 onwards. What is striking in comparison to figure 1 is that the majority of tweets originate from Twitter native sources. Even though less than 1 percent of all sources are native, a striking majority of all tweets are generated with these few sources, suggesting that few sources dominate Twitter use practices. Looking at non-native sources, we see a rise in tweets from non-native up until 2015 and a decline afterwards, suggesting that there is a decrease in the variety of third-party sources on the platform—a claim we will return to later in the paper. This indicates that sources follow a long tail distribution (Anderson 2004) with few, largely native sources being used many times and the majority of sources only appearing around 1-5 times within the dataset. Therefore, we continue with a focus on the top 10 sources which generate the majority of all tweets in our dataset, and particularly on the 20 most used non-native sources. We are interested in what actors these sources are tied to and whether or not they enable different ways of being on Twitter and different valuations of platform functionality which may cause frictions.

In the next step, we ranked the 10 most used apps from 2009 until 2021 using the tool PyCatFlow. Figure 4 shows them ordered based on the number of tweets (normalised) created per source. The links between the sources show which source remained within the top 10 over the years. To further explore the different types of apps, the spectrum and development of alternative interpretations and use practices, we categorised the apps according to the functionalities they facilitate, whether they are native or non-native apps, and according to the device or operating system they can be installed on. We did so by researching the sources, engaging with their web presence or consulting tutorials, and identifying their main use purpose through emergent qualitative coding. This resulted in 5 different app categories: alternative device specific twitter applications, automation, cross-posting, native device specific twitter applications, and professional applications. The categories are differentiated by colour. Looking at figure 4, a key finding is that the year 2009 diverts substantially in its source composition—featuring barely any native sources except for Twitter Web Client and Twitter SMS and comprising of many specific sources such as a radio show hosting platform (BlogTalkRadio) and quizzes (LOL quiz) developed by third parties. The most used source is Twitter Web Client and the second most used source in the 2009 random sample is Twitter SMS. Tracing their presence across the years shows that source distribution is informed by the popularity and use of hardware devices and characterised by the decline of web and alternative devices (SMS) in favour of mobile practices. In 2012, Twitter for iPhone features as the most used source and remains such until 2021. However, it is important to remind that we are looking at an English speaking random sample and that the iPhone is the most popular device in the US. In the same year, Twitter for Android features as the third most popular source, in 2013 it became the second most used, placing Twitter for Web on place three. In 2014, Facebook was the second most used app, but from 2015 Twitter for Android held this rank. We can see the rise and fall of devices: Twitter for Blackberry for instance scores fourth from 2012-2014, followed by a decline in the ranking. The source metric thus inflects the rise and demise of the popularity of devices and other software, such as, for instance social media platforms. Some platforms gained traction around 2013, such as Facebook and Instagram. Facebook remains one of the most popular sources, but rapidly lost popularity from 2017 and disappears in 2020 (figure 4). Twitter for SMS disappeared from the top 10 after 2012. These findings suggest that first, there is an attempt at (seamlessly) integrating and catering to changing device cultures. Second, it becomes apparent that what we are studying when engaging with Twitter data also contains data from other platforms, such as Facebook or Instagram, which comes with its specific publics, contexts, and use practices. While cross-posted data appears to be made interoperable in seamless ways, it may open up avenues of frictions—through interpreting platforms differently.

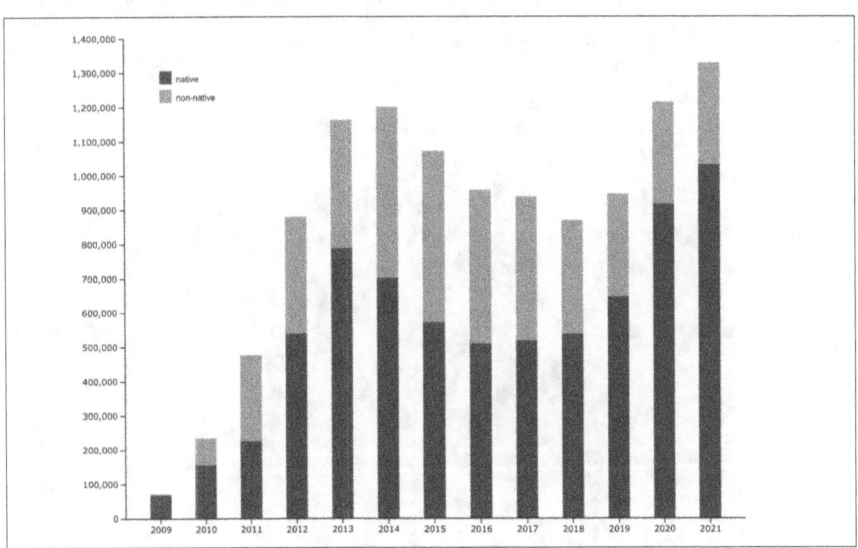

Figure 3: Total number of tweets per year from native and non-native sources.

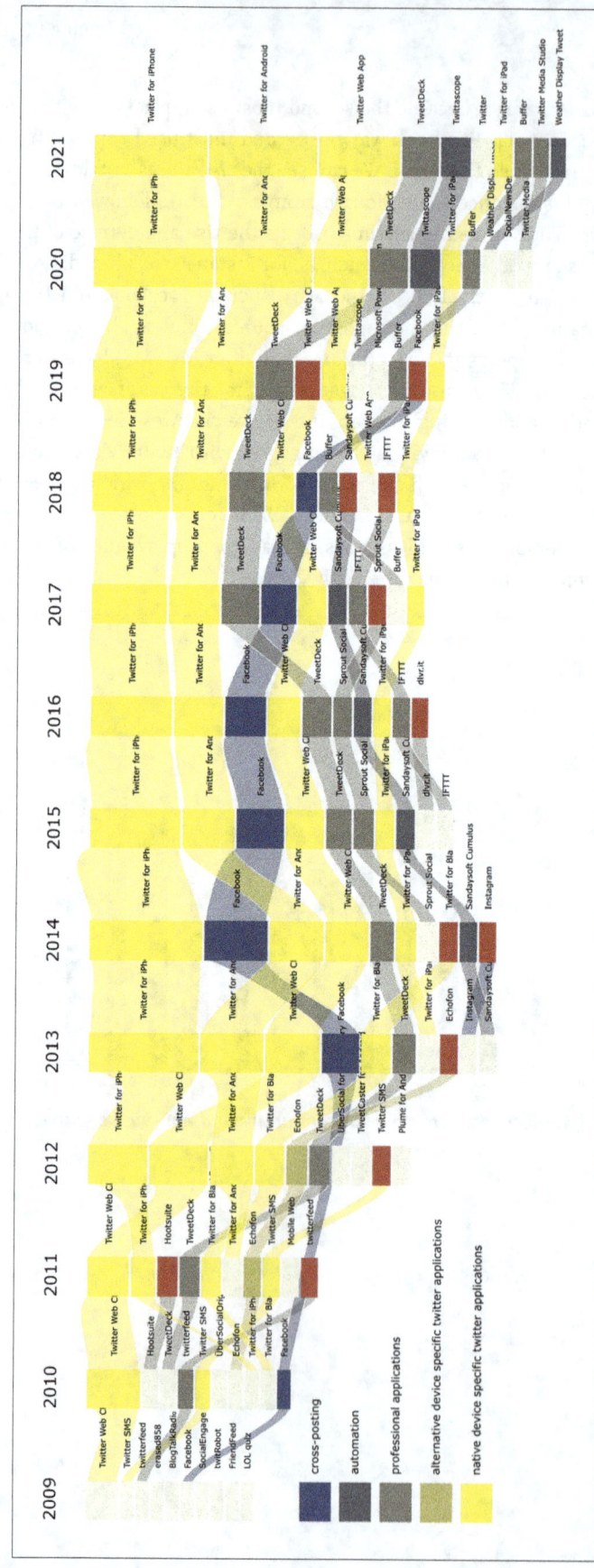

Figure 4: The rise and fall of the 10 most used sources from 2009 until 2021.

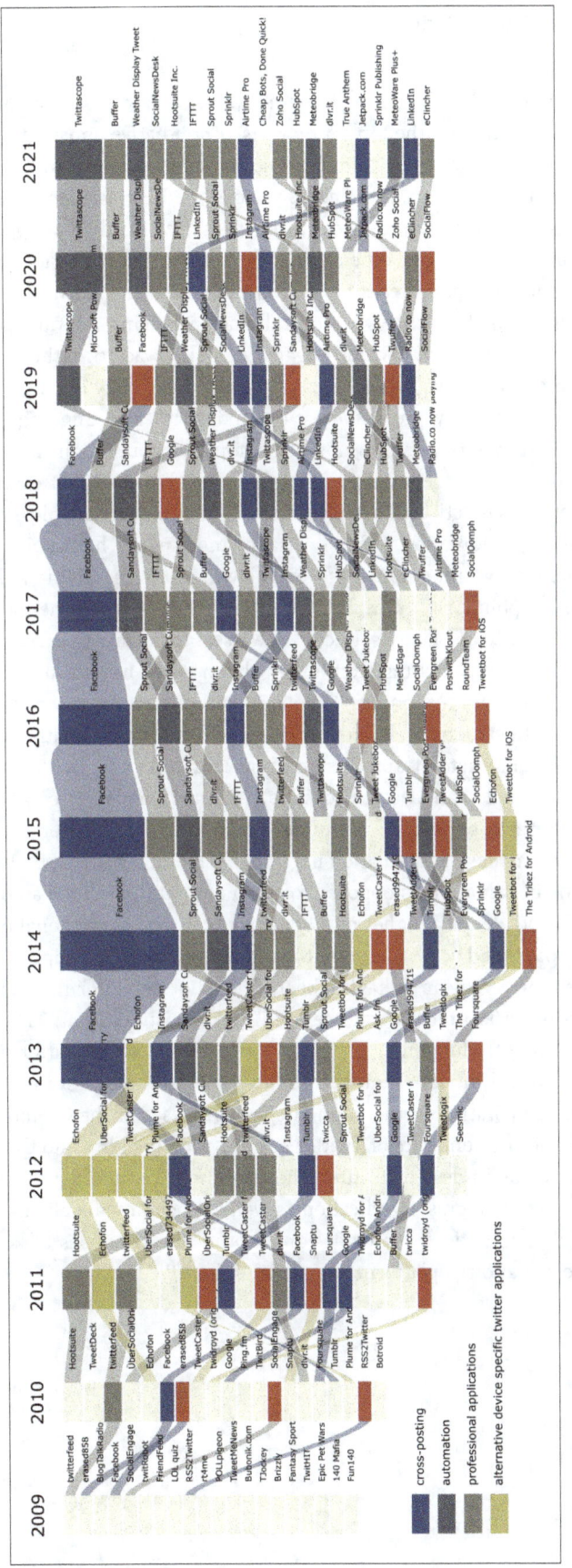

Figure 5: The rise and fall of the 20 most used non-native apps from 2009 until 2021.

To further investigate the spectrum of non-native sources for potential indicators of frictions, we also ranked the top 20 most used non-native apps (figure 5) and differentiated their categories by colour. Some source types maintain a presence over many years in the top 20, most notably social media management software and clients. Hootsuite for instance became the most used third-party app in 2010, and remains present until 2021, others such as Sprout Social, twitterfeed and dlvr. it remain present over many years too. Hubspot, Buffer and Sprinklr enter the top-20 later (figure 5). This shows the overall and increasing relevance of social media management apps for Twitter engagement since 2009. Other practices, such as tweeting from blogs or RSS feeds have their currency during a specific time—RSS2Twitter is only present in 2009 and 2010. The ongoing presence of automation software is worth to note, as automation builds on the technical seamlessness of software generated data production, but is a controversial and potentially frictitious practice within platforms. Twitter has historically supported certain forms of automation, whilst disallowing spam, harassment, mass automated interaction, and automation for following growth. Dlvr.it and IFTTT gained increasing popularity from 2010-2015 when they entered the top 20 and remain present until 2021. These services allow users to perform a variety of automation tasks, from cross-posting from other platforms or news sources to automatically retweeting and responding to content without necessarily enabling the creation of bot infrastructures. Moreover, interfaces of private weather stations, which enable the automated transmission of measured data to Twitter accounts, are present from 2012 (Sandaysoft Cumulus, Weather Display Tweet) and from 2015, the app Twittascope was used frequently to automatically generate and post horoscopes. Such modes of automation have not been problematised by Twitter or caused frictions in valuation as opposed to spam and scam oriented automation. However, we did not detect a higher number of sources that suggest enabling fully automated or bot related activity among the top 20 of most used apps. Yet, a few sources in the top 20 appear as having been deleted or deplatformised either by their operators or by Twitter (listed as "erased" in the visualisation) These traces might point at the introduction of frictions in valuation that the platform sought to discontinue. We will further inquire into these special cases later in the paper.

This initial exploration of the popularity of sources and the composition of the top sources of thirteen years of Twitter has provided insights into the embeddedness of platforms in device cultures, the relevance of other platforms as key stakeholders for content cross-syndication as well as social media clients and the diverse range of automation. It provides an account into the types of key actors involved in the valuation of platform data through its API.

Native and Non-Native Sources

To inquire further into alternative interpretations and practices, we took a more detailed look at the development of the app categories. Focusing on the type of actors provides a first indication of how platforms can be engaged with from the different sources and what type of valuation of functionality and data they may entail. We visualised the usage of these app types over time (figure 6).

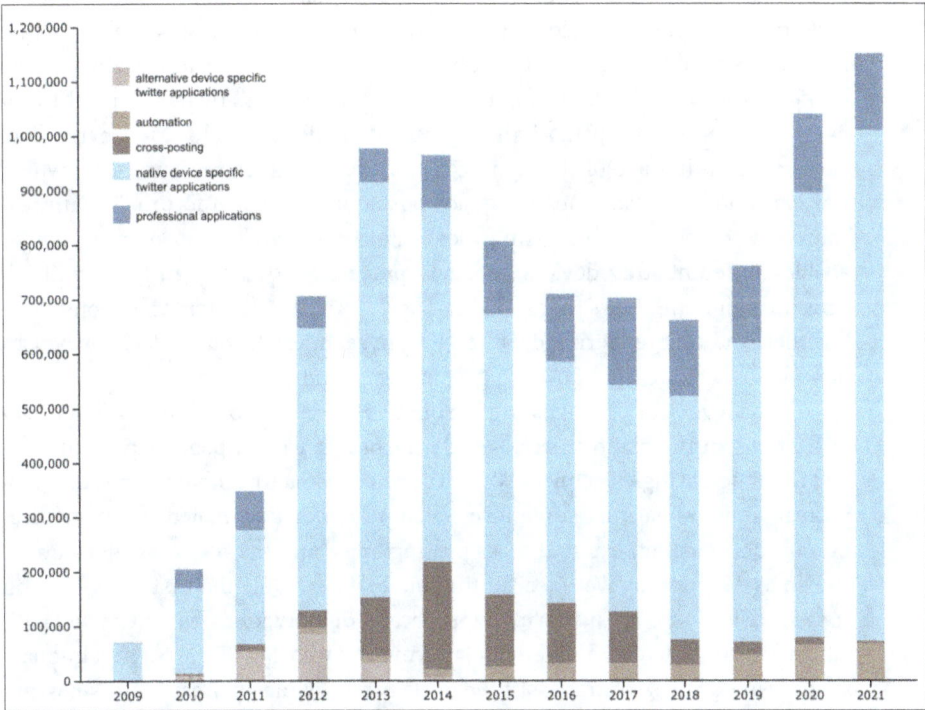

Figure 6: Categories of the 20 most used apps from 2009-2021.

Figure 6 illustrates how in the early years of the platform until around 2013, when native mobile clients were only gaining popularity, alternative device specific twitter apps, mostly for mobile devices like Blackberry or iPhone, were used a lot (2010-2013), whilst they declined thereafter or have been purchased/banned to be folded into native Twitter apps. In 2012 using Twitter from tablets became more relevant, as the increase of Twitter for iPad illustrates (figure 4). Twitter for Android Tablets became popular in 2014 (below the top 20), but disappears from our sample from 2019. The source merges with Twitter for Android. Between 2010 and 2015, content posted via Twitter buttons on external websites was captured as posted with "Twitter for Websites", classified as "cross-posting" here. Buttons on external websites facilitate a "decentralisation of data mining and the recentralisation of data processing within platforms" (Gerlitz/Helmond 2013: 1361). External user activities can be turned into data without major seams. Until 2015, these buttons also displayed the number of shares of the corresponding URL on the external page and this info was made available via an unofficial API endpoint. In this sense, the Twitter button can be considered a productive seam by explicating its usage stats that webmasters can deploy for displaying and analysing the circulation of their content. From November 20, 2015, Twitter changed the design of the button. It removed the share-counter from websites and deprecated all respective endpoints, including the source "Twitter for Websites". Blackboxing this metric may remove a seam, yet also points to a friction in valuation, as webmasters and researchers have an interest in the button analytics while the platform aims to take back control over how its data is retrieved and evaluated: Twitter stopped third-party developers from using an undocumented API method for retrieving data and from making use of the share count as performance measurement, which was explained in an accompanying blog post and a developer forum. The unified source metric becomes increasingly less informative, and at this point no longer enables differentiating devices and data processing becomes fully centralised. This little vignette shows that seams can be a site where different valuations come together, and that rendering data flows more seamless through blackboxing can be a platform strategy for governing valuation frictions.

The category of cross-posting (coloured in brown) points to a different set of frictions in the platform ecology. Cross-posting gained popularity until 2014 and then increasingly declined. We can differentiate four different types of cross-posting apps: social media platforms that allow for (automated) cross-syndication of their content, external cross-posting apps, and the native Twitter button, shown as "Twitter for Websites" in the source data. While the first allow sharing content tailored to one platform automatically onto Twitter, the latter two facilitate publishing content to different platforms and websites. They potentially enact seamlessness and seamfulness at the same time—while automated cross-posting enables seamless data flows from one platform to another, translating the content may introduce seams—hashtags may not be used in the same way, captions may be longer, presentation of content (image/video focused or text focused) may be different, links may or may not be clickable.

The rise and fall of the cross-posting category is influenced by the popularity of social media platforms from which content was cross-posted. The generally high prevalence of these platforms as third-party sources shows how Twitter is supportive of such data interoperability. By facilitating cross-posting, Twitter became a collecting basin for references, different content-types as well as practices and debates unfolding on other platforms. Figure 5 illustrates the importance of content shared from Facebook and its rapid decline. While it was the second most used app in 2014, ranking higher than Twitter for Android and the Twitter Web Client, it disappears from our samples completely in 2020. From 2017, Facebook significantly lost considerable shares of the overall number of tweets: While in 2017 Facebook published 8 percent of all tweets in our sample, in 2019, it only accounted for around 1,5 percent. Before July 2017, a large percentage of cross-posted Facebook posts were photos without a description text. A description was then automatically attached on Twitter ("I posted a new photo to Facebook"), followed by the Facebook URL. These posts disappeared in 2017. This is explained by a change in Meta's content strategy: In June 2017 they rolled out new posting possibilities, now focusing on albums instead of single photos, leading to a disappearance of single photo content with automated descriptions from Twitter. Cross-posting photos became a little less seamless—the automated photo descriptions disappeared—as a side-effect of Meta's changes in the valuation of its content. In 2020, Facebook's Twitter integration was then shut down completely, and cross-posting turned from seamless to seamful. Users speculated that this is the result of Meta's attempt to avoid duplicate content from Instagram and Facebook. Instagram's cross-posting feature, meanwhile, was maintained. However, there is no official documentation about the removal of Facebook's cross-posting feature confirming this assumption. The removal of the cross-posting integration can be understood as the removal of a seam: Cross-posting from Facebook may be continued via other cross-posting tools, while visible traces of its origin from Facebook disappeared. The vanishing of an analytical seam points to a friction in valuation introduced by the external stakeholders. Tracing the popularity of particular sources over time sheds light on how seams may be introduced by other actors and how data flow admission between big platforms relies on the strategies of the involved parts.

Apps for professional social media practices (coloured in dark blue), including marketing, customer service, data analytics, and sales, gained relevance from 2014. The most important type of tools within this category are social media management apps. These apps aim to facilitate a seamless spread of content on different platforms and websites. As shown in figure 4, some clients were even present in the top 10 ranking for multiple years. These sources often comprise paid-for software that enables professional social media management, including posting plans, collaborative content creation, cross-platform posting, and additional audience and performance analytics. The analytical functions of management apps facilitate a seamless interlocking of evaluation metrics and cross-platform content spread. Metrics produced on the different platforms are aggregated and commensurated in this type of management software and used to derive generalised recommendations. They also make data ready for the integration into the quantified management of companies (cf. McCosker 2017): Marketing performance metrics, thus, can become part of the overall business performance analytics that integrate numbers from very different origins, like sales figures or customer relation metrics. This type of seamlessness and data reinterpretation is tolerated and even promoted by Twitter as it elevates the status of Twitter data: From 2015, the platform established a partner program, including partnerships with Sprinklr or Sprout Social, which enabled privileged data access and visibility, but most importantly a stability that common third-party apps didn't have, as shown by their sudden deprecation in 2023.

Apps that facilitate automated tweet production and publishing (light brown), like games posting the achievements of players to their Twitter account, or automatically generated horoscopes, are constantly prevalent in our sample and even gain relevance from 2018 onwards. They are relevant in the context of tracing seams, as they enable highly heterogeneous content to be folded into a Twitter-adjusted format and posted on the platform. Among the automators are weather forecast apps, like Sandaysoft Cumulus, becoming popular in 2012, and Weather Display Tweet, joining the top 20 of non-native apps in 2016. Both apps automatically tweet measurement values from private weather stations and are used to set up weather forecast accounts that publish updates at regular intervals. Although the permanent prevalence of weather apps in sources suggests that Twitter did not object to this type of automation, the development of Sandaysoft Cumulus indicates a friction in 2019, when the number of tweets suddenly decreased. Users reported a rate limit problem in a Cumulus forum in 2019, pointing at an interrupted posting functionality and explaining it by Twitter's changed protocol requirements regarding client-server-connections that Sandaysoft Cumulus did not fulfil. Put differently, the platform introduced a technical-regulatory seam for data exchange addressing developers. Twitter's developer documentation is not completely archived in 2019, but a comparison of an early version from 2019 and a version from 2020 suggests that a change took place between these two points in time. Namely, Twitter started requiring a TLS (Transport Layer Security) 1.2 cryptographic protocol that some versions of Sandaysoft Cumulus did not incorporate. The entries from Cumulus' forum suggest that only the older Cumulus 1 stopped working, while cross-posting from the newer version Cumulus MX was still possible, as it probably incorporated the newer TLS version. This is also indicated by our data from 2020 and 2021: Tweets sent with Sandaysoft Cumulus still appear in our samples, but they decreased significantly in volume. The source metric, however, does not allow distinguishing between version 1 and MX.

The increase of the "automation" category from 2018 onwards can mostly be traced back to a single app, namely Twittascope that allowed the automatic publishing of horoscopes from tarot.com. Our sample data shows that the accounts that use Twittascope often post in a very regular rhythm, in some cases several times a day, which explains the high prevalence of tweets sent with this app. Twittascope appears in our sample from 2010, but increased in popularity from 2018. The high amount of tweets in our dataset is also influenced by the fact that many users set monthly horoscopes to the first day of a month.

Various apps appear as "erased", as discussed in the previous section of the rise and fall of sources, followed by an id composed of numbers or numbers and letters, which means the app has by now been deprecated. Erased734497 for instance, was popular in 2011, but decreased in popularity until it disappeared after 2014. Tweets archived in the Internet Archive's Wayback machine indicate that it's the app ÜberTwitter [sic], belonging to UberMedia who also owned several other apps, like UberSocial for Blackberry. ÜberTwitter and two other apps of

UberMedia were suspended in 2011. The platform saw the apps' use of the tweet-elongation tool tmi.me that enabled users to post tweets longer than 140 charac-ters as a violation of its Terms of Service. Additionally, trademark infringement was claimed against ÜberTwitter due to using the brand name Twitter in its app name, as explained by UberMedia's owner Bill Gross in a Quora post. The depre-cation of UberMedia's apps must be considered in the context of the competitive relationship between UberMedia and Twitter (Halliday, 2011). Many alternative clients belonged to UberMedia in 2011 and in May, Twitter outbid UberMedia for the purchase of TweetDeck (Arrington, 2011). Friction, in this case, resulted from Twitter's attempt to retain the sovereignty over points of access to the platform. While interoperability and its promise of seamless data exchange is supposed to foster innovation, it also bears the risk of external software operators dominating the app ecosystem.

Linking these observations back to the question of seamless and seamful valuation, the findings so far suggest that we face a complex entanglement and intersection: allowing for external sources to produce content for the platform opens up possibilities of technical seamlessness, however, may introduce seams, if content from one platform or website is fitted to another, like shortened links or automatically created replacement texts. These seams may serve as analytical entry points to trace frictions in data valuation. Technical seamlessness is influenced by Twitter's market interests—by promoting business models that add value to data on the one hand (social media management apps), and by attempting to maintain control alongside other large platform companies on the other hand (UberMedia). It is negotiated by both platforms and apps and their respective interests, like avoiding duplicate content, differentiating the purpose of two platforms, or main-taining security standards. We will explore this in more detail in the next section engaging with the practices that emerge from different sources.

Sources and Their Practices

In the next step, we inquired into the different ways users take up the different functionalities of third-party apps and make them valuable. Put differently, we explore how users deploy the interpretative flexibility of source and platform grammars to unfold specific ways of being on Twitter. For this purpose we created source profiles based on source specific use of platform functionalities with the top 20 sources in each year and particularly compared the years 2011 and 2021 (Figure 7 and Figure 8). We calculated the average number of tweets containing the features hashtag, URL and mention, and whether tweets are retweets, replies or quote tweets (introduced in 2020) and then differentiated these numbers by adding a colour scheme: Low values are coloured in light beige, values until 40 percent increasingly become darker and from 40 percent until 100 percent they tend towards blue.

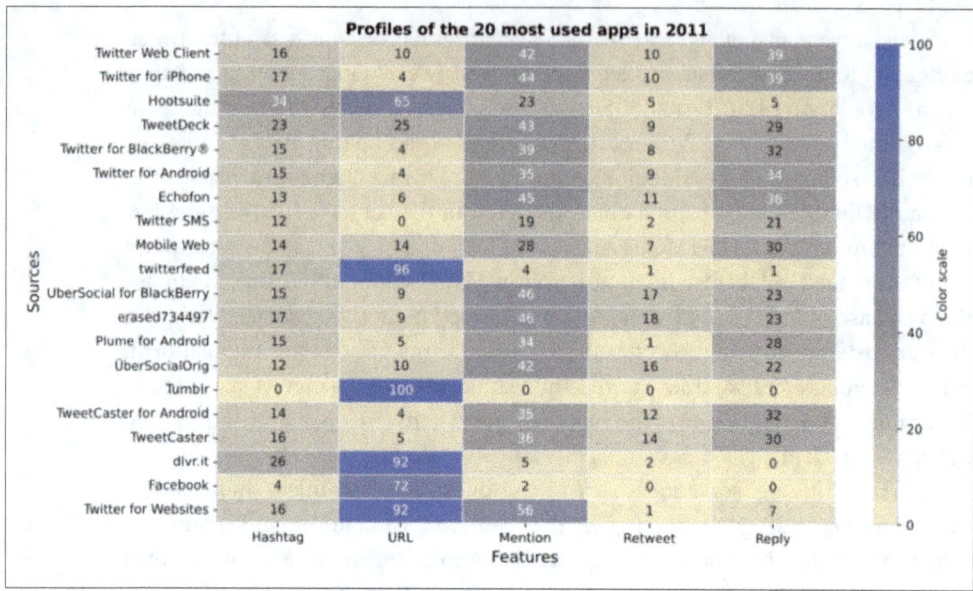

Figure 7: The share of features in tweets by the 20 most used apps in 2011.

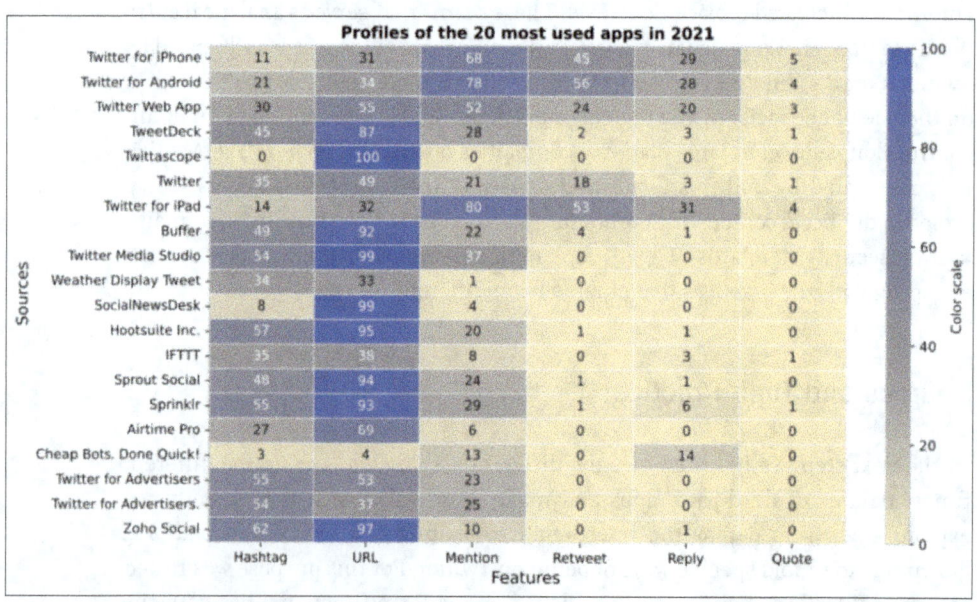

Figure 8: The share of features in tweets by the 20 most used apps in 2021.

The profiles point to three different app groups: Group A include apps with tweets that (almost) always contain URLs, while showing very few signs of interaction through retweets and replies. Group B contains app profiles with a mixed uptake of all platform features, especially including interaction metrics. Group C includes apps with a medium-sized share of hashtags, URLs and mentions in tweets, while (almost) never containing retweets or replies, that is tweets from these sources do rarely respond to or engage with other tweet content. In 2011, group A comprised cross-posting apps and platforms: Facebook, Tumblr or Twitter for Websites. With twitterfeed, Hootsuite and IFTTT, the cluster also includes social media management apps. The apps from group A largely facilitate posting external content to Twitter, either from a specific website or platform, or simultaneously on various platforms and websites. Within the 20 most popular apps, we can observe an increase of group A until 2021. It still consists of social media management apps, like Sprout Social, Zoho Social, Hootsuite or Social News Desks, but now increasingly also of native social media management apps, like Twitter Media Studio and TweetDeck. Other platforms however, disappeared.

Group B does not show a clear tendency with regard to one feature, as group A does with regard to URLs. It includes native Twitter apps, like Twitter for Android or Twitter for iPhone, but also alternative mobile clients like UberSocial for Blackberry or Echofon. In 2021, group B only consists of native apps, alternative clients have disappeared. At the same time, group C became more relevant, which hasn't been part of the top 20 in 2011. Group C is characterised above all by the absence of replies and retweets, while not showing the same tendency towards containing URLs as group A. Examples are Weather Display Tweets, Twitter for Advertisers, and IFTTT. Overall, until 2021 replies, retweets, and quotes, that is interaction with Twitter content, are almost exclusively produced by native apps. Third-party apps tend to include external content on the platform and spread it via hashtags within the platform, as indicated by the increase of group A. Over the years, we can conclude, that practices of third-party apps have developed into a rather uniform direction—in 2021 they were mostly used to strategically spread and broadcast content –, while interactive features have become the exclusive realm of native apps.

Negotiating the Seams:
Platform Governance and Valuation Frictions

The current Twitter/X frontend presents all tweets as equal. In 2023, it even removed the last sign of possible heterogeneous origin—or seam—by no longer displaying the source metric. This change can be understood as a move towards a more seamless platform experience, giving little insights into the heterogeneity of tweet origin, the diversity of practices, and platform use cases. On a technical level, however, facing its diverse developer ecology, the platform moved away from a seamless approach by gradually controlling, restricting, and shutting down access to its data and functionality via APIs, rendering API access seamful for developers. This illustrates how seamfulness and seamlessness often occur concurrently, and how each may facilitate the other. Prior to this comprehensive shift in the platform's approach to interoperability via its API, apps elevating the status of Twitter data by enriching it with data from other contexts and transforming it into relevant marketing measures (social media management tools) were fully established. At the same time, automated content production remained tolerated.

Our historical engagement with Twitter sources allowed us to look at both stakeholders and capacities of platforms to be built on top. It enabled us to trace seamless and seamful data flows and their entanglement with frictions in valuation. Such perspective allows us to revisit the notion of seams in the context of social media platforms, especially when treating seams not only as markers of transparency, but as instances of configurability, control and uncertainty:

(1) HCI and ubiquitous computing largely focus on technical seams, which, in the context of platforms, are enacted through defining/deleting API endpoints, limits to access to post, rate limits, depreciation of connection or altering of content when posting to the Twitter API that regulate data flows. It is here that it becomes clear that seams do not have to equal frictions but are rather boundary objects (Star & Griesemer 1989) data have to conform to in order to enable exchange between platforms and sources. In the case of Twitter, such technical seams can become sites where valuation frictions occur—for instance when rate limits are exceeded through automated activity or when access to data endpoints in the platform API are deprecated.

(2) In addition, platforms can enact socio-political seams by disallowing certain keywords and content, but also use practices and entire sources to configure and control the content on the platform. These seams can be found in the developer policies. These use cases detail how the platform deals with, supports or prohibits spam as well as automation rules. The later are particularly interesting as Twitter explicitly invites for form of automation that "automatically broadcast helpful information in posts", "[r]un creative campaigns that auto-reply to users" or "[t]ry new things that help people (and comply with our rules)" (ibid.). The line between desired and unwanted automation, however, is not entirely clear, as users are asked to be "[b]e extra mindful of our rules about abuse and user privacy" (ibid.) and not to share misleading links or sensitive media, leaving a certain openness in evaluation in regards to the content shared. Here, the seams of automating Twitter at the same time establish a friction in valuation, as what is considered unwanted automation does not comply with Twitter's desired use scenarios and may lead to a deprecation of access. In addition, Twitter has a set of rules what type of posts, interaction, and media it is not supported on its platform. This includes among other things violence, all forms of abuse, illegal goods, harassment, private information, non-consensual nudity, account compromise, spam, synthetic and manipulated media, copyright infringement.

(3) In addition, platforms can introduce economic seams by purchasing sources, raising fees, creating paid-for partnerships (for a study on platform partners, see van der Vlist & Helmond 2021), or discontinuing third-party mone-tisation. In the case of Twitter, the change to X came with the introduction of premium paid for accounts. Twitter premium for users allows for different ways of

being on the platform by enabling the capacity to edit tweets after posting, longer posts and media uploads, verified badges, and reply priorisation. Equally, Twitter introduced different paid for access tiers for developers which allow to widen the seams of posting and getting tweets to and from the API. Seamless data exchange is therefore also a question of financial investment, as access to Twitter's Enterprise API starts at 42.000 $ a month.

(4) But beyond the platform itself, other actors can also contribute to seams, namely through interpretative or practice based seams, which introduce new ways of deploying platform functionality or interpreting its action possibilities, as discussed in the many examples of third-party sources in this paper. Seams may be enacted through means of re-situating content via cross posting across platforms, allowing content created for the logic of one social media to enter another platform. Here, the case of automatically posting from Facebook to Twitter as discussed above is indicative. The moment Facebook shifted its support from individual image posting to album posting, this automation possibility was no longer supported. Cross-posting across platforms thus also enables cross-platform seams where the policies and content strategies of one platform inform others. Each platform has its specific culture of engaging its features, hashtags, media or mentions may have a different meaning or be part of different use and also valuation regimes - opening up the possibility for valuation friction.

(5) Similarly, interpretative seams and frictions may also be created when tweets consisting of highly heterogeneous practices are combined in acts of topical data collection for research, marketing, or other analytical purposes. Previous research engaging with the source metric (Gerlitz & Rieder 2013) has already posed the question how comparable tweets sent manually by human users are to those produced automatically by smart devices, cross posted content from the web or automated bots? Here, research renders the heterogeneity of data more visible.

Drawing on platform research, the paper shows that platforms are by no means seamless intermediaries. Taking on the HCI and infrastructure studies definition of seams as moments of configuration, governance or translation it became clear: Seams can, but do not necessarily have to lead to frictions in valuation. There are cases when seamlessness becomes a source of friction—for instance when the source metric is deprecated. In the case of Twitter sources, frictions occur if sources or their practices do not align with the platform rules or strategies. Rate limits for instance pose a seam, but only become a friction if they limit the activities of third parties or are being breached. Tracing the relation between native and non-native apps over time has shown the rise and fall of popularity of source software—as well as the diversity of platform responds to this. Twitter/X reacted to source popularity in at least three ways: (1) by merging different sources (native and non-native) into one, as in the case of Tablet and Android, (2) by purchasing popular third-party sources such as TweetDeck and maintaining them under their original brand name to capitalise on their popularity and (3) by discontinuing them if they pose a threat to Twitter's business model. Turning to seams in the case of the source metric allowed us to unfold a specific platform-ecological perspective on possible sites of friction in regards to platform APIs.

Conclusion

Within this paper, we explored the relevance of Twitter's source metric as an entry point to trace seams as potential sources of frictions in platform valuation. The starting point has been Elon Musk's announcement to stop displaying the source metric both underneath each tweet and in the API data as well as his suggestion that it only provides information about the device from which people tweet. Considering the fact that the majority of tweets originate from Twitter for iPhone, Twitter Web Client, or Twitter for Android may indeed suggest that the metric mainly tells about the device used. However, as we have shown in this paper, the metric offers an entry point to explore the diverse and highly seamful entanglement between the platform, third-party developers, and their specific valuation of Twitter data. Our aim was to unfold the analytical potential of this metric for empirical platform research and to show how it can function as a lens to explore seams and frictions in platform valuation. We did so by offering a historical perspective on the source metric. Drawing on random English tweet samples from 2009-2021, we analysed the distribution of sources within these tweets, the rise and fall of categories of sources, and their popularity and profiled their use practices.

Our insights showed the changing relation between Twitter's native and third-party sources, the different ways in which Twitter responded to the popularity of sources as well as activity and practice profiles of sources. Sources, our findings indicate, can be characterised by distinct use practices and thus enable different interpretations and valuations of what the platform can be used for.

Seamlessness and seamfulness did not emerge as oppositions, but as relational and dependent on another, as opening the platform to seamless data integration and interpretation is the foundation for new seams but also potential frictions to emerge. The historical perspective allowed us to shift perspective from individual, seemingly seamless and personalised timelines to anonymised historical aggregates of average practices. We looked at Twitter not through the lens of a user but approximated the perspective of the platform. Negotiating sources emerged as a key site of platform politics between the platform's technical capacities and regulation of stakeholder relations and politics.

Reconstructing the use of sources allowed us to show the heterogeneity of Twitter data in regards to Tweet origin, stakeholders and use practices. We propose that the source metrics offered a way of re-situating appearingly comparable, seamless data in the usually obfuscated and highly seamful context of its making. Here we follow recent suggestions that digital data is informed by the situation of its making, whilst these situations are usually obfuscated and difficult to trace (cf.

Clarke et al. 2018; Dieter et al. 2019; Rettberg 2020). Such situated perspectives are also relevant to account for valuation friction, as the situated interplay between actors, data, and seams may result in local and situated frictions. Removing the source metrics not only renders tweets and their data more flat and seamless, it also makes it more difficult to situate data production (Rettberg 2020) and inquire into its frictions. The historical overview was an attempt to re-situate Twitter data, in regards to the origin of its making, the actors involved, but also the historically situated context which is informed by the popularity of other platforms, device cultures and practices of use. The activities of Musk and X, however, show that the platform does invest in seamfulness. As long as platforms like Twitter/X focus on rendering these frictions invisible and platform data seamless, it remains the role of researchers to re-introduce seams as they offer methodological access points to reflect on the distribution of agency between platforms and their stakeholders and to advance critical perspectives on platform police and their political economy (Zuboff 2019).

List of References

Alaimo, C./Kallinikos, J. (2016): "Encoding the Everyday: The Infrastructural Apparatus of Social Data." In: C. Sugimoto/H. Ekbia/M. Mattioli (eds.), Big Data is not a Monolith: Policies, Practices, and Problems. Cambridge MA: MIT Press, pp. 77-90.

Anderson, C. (2004): "The Long Tail." (1 October 2004). Retrieved from http://www.wired.com/wired/archive/12.10/tail.html (accessed: December 12, 2023).

Arrington, M. (2011): "Twitter To Buy TweetDeck For $40 Million—$50 Million." (2 May 2011) Retrieved from https://techcrunch.com/2011/05/02/twitter-to-buy-tweetdeck-for-40-million-50-million/.

Beer, D. (2016): Metric Power. London: Palgrave Macmillan.

Bijker, W. E./Hughes,T. P./Pinch, T. F. (1987): The Social Construction of Technological Systems. New Directions in the Sociology and History of Technology Edited. Cambridge and London: MIT Press.

Bogost, I./Montfort, N. (2009): "Platform Studies: Frequently Questioned Answers." Digital Arts and Culture 2009, December. Retrieved from https://escholarship.org/uc/item/01r0k9br.

Boltanski, L./Thevenot, L. (1991): On Justification. Economies of Worth. Princeton and Oxford: Princeton University Press. https://doi.org/10.1017/CBO9781107415324.004.

Bowker, G./Star, S. L. (1999): Sorting Things Out: Classification and Its Consequences. Cambridge, MA; London: MIT Press.

Bruns, A. (2019): "After the 'APIcalypse': Social Media Platforms and Their Fight Against Critical Scholarly Research.", Information, Communication

& Society, 22(11), pp. 1544–1566. Available at: https://doi.org/10.1080/13691 18X.2019.1637447.

Callon, M./Muniesa, F. (2005): "Peripheral Vision: Economic Markets as Calcula-tive Collective Devices". Organization Studies, 26 (8), pp. 1229–1250. https://doi.org/10.1177/0170840605056393.

Chalmers, M./MacColl, I./Bell, M. (2003): "Seamful Design: Showing the Seams in Wearable Computing." 2003 IEE Eurowearable, pp. 11–16. https://doi.org/10.1049/ic:20030140.

Clarke, A. E./Friese, C./Washburn, R. (2018): Situational Analysis: Grounded Theory after the Interpretive Turn. Second edition. Los Angeles: SAGE.

Dieter, M./Gerlitz, C./Helmond, A./Tkacz, N./van der Vlist, F. N./Weltevrede. E. (2019): "Multi-Situated App Studies: Methods and Propositions". Social Media + Society, 5 (2). https://doi.org/10.1177/2056305119846486.

Dourish, P./Bell, G. (2007): "The Infrastructure of Experience and the Experience of Infrastructure: Meaning and Structure in Everyday Encounters with Space", *Environment and Planning B: Planning and Design*, 34(3), pp. 414–430. https://doi.org/10.1068/b32035t.

Espeland, W. N./Stevens, M.L. (1998): "Commensuration as a Social Process". Annual Review of Sociology, 24 (1), pp. 313–343. https://doi.org/10.1146/annurev.soc.24.1.313.

Gawer, A. (2015): "What Drives Shifts in Platform Boundaries: An Organiza-tional Perspective." Druid Summer Conference 15/2015. Retrieved from http://druid8.sit.aau.dk/druid/acc_papers/yslbxh6uho6lntrgqj23dme9l2bn.pdf.

Gerlitz, C. (2016): "What Counts? Reflections on the Multivalence of Social Media Data." Digital Culture & Society, 2 (2), pp. 19–38. https://doi.org/10.14361/dcs-2016-0203.

Gerlitz, C./Helmond, A./van der Vlist,F.N./Weltevrede, E. (2019): "Regramming the Platform: Infrastructural Relations between Apps and Social Media." Computational Culture, no. 7 (October). Retrieved from http://computational-culture.net/regramming-the-platform/.

Gerlitz, C./Rieder, B. (2013): "Mining One Percent of Twitter: Collections, Base-lines, Sampling". M/C Journal 16 (2). https://doi.org/10.5204/mcj.620.

Gerlitz, C./Rieder, B. (2018): "Tweets Are Not Created Equal: Investigating Twit-ter's Client Ecosystem". International Journal of Communication 12, pp. 528–47. https://doi.org/1932–8036/20180005.

Gerlitz, C./Weltevrede, E. (2019): "What Happens to ANT, and Its Emphasis on the Socio-Material Grounding of the Social, in Digital Sociology?" In: C. Roberts/I. Farias/A. Blok (eds.), Routledge Companion to Actor-Network Theory. London and New York: Routledge, pp. 345-356.

Gillespie, T. (2010): "The Politics of 'Platforms'." New Media & Society, 12(3), pp. 347–364. https://doi.org/10.1177/1461444809342738.

Gorwa, R. (2019): "What Is Platform Governance?" Information, Communication & Society, 22 (6), pp. 854–871. https://doi.org/10.1080/1369118X.2019.1573914.

Halliday, J. (2011): "Twitter Suspends UberTwitter and Twidroyd Apps, Citing Issues 'Affecting Many Users'." (19 February 2011). Retrieved from https://www.theguardian.com/technology/blog/2011/feb/18/twitter-digital-media.

Helmond, A. (2015): "The Platformization of the Web: Making Web Data Platform Ready". Social Media + Society, 1 (2). https://doi.org/10.1177/2056305115603080.

Inman, S./Ribes, D.(2019): " 'Beautiful Seams': Strategic Revelations and Concealments." Proceedings of the 2019 CHI Conference on Human Factors in Computing Systems, 1–14. CHI '19. New York, NY, USA: Association for Computing Machinery. https://doi.org/10.1145/3290605.3300508.

Johnson, B. (2007): "Glitch Leaves 'Private' Twitter Users Exposed to the World." (24 May 2007). Retrieved from https://www.theguardian.com/technology/blog/2007/may/24/twitterglitch

McCosker, A. (2017): "Social Media Work: Reshaping Organisational Communications, Extracting Digital Value", Media International Australia, 163(1), pp. 122–136. https://doi.org/10.1177/1329878X17693702.

Morstatter, F./Pfeffer, J./Liu, H. (2014): "When Is It Biased? Assessing the Representativeness of Twitter's Streaming API." arXiv. Retrieved from http://arxiv.org/abs/1401.7909.

Plantin, J.-C./Lagoze, C./Edwards, P. N./Sandvig, C. (2016): "Infrastructure Studies Meet Platform Studies in the Age of Google and Facebook." New Media & Society, 20(1), pp. 293-310. https://doi.org/10.1177/1461444816661553.

Poell, T./Nieborg, D./van Dijck, J. (2019): "Platformisation". Internet Policy Review, 8 (4). Retrieved from https://policyreview.info/concepts/platformisation.

Power, M. (2004): "Counting, Control, and Calculation: Reflections on Measuring and Management". Human Relations, 57 (6), pp. 765-783.

Puschmann, C./Burgess, J. (2013): "The Politics of Twitter Data". HIIG Discussion Paper Series No. 2013-01, Retrieved from https://ssrn.com/abstract=2206225. https://doi.org/10.2139/ssrn.2206225.

Rettberg, J. W. (2020): "Situated Data Analysis: A New Method for Analysing Encoded Power Relationships in Social Media Platforms and Apps". Humanities and Social Sciences Communications, 7 (1), 5. https://doi.org/10.1057/s41599-020-0495-3.

Robinson, D. (2016): "Text Analysis of Trump's Tweets Confirms He Writes Only the (Angrier) Android Half." (9 August 2016). Retrieved from http://variance-explained.org/r/trump-tweets/.

Rochet, J.-C./Tirole, J. (2006): "Two-Sided Markets : A Progress Report". The RAND Journal of Economics, 37 (3), pp. 645–667. https://doi.org/10.1111/j.1756-2171.2006.tb00036.x.

Star, S. L./Griesemer, J.R. (1989): "Institutional Ecology, 'Translations' and Boundary Objects: Amateurs and Professionals in Berkeley's Museum of Vertebrate Zoology, 1907-39". Social Studies of Science, 19(3), pp. 387-420.

Stark, D. (2009) The Sense of Dissonance: Accounts of Worth in Economic Life. Princeton, N.J.; Woodstock: Princeton University Press.

van der Vlist, F./Helmond, A. (2021): "How Partners Mediate Platform Power: Mapping Business and Data Partnerships in the Social Media Ecosystem." Big Data & Society, 8 (1). https://doi.org/10.1177/20539517211025061.

van der Vlist, F./Helmond, A./Burkhardt, M./Seitz, T. (2022): "API Governance: The Case of Facebook's Evolution" Social Media + Society, 8(2). https://doi.org/10.1177/20563051221108622

van Dijck, J.V. (2011): "Tracing Twitter: The Rise of a Microblogging Platform", International Journal of Media & Cultural Politics, 7(3), pp. 333–348. https://doi.org/10.1386/macp.7.3.333_1.

van Dijck, J./Poell., T. (2016): "Understanding the Promises and Premises of Online Health Platforms", Big Data & Society, 3(1), pp. 1-11. https://doi.org/10.1177/2053951716654173.

van Dijck, J./Poell, T./de Waal, M. (2018): The Platform Society: Public Values in a Connective World. Oxford: Oxford University Press.

Vatin, F. (2013): "Valuation as Evaluating and Valorizing." Valuation Studies, 1(1), pp. 31–50. https://doi.org/10.3384/vs.2001-5992.131131.

Vertesi, J. (2014): "Seamful Spaces: Heterogeneous Infrastructures in Interaction." Science, Technology, & Human Values, 39 (2), pp. 264–284.

Weiser, M. (1999): "The Computer for the 21st Century." ACM SIGMOBILE Mobile Computing and Communications Review, 3 (3), pp. 3–11. https://doi.org/10.1145/329124.329126.

Wiggers, K. (2023): "Twitter Officially Bans Third-Party Clients After Cutting Off Prominent Devs", (20 January 2023). Retrieved from https://techcrunch.com/2023/01/19/twitter-officially-bans-third-party-clients-after-cutting-off-prominent-devs/.

Zuboff, S. (2019): The Age of Surveillance Capitalism: The Fight for a Human Future at the New Frontier of Power. First edition. New York: Public Affairs.

On "Super Likes" and Algorithmic (In)Visibilities

Frictions Between Social and Economic Logics in the Context of Social Media Platforms

Christian Schulz

Abstract

This article explores the frictions between social and economic logics intertwined in the like button. Using a media archaeological perspective, this will first be demonstrated by a forgotten Facebook feature: the "zeldas". These zeldas represented a form of currency within the platform that users could purchase for real money and give as a "super like" for posts. Depending on the number of zeldas in their account, users were free to choose the amount of zeldas they wanted to give for a post. However, indeterminacy of semantic meaning is crucial for creating sociality on platforms, and this project, which can be described as being similar to the potlatch, no longer offered room for this necessary vagueness. In other words, the social logic of the like button with the thumbs-up icon was undermined, even though the zeldas would certainly have enabled more precise user profiling in the algorithmic backend and insofar would have added more economic value to the platform. In the history of the like button, the zeldas represent a source of friction between social and economic logics and show that this conflict is inherent to the development of algorithmic feeds. This case study can therefore be extended to recent developments. Referring to two netnographic observations of influencers who supposedly purchased likes and followers on Instagram, the paper then aims to show that the more semantically explicit a platform unit is, the higher the proportion of economic logic in it, at the expense of the social value of platforms. This is associated with another source of friction between supposedly "authentic" and "fake" user behaviour, which is not only perceived by users as part of an affective attunement and leads to practices of (self-)evaluation and (self)justification. The platforms also use this problematic friction as a justification of neutrality, thereby cementing a narrative of individualisation.

Keywords

Social Media, Like Button, Facebook, Algorithms, Instagram

DOI 10.14361/dcs-2023-0204

DCS | Digital Culture and Society | Vol. 9, Issue 2 | © transcript 2025

Introduction: Social Media Between Social and Economic Logics

Taken literally, social media are media that are used to negotiate the "social", i.e. to establish relationships with other people or to keep them at a distance. Social media can thus be traced back to the oldest human societies. One example is the reciprocal exchange practices of the Trobriand people with shells in the Kula ring, described by Malinowski (2005). These exchange practices in the form of "the gift" (Mauss 2002) have also been repeatedly mentioned in various social media discourses since the early 1990s (e.g. Rheingold 1993, Miller 2011, Jenkins/Ford/Green 2013).

Even in these societies, gifts were imbued with both social and economic logics. Kula, a form of bartering between the tribes of a large area in the south-west Pacific, is one example of this. The tribes constantly exchange two types of objects with each other in a closed cycle: bracelets made of shells (mwali) on the one hand and necklaces made of red shells (soulava) on the other (Malinowski 2005: 62). According to Marcel Mauss, who generalised Malinowski's ethno-graphic observations, socialisation in early societies took place through such gifts, which are theoretically voluntary, but have an inherent compulsion to reciprocate. This is why, in his famous essay, Mauss describes the gift as a "total social fact" and thus as the origin of every form of sociality (2002). Nonetheless, the soci-alities negotiated via gift practices are always interwoven with an economic logic, and Malinowksi made clear that the two spheres of the social and economic in the gift are not easy to separate due to the many transitions and gradations that can also lead to friction (Malinowski 2005: 135).[1]

Such frictional relationships are also central in the context of social media platforms. Here, too, social and economic logics are inextricably linked. Never-theless, there are different frictions between the economic (business) interests of platforms and the social logics that are responsible for creating and negotiating sociality on the platform (e.g. liking, commenting). However, according to Anna Tsing, social and economic logics can be separated for analytical purposes (Tsing 2015: 122). In this article, I will illustrate a few such frictions between social and economic logics in the context of social media in more detail.

The first part of the article is based on a media archaeological approach and shines a light on a largely forgotten tech-historical episode in the history of the like button on Facebook: the "super likes" that were referred to as "zeldas". These "zeldas", which were implemented in 2009 only in A/B test[2] procedures

---

1   The Trobriand distinguish between *kula*, the socialising exchange, and *gimwali*, the barter with other tribes that do not belong to the Kula archipelago (Malinowski 2005: 135).

2   A/B Testing is a widely used method in software development and a way to compare multiple versions of a single variable, for example testing a subject's response to vari-ant A and variant B.

in addition to the like function with the thumbs-up icon, reflect a central friction between economic platform logics and logics of negotiating sociality. Based on the case study of the zeldas, I will show that if they had been implemented, the zeldas would probably have eroded the social value of the standard like button with the thumbs-up icon by allowing posts to be assigned a precise value. Following Paßmann and others (e.g. Paßmann 2018: 148; Paßmann/Schubert 2020: 2951, Sumner/Ruge-Jones/Alcorn 2018: 1452), this would likely have undermined the indeterminacy of the like button, which is so central to the negotiation of the social, thus pitting the economic logic of the platforms against the social logic of the users. Interestingly, more recent developments in social media platforms show a similar tendency towards a determination of platform units. Since 2015, a disambiguation or semantic closure has been observed, which is particularly evident in the cross-platform spread of the like button with the heart icons (Gerlitz/Herma/Kyrimi 2015). But here the underlying algorithmic organising principle erodes the social logic, whereas in the case of the zeldas it would have been the user practices. It will be argued, that the higher degree of semantic determination of platform units is intertwined with an algorithmisation of social media from the very beginning. Insofar as this reflects a central friction between social and economic value production on social media platforms that has a concrete impact on user behaviour.

The second part of the article uses two netnographic vignettes to examine algorithmic (in)visibilities of two influencers on Instagram and their supposed purchase of likes and followers. Behind both cases is an algorithmisation of social media, reflected in the attempts of platforms to obtain an exact data image of users. I argue that this leads to further friction between social and economic logics at the user level. The cases of the two influencers will illustrate how algorithmic feeds and the semantic closure of platform units have led the followers to demand authenticity from the influencers, who, for their part, remain subject to the economic logic of the platform if they want to continue to show up on users' feeds. Finally, I will use the case of Instagram to describe how social media platforms are continually adjusting their policies to account for both social and economic logics, creating problematic narratives of platform neutrality. The study will conclude by tying together the strands in a brief summary.

Facebook's *Project Zelda*

The history of the like button has often been described relatively cursorily (e.g. Gerlitz/Helmond 2013), but it requires an adequate methodological approach, in part because it is difficult to reconstruct the like button's genealogy through the various precursors and influences in the form of social buttons, bookmarking services (e.g. Digg, Reddit) and web counters, among others. A media archaeological approach is particularly suitable for this purpose, as it makes contingencies visible (Schröter 2020) and, in the present case, can provide information as to why the like button was implemented in this way and not otherwise. However, official sources regarding the implementation of the like button are relatively sparse. This applies even more to the largely unknown function of "super likes" on Facebook. Various patents describe the social graph and the timeline, and the algorithmic feed, but without mentioning specific details like the "super likes". However, information about "Project Zelda" was gained through detailed media archaeological research on the history of the like button. The technology forum Quora is a central medium for developers, project managers, and start-ups in general in Silicon Valley, and I used it to collect various entries from programmers involved in the development of the like button. In addition to a timeline for the introduction of the like button by the current technical director at Meta, Andrew "Boz" Bosworth (2014), there are two entries (including screenshots) by Thomas Whitnah (2013a; 2013b), programmer and technical director at Facebook from 2007 to 2017, in which he describes the test rollout and the functionalities of the zeldas. The media archaeological approach dictates, however, that even when the source material is sparse, the gaps are not to be filled with a coherent narration. Instead, the existing material will be made theoretically productive in the following (Schröter 2020).

The now ubiquitous like button was globally rolled out by Facebook in 2009. Despite its seeming simplicity, the development took two years (Bosworth 2014). In the course of this, there were also experiments with a virtual currency, known as "zeldas", shortly before the final release between December 2007 and November 2008. As Whitnah writes in one of his entries, a new "universal feedback interface" (UFI) was developed for the like button in the second half of 2008. This UFI allows users to react directly to posted content in supposedly real time and largely corresponds to what is now the feed or its graphical user interface (GUI) in the form of a never-ending list (Whitnah 2013a). According to Whitnah, the UFI was implemented in all areas of the GUI within a week in preparation for the final like button rollout, but initially without the button itself (ibid.). The designer Soleio Cuervo, who was significantly involved in the final phase of the like button development, presented this new UFI for the first time during an internal presentation on the aforementioned zeldas. These zeldas, probably named after the popular video game of the same name by Nintendo, represented a form of currency within the platform that users could purchase for money and give as a kind of "super like" for posts (Whitnah 2013b).[3] Depending

3   Both the dating app Tinder (since 2015) and TikTok (since 2021) now have a feature referred to as "super likes", but these have little to do with the principle behind the zeldas outlined here. However, there is a similarity between the "gifts" on TikTok (in the form of diamonds) and the zeldas, which users can give to other users if they like their live streams. In this respect, it is interesting that TikTok exclusively links these gifts to live streams, a point that would be worth an in-depth reflection elsewhere.

on the number of zeldas in their account, users were free to choose the amount of zeldas they wanted to give for a post (Fig. 1).

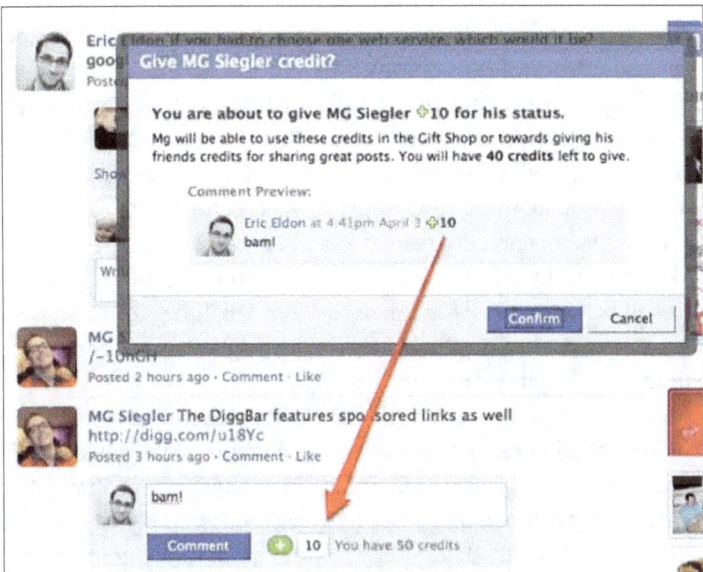

Fig. 1: Facebook's Project Zelda (Source: https://www. quora.com/What-does-Facebook-refer-to-as-UFI-and-what-is-the-acronym-for-Is-this-the-like-comment-section-or-the-photo-details-Is-this-term-used-internally/answer/ Tom-Whitnah)

This currency was rolled out in form of A/B test procedures (only displayed to a small group of users) during the final phase of the like button development, but it was never officially implemented (Whitnah 2013b). Nevertheless, according to Whitnah, the project seems to go back much further in Facebook's history, as he calls it "the codename for a long forgotten project" (Whitnah 2013a). Although this statement can make the zeldas appear to be simply a continuation of the virtual gifts feature first tested by Facebook in spring 2007, where users could send various stickers to other users in a similar way for money (Arrington 2007), the situation is more complex.[4]

In his platform biography authorised by Facebook, David Kirkpatrick reveals that Mark Zuckerberg discussed the "potlatch" in an evening conversation with with him (Kirkpatrick 2011: 287). Although Zuckerberg did not explicitly refer to Marcel Mauss (2002), who described this extreme form of a combative reciprocal

---

4   Significantly, the virtual gift store was then shut down a little over a year after the like button was rolled out, according to the priority of the news feed and like button. See Kincaid 2010.

exchange practice, a closer look at Mauss' descriptions is helpful. The potlatch is a system of ostentatious gift distribution in the context of which gifts are given to guests who always belong to a different group than the hosts. These gifts are perceived as payment for a service rendered by the guests, which, in addition to having a material aspect, fulfils above all a legal function: it consists in testifying to and symbolically conveying the transfer of titles, names, or even privileges within the group of hosts (Hamberger 2012). This function is crucial for the reproduction of the group and, therefore, for sociality. Mauss described this practice as a "monstrous product of the system of presents" (Mauss 2002: 54). In the context of archaic societies, this practice sometimes did not even stop at a ruinous expenditure or killing and in this way established a relationship of exchange that was further fuelled by the rivalrous moment (see also Quadflieg 2019: 217). Similarly, Kirkpatrick quotes Zuckerberg in his book: "'The highest status goes to those who give the most away'" (Kirkpatrick 2010: 287).

Such gifts, the size of which could have been determined by the users themselves, would also have been possible with the currency of the zeldas on Facebook and may have been the central idea behind this experiment. Zuckerberg envisioned a gift economy based on complete transparency, in which everyone could see everyone else's posts (ibid: 287). A first attempt to implement this was made a short time later in the context of Beacon.[5] With Beacon, online purchases, comments, and posts by Facebook users on external third-party websites participating in the system were made visible to other Facebook users using web cookies. It is interesting to note that Facebook had already used the Beacon system to test the dynamics of user influence on other users. Against this backdrop, it is not surprising that Project Zelda was again discussed internally during developing the like button. After all, the news feed was supposed to enable just that on the user level as a system for creating order: every user was to see all relevant posts.

Given this, the question arises as to why Facebook decided not to roll out the currency of the zeldas as super likes beyond small A/B test procedures. The question becomes more pressing in light of Zuckerberg's statements that for him, this system also represents an alternative to the existing market economy, which is not coincidentally reminiscent of the early network utopias of the 1990s (e.g. Barlow 1996). Zuckerberg uses similarly utopian rhetoric when he sees in his like-feed system nothing less than the possibility of simulating in the platform context what would also be possible on a societal level: an alternative economy. He describes this to Kirkpatrick as follows:

---

5   Beacon was an advertisement system that sent data from external websites to Facebook for the purpose of allowing targeted advertisements and allowing users to share their activities with their friends.

"When there's more openness, with everyone being able to express their opinion very quickly, more of the economy starts to operate like a gift economy. It puts the onus on companies and organisations to be more good, and more trustworthy. It's really changing the way that governments work. A more transparent world creates a better-governed world and a fairer world." (Kirkpatrick 2010: 287f.)

This reveals the naïve belief in progress with regard to the positive efficacy of its own technologies, which is quite typical for Silicon Valley advocates. However, it also brings up the associated problems such as scaling with regard to a globally functioning economic system. This is the case because, according to Zucker-berg, the like-feed system is nothing less than a simulation of an alternative gift economy on a societal level. Situating Project Zelda in this context may therefore not only allow us to find out why the project was never realised beyond A/B test procedures. Rather, a central friction between social and economic logics already seems to be emerging here which is also important for understanding the functioning of contemporary algorithmic social media.

Taking a closer look at this requires a somewhat more precise recourse to Marcel Mauss and the relationship between gift and money that he addresses or, in other words, the relationship between ritual-social and exchange-oriented-economic logic. As pointed out in the introduction, social and economic logics in the context of social media are always mutually dependent and cannot be separated. Although this position can be found in Malinowski's work (2005) and is also predominant in research on the gift, it is not uncontroversial and there are other positions.[6] Marcel Hénaff, for example, strongly advocates for a distinction between social and economic logic (2010: 313). Additionally, for the present context, it makes sense to keep this distinction for analytical purposes, as suggested by Anna Tsing (2015: 122). Tsing sees the dichotomy of gift and commodity economies, for all their conflations, as a heuristic tool to better capture certain aspects of this relationship analytically (ibid: 122). With regard to archaic societies, Malinowski, to whom Mauss refers as a central source in his essay, uses the concept of money primarily as a measure of value to determine worth (Mauss 2007: 104). In his *Manual of Ethnography*, Mauss writes: "Economic phenomena are defined [...] by the presence of the notion of value" (Mauss 2007: 98). This notion of value refers to a general concept of value. According to Mauss, and here he differs from Malinowski, a general notion of value is also a prerequisite for the potlatch as an extreme form of gift practices. Without a vague "price concept" of any kind, the potlatch system would simply collapse, because the inherent overbid-ding structure could not be perceived as such by the parties involved (Quadflieg

---

6   There is a long debate in cultural anthropology about the separation of "gift" and "commodity", which corresponds to the separation into social and economic logic. For an overview, see Rus 2008.

2019: 245). Thus, such a concept of value is a logical precondition for an exchange to be possible at all, whether in the form of gifts or commodities (ibid: 245).

It is this connection between the "total social fact" (Mauss 2002) of giving and the fact of money—in short, the relation between social and economic logic—that shows a parallel between what Zuckerberg wanted to simulate with his like-feed system and what he believed was possible on a societal level. However, I suggest that Project Zelda indicates that this transfer did not succeed so easily and poses a whole series of problems, not only in terms of scaling, but also in terms of algorithmisation. This is largely because of the monetisation strategy of the platform that stands behind it. The unrealised project, which was basically intended to allow users to outbid each other in the sense of a potlatch, was tested between December 2007 and November 2008. In a short chronology about the development of the like button by one of the central programmers, Andrew "Boz" Bosworth (2014) wrote that during this period, smaller implementations were tested internally by both the news feed team and the ads team. These were only displayed to the users who participated in the test and were not publicly visible to everyone else. However, Bosworth stated that the test proved inefficient due to the functionality of the feed (ibid.). It is more than likely that one of these tested implementations was the zeldas, so Bosworth's following statement is particularly interesting. In the very paragraph which addresses the period between December 2007 and November 2008, he writes: "'The ads team implementation [...] helps demonstrate that clicks do not always correlate with a user-supplied quality score [...]'" (Bosworth 2014). Basically, Bosworth is addressing nothing more than an indeterminacy or disambiguation in the semantic meaning of likes. That is, users click on the like button for various reasons (appreciation, bookmarking, irony, etc.). And exactly this indeterminacy in semantic meaning is crucial for establishing sociality on the platform according to Paßmann and others (e.g. Paßmann 2018: 148, Paßmann and Schubert 2020: 2951, Sumner, Ruge-Jones and Alcorn 2018).

According to the programmer Thomas Whitnah (2013b), in the test runs of Project Zelda, it was possible to react to shared content via likes and super likes (i.e. the zeldas) (see Fig. 1). It is likely that in that context, the zeldas, with their money-like units, would have undermined the like function with the thumbs-up icon. This would have led to liking no longer being vague and would have meant that it had less social value. This is because users could have used the zeldas to give an exact amount of likes for a post, which would have granularised the gesture of liking to a certain extent through the various self-selected amounts, severely impairing interpretative flexibility. After all, who would spend money to buy super likes only to use them ironically or as bookmarks? This is at least highly doubtful, because this ambiguity of meaning, as one of the central features of the like button, would no longer have existed with such a very concrete economisation of the social, or at least only to a very limited extent. In other words, the zeldas would have undermined the indeterminacy of likes, which is so crucial for sociality on social media platforms. Because the zeldas were implemented in the tests in addition to the regular like button (hence the "super likes"), they can be read not only as an economisation of the social, but rather as an undermining of social logic. The super-like feature would have allowed users to set a very specific, self-selected amount for a post. This would have given Facebook and its algorithms much more precise information about how much value users attributed to a certain piece of content. As a result, Facebook would have obtained a much more accurate data profile regarding its users' preferences.[7] This would certainly have served the platform's economic interests when displaying appropriate advertising for users. At the same time, however, there would have been a significant risk that users would have surrendered to an economic logic of overbidding, which in turn would have undermined the social value. This can be perfectly summarised with a quote from a text by Anna Tsing in which she reflects on the relation between commodities and gifts: "'Assessment work erases gifts'" (Tsing 2013: 39). Or to put it another way, the granularity of super likes would have gradually erased the platform's social logic.

Semantic Closure in the Meaning of the Like Button

These two functions, the like button in the form of the thumbs-up icon and the clearly definable zeldas, represent an initial pivot in the history of the like button, highlighting the friction between economic and social logics and showing that this type of friction is inherent in the development of algorithmic (news) feeds. Interestingly, however, the implementation of such a like-feed system on almost all platforms is associated with a semantic closure (and thus a loss of vagueness) or disambiguation in the meaning of the like button. This fundamental friction, which to a certain extent arose from the "super like" and the goal of obtaining more precise user data, is now returning across platforms in the form of an alignment of the like button with the heart icon.

First, it is important to emphasise again that these logics, despite the distinction made here for analytical purposes, are not separable. Social logics always have economic logics at work and vice versa. The potlatch as an extreme example illustrates this, since with this outbidding competition, sociality is nevertheless also negotiated, albeit in a highly aggressive way. However, with reference to the

7   There are studies (most prominently Kosinski/Stillwell/Graepel 2013) that show a fundamental correlation between just a few likes and a precise data profile, including sexual orientation or alcohol dependency. However, the models in these studies have proven to be low performing (e.g. Sumpter 2018) and inaccurate and must therefore be regarded as part of a Cambridge Analytica PR narrative, not least because the main authors of the studies were leading figures in the company at the time.

platform units and the latest developments in the area of the like button with a cross-platform institutionalisation of the heart icon, it can be formulated: the more semantically closed a platform unit is, the higher its proportion of economic logic. This is precisely what the introduction of the algorithmic feed on other social media platforms and the accompanying observable changes in the semantic closure of the like button with the heart icon seem to show.

Twitter/X can be taken as a prime example of this. In 2015, in the course of the change from a chronological timeline to an algorithmically curated timeline based on popularity and relevance, Twitter/X changed the "fav" (star icon) button to a heart button, which was described as a like button. Research on fav practices has shown that the fav button was characterised by a structural interpretative flexibility that went far beyond "faving" (e.g. Meier, Elsweiler, and Wilson 2014, Paßmann 2018). In that sense, the heart icon represented a semantic closure in the meaning of the like button, because it is much harder to like something ironically with the heart icon than with the thumbs-up icon, or it is sometimes even impossible due to the more emotional/affective connotation that goes along with the heart icon (Schulz 2023b: 144-148). This change annoyed large parts of the Twitter community (Parkinson 2015). In a video that accompanied the introduction of the like button, Twitter then highlighted precisely this interpretive flexibility (Fig. 2), showing that such considerations of indeterminacy and vagueness play a central role within the platforms (Kumar 2015). However, in contrast to Twitter's statements and following Carolin Gerlitz et al. (2015), this also limits the indeterminacy or ambiguity of liking on Twitter, as the focus is exclusively on positive affects. This means that certain liking practices that do not fit this positive connotation are no longer possible.

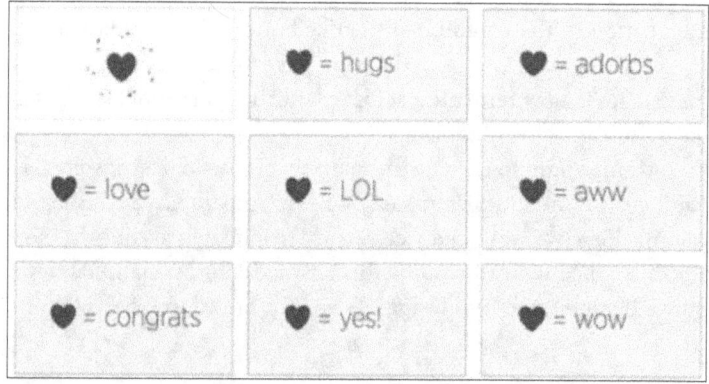

Fig. 2: Possible meanings of hearts on Twitter/X
(Source: https://www.pinterest.de/pin/
news-about-twitter-hearts-on-twitter-58054282674429041)

In line with this disambiguation in semantic meaning, Facebook introduced further emoji reactions in early 2016, adding five more emotional reactions to the standard like: love, wow, haha, sad, and angry. The heart icon was introduced as the "love" reaction. With the beginning of the COVID-19 pandemic, a hug emoji was also introduced in April 2020 (with a smaller heart icon) (Fig. 3).

*Fig. 3: Facebook reactions since April 2020 (Source: https://
www.meedia.de/marken/neue-reactions-auf-facebook-und-
im-messenger-verfuegbar-25aa126aa064c853fda6057b89a8d9
af)*

On Instagram, the heart has always been the standard icon for the like. Instagram now also allows quick access to emojis, at least in the comments section. However, the regular like on Instagram directly under a post still consists of the heart icon, which is even more closed and affective in its semantic meaning than the Facebook like in the form of the thumbs-up icon or the former Twitter fav with the star icon. Nonetheless, what can be observed here is an alignment in the symbolism of likes on all major platforms in the form of the heart icon, which means that there is a tendency toward closure in the semantic meaning across platforms. This is quite directly linked to the introduction of algorithmic feeds and in some ways can be seen as a return to the granularity that the zeldas would have enabled years earlier.

The like button with the little heart icon gives the platform algorithms a clear (positive) signal and thus reduces the ambiguity of user reactions. This is certainly the most obvious and ambitious on Facebook, where the heart icon was introduced along with some other emojis that allow Facebook to create a more accurate data profile of its users. In addition, the integration of the same like button as on Instagram (heart icon) potentially enables cross-platform merging of user data in one social graph at Meta/Facebook. So what can be observed here across platforms is a tendency to disambiguate likes, which can also be described as granularisation (from a platform perspective). The crucial difference to the zeldas here is that the semantic closure is accompanied by an affective attunement, which users may experience differently depending on their situation.[8] However, all users of a platform have the same like and/or emojis buttons that shape this affective attunement and have to deal with the same algorithmic logics behind it.

This leads to an intensification of the friction between social and economic value production. However, this fundamental friction, which to a certain extent

---

8   I borrow the term 'affective attunement' from Jan Slaby. According to Slaby affective attunement means that the world of subjects can only be meaningfully experienced and described in a form of radical situatedness (Slaby 2017: 11).

arose from the "super like" and the aim of obtaining more precise user data, is now returning across platforms in the form of an alignment of the like button with the heart icon. At the user level, this is then reflected in economies of visibility and further frictions between "authentic" and "fake" user behaviour. This manifests itself both in users' insecurities or mistrust of the platform and its algorithms and of each other, and leads to practices of (self-)evaluation and (self-)justification. I will now try to show this using two small netnographic vignettes of influencer practices on Instagram, because social and economic logics culminate to a certain extent in the social figure of the influencer (Hund 2023: 98), which is why they are particularly suitable for analysing this point of friction at the user level.

"That's the Algorithm! Sometimes it Just Does What it Wants"

The empirical vignettes in this section are based on a larger netnography (Kozinets 2009), which I conducted from 2016 to 2018 and for which a total of 100 Instagram influencers from Germany were netnographically observed periodically. This netnographical approach specialises in the (participatory) observation of online interactions of specific users or groups, but does not exclude offline interactions (e.g. interviews). The study included phases of passive observation and direct interaction with these influencers, focusing on their selfie practices. The corpus was compiled using a now defunct third-party tool (*InfluencerDB*), which could filter Instagram accounts according to various search criteria (e.g. hashtags, geodata). As the focus of the larger netnography was on selfie practices, the two actors discussed in this section were also included in the corpus via a search with the tool for the most frequently used hashtags together with selfies at the time. Both users frequently posted selfies and were observed (participant observation) during the period between 2016 and 2018 (see also Schulz 2023b: 293–300).

In October 2017, I observed a discussion between the food blogger @alltags-gold and her followers on her account, which was a perfect example of economies of visibility. These economies of visibility are the result of the friction between social and economic value creation, as fed by the changes outlined in the previous section and generated by the platforms due to the algorithmisation of social media. In this respect, it is precisely this implementation of algorithmic feeds (and the cross-platform proliferation of the little heart icon that symbolises this) that leads to distrust and demand for "authenticity" on the part of users, as these two empirical vignettes will attempt to show.

The user @alltagsgold posted a selfie on October 7, 2017, which has since been deleted, presumably showing her in her bedroom. She was wearing casual clothes with a hoodie, and in the background, there was a mirror that showed that the shot was a selfie. The caption said: "I'm a little perplexed why your comments and likes have dropped so much lately. Are you even seeing my posts anymore? [...] Are you guys having similar problems?"[9]

What initially looked like a personal address to followers about the lack of engagement on their part turned out to be a reaction to the lack of likes and comments in the wake of the feed change, as the following comment from a follower showed: "I feel the same way. I'm also very sad. I feel like Instagram has changed something again. I still see your photos, but super delayed and not always, I guess". The strange feeling that the platform must have changed "something" was ubiquitous, as further comments under the posted selfie revealed: "I'd just be interested to know what the reason is", @alltagsgold wrote in response. And, according to another follower, in general "'it's unfair, because sometimes you put so much effort into a photo, which then gets so few likes'". A third follower finally pointed out: "That's the algorithm! Sometimes it just does what it wants".

In a way, this last remark suggests a kind of temporary loss of control over "the" algorithm, which sometimes simply "goes nuts" and then just does what it wants. This humanises the algorithmic systems in the users' imaginations (Bucher 2018: 113-116, Schulz 2023a). What is rather interesting here is that the statement suggests control over "the" algorithm (and that means the platform) as the normal state, and that it is only through this moment of apparent irritation that agency is delegated to the algorithm. The gesture of humanisation in the users' imaginations with an autonomous will ("sometimes it just does what it wants") attributed to the technology serves here as the simplest conceivable form of an explanation for the visibility problems lamented by @alltagsgold.

But besides this supposedly simple explanation of increasing algorithmic invisibility, this discussion reveals even more. Another follower, also a food blogger according to her profile information (but with far fewer followers than @alltagsgold), was much more sceptical and asked in the comments under the selfie how she got so many followers in the first place. To this @alltagsgold responded: "I've been posting for a long time & also often recipes, so the followers went up quickly for a while [...]. However, I think that many followers are bots or have never made themselves known in any way".

@alltagsgold's answer that many of her followers are "bots" implicitly addressed a central problem of social media platforms after their algorithmisation to increase economic value production: the loss of trust in the functioning of the platforms and their algorithms, as well as in the motives of other users. The fact that it is supposedly no longer easy for users to recognise whether real people are behind user accounts and, above all, what motivations these people may have, has a lot to do with the spread of algorithmic organising principles and unambiguous signals from users (nothing else is represented by the cross-platform spread of

---

9   All of the following quotes from this second case study are originally in German and
     I have translated them.

the heart icon) in the context of social media. The aim here is not to expose @alltagsgold in any way or even accuse her of possibly purchasing likes or followers. This question is secondary for media theoretical purposes. What is much more interesting from a theoretical perspective is that the explanation given by the user for the supposedly limited visibility is based on another source of friction within the tension between economic and social value production: the problematic and rather artificial dichotomy of authentic vs. fake. This dichotomy leads to a friction between (self-)evaluation and (self-)justification between influencers and their followers. But even more important, it marks a shift from social to primarily economic logics in the form of a desirable algorithmic visibility that emerges in this example and reproduces to a certain extent the structural problem of social media platforms identified in the first part with Project Zelda. However, where the potlatch-like system of super likes would have left no room for indeterminacy and thus a social logic through users' overbidding practices, it is now the algorithmic feed and the hearts inextricably linked to it that limit these ambiguities and create distrust among users. Social logic is increasingly undermined as a result, as from now on the users focus on evaluating and justifying visibility or invisibility. This is illustrated best by another user.

"I'm Telling You: Everyone is Doing it!"

At the beginning of August 2018, I observed a series of Instagram stories by an influencer named @anna_ix_, of which I took screenshots. She posted several story clips in which she took a stand on the issue of purchased reach and justified to her followers why many of them are from Brazil and speak Portuguese. During this, she admitted that she bought likes a few months ago and that the followers were most likely obtained through tools that automatically give likes and follow other accounts. She stated: "I don't think there are any bloggers anywhere who have never done this, because there are just too many of us now. I'm telling you, everyone is doing it" In particular, the discrepancy between the high number of followers and the constant interaction rates on her posts was a problem for some of her followers, to which she resolutely replied that she could not explain it. All she could say was that it was up to everyone whether or not they chose to believe her. "All of you know how hard it is to grow on Instagram, and I think many of you just don't have enough patience", she stated in an attempt to deflect the problem from herself.

However, in terms of media theory, it is not the number of followers that is interesting at this point, nor whether they were dwindling. The interesting thing here is rather the fact that @anna_ix_ is urged by her followers to explain her statistics and in particular the many followers from Brazil, as she states in one of her story clips. This stands in contrast to the first example of @alltagsgold, as in this case a comment only critically inquired how the user got so many followers at all. The fact that @anna_ix_ had to justify herself to the followers who confronted her with her statistical inconsistencies is only possible because a few of her followers probably use easily accessible software tools and apps and closely scrutinise the likes and followers.[10] How else could they have had such detailed statistics on @anna_ix's account?

So what the followers of @anna_ix_ are also addressing is a more or less precise knowledge of the effectiveness of the algorithms and how they work. This knowledge is disseminated by official Instagram blog posts (e.g. Mosseri 2021) or multipliers such as influencers with high reach (e.g. Gevinson 2019). Thus, the users imagine how the algorithm functions and how this affects rankings (Bucher 2018: 113-116, Schulz 2023a). In addition, these user assumptions about the functioning of the algorithms subsequently lead to users buying likes and followers or using certain tools to optimise reach (automated follow-unfollow) for the purpose of achieving a better ranking and associated visibility in the explore feed. Here, the loss of trust among users already noted in the first example, is exacerbated and leads to a climate of distrust that undermines social logic in the long term.

Instagram Platform Guidelines, Policies and Strategies

Instagram is well aware of this practice. In the wake of the alleged Cambridge Analytica scandal in 2018, Instagram frequently announced restrictions on the API (application programming interface), which is the interface for developers of third-party apps (Gummadi 2018). During this process, Instagram also repeatedly stated that comments from social bots and purchased likes would soon no longer be possible. So far, however, such an undertaking has not been successful in the long term, and we should have serious doubts as to whether it should be banned at all from the platform's point of view. After all, this practice also generates many follow-up interactions, albeit in the short term. It is therefore likely that, even if the platform were to take action against this type of fraud, in the end, only the so-called clickworker industry, with its mostly inhumane working conditions, would benefit. This can happen in two ways: on the one hand for platforms in the form of outsourced content moderation (Gillespie 2018, Roberts 2019), and on the other hand for account farms that generate fake profiles (verified by cell phones) with false identities and resell them to click farms, from which they reach influencers in the form of purchased likes and followers (Clark 2015). This aspect illus-

---

10   For example, there is a free version of the easy-to-use tool *HypeAuditor*. This is a software tool that has been available since 2018 and is primarily used by companies in the field of influencer marketing. It is dedicated to the precise analysis of accounts and their reach and aims to enable companies to identify accounts with purchased reach followers and likes without much effort. See also https://hypeauditor.com/

trates once again that the underlying structural problem is more complex and is not primarily concerned with social bots or "dishonest" users who use apparently questionable software tools to gain more reach. Rather, the problem is inherent to platforms based on algorithmic organising principles, and that is precisely why Instagram has repeatedly taken public action against bot factories and click farms, to avoid risking user migration to other social media platforms. What we can observe here is a problematic economy around liking, which is constantly being penalised by the platforms. Ultimately, however, it is precisely the algorithmic visibility regime installed by the platforms through the like-feed system that creates certain economies, such as influencers and clickworkers, both of which undermine the sociality of platforms in different ways. Instagram's changes to an algorithmic explore feed and the controversies surrounding supposed authenticity are effects of this, as they manifest the various frictions between the social and the economic. Therefore, that it is precisely these frictions that force the platforms to constantly balance the conflict between social and economic logics of value creation.

In this respect, it makes sense from the perspective of the platforms that, as part of an A/B test, the number of likes received by selected accounts has no longer been visible since the end of 2019 (Constine 2019) and that it is now possible for users to deactivate the number of received likes from other accounts in the account settings. The more recent revelations surrounding the Facebook leaks (Haugen 2023) show that Meta is aware of the negative effects of algorithmic feeds, indicating that these additions to the account settings (such as deactivating received likes) must also be seen primarily as a PR campaign. This seems to be, in part, Instagram's way of picking up on what media artist Ben Grosser has been developing since 2012 with the Demetricator tool for Facebook, Twitter, and Instagram (Grosser 2014). Nonetheless, this does not change the way the algorithmic ranking system works because the number of hearts is, of course, only hidden on the GUI of the respective users, and thus only at the frontend of the interface.

I argue that these kinds of PR campaigns (such as hiding likes in the interface) by Instagram correspond to a narrative of platform neutrality intended to deliberately present itself as a morally superior authority. For example, Instagram specifically targets the aspect of authenticity when deleting bot accounts, provided users are notified.[11] This insistence on authenticity is often accompanied by talk of "organic growth", which even the corresponding third-party apps now use to advertise the quality of their bots.[12] In this way, Instagram ultimately establishes a narrative based on the problematic dichotomy of authenticity vs. fake or organic vs. artificial, which not only obscures Instagram's own business interest, but also

---

11 "Reducing inauthentic activity on Instagram" (19 November 2018). Retrieved from: https://abo ut.instagram.com/de-de/blog/announcements/reducing-inauthentic-activity-on-instagram

12 "16 Best Instagram Growth Services for Organic Followers" (Updated 17 October 2023). Retrieved from: https://seodigitalgroup.com/best-instagram-growth-services/

attempts to negate its curatorial role, reproducing a narrative of neutrality that is characteristic of so many platforms. Caitlin Petre et al. aptly refer to this behaviour as "platform paternalism" and note very similar strategies at Facebook and Google as well (Petre/Duffy/Hund 2019). According to this narrative of neutrality, only third-party apps and the users who use these apps for likes and follower purchases are to be held responsible for undermining trust and, therefore, the social logics on the platform. The API restrictions announced (and sometimes implemented) at regular intervals, which would render such third-party apps functionless, illustrate that such one-sided narratives do not necessarily create more trust among users. This is why influencers increasingly use strategies that minimise dependence on changes on the platform side or third-party apps.

Against this backdrop, it was probably no coincidence that influencer @anna_ix_ invited other high-reach influencers to a meeting in Düsseldorf at the end of August 2018, as I observed in another story series. The meeting was organised at short notice, according to @anna_ix_, interestingly shortly after another announcement from Instagram that core API features for such tools would be limited until December 2018. For this meeting, two entrance tickets were raffled off via Instagram story in the days prior. In addition to food and goodie bags for the participants, the informal offline event allowed attendees to get to know one another (most of them did not know each other offline before). This meeting also aimed to create synergy effects among each other in terms of followers, which would ultimately reduce the dependence on the corresponding software tools.

In addition, there are two mysterious fanpages for @anna_ix_, one of which has existed since July 2018 (first visible post on 9 July 2018). The other account has existed since April 2017 (first visible post on 9 April 2017), when @anna_ix_ did not yet have 1,000 followers. This suggests that @anna_ix_ runs or has run the latter fanpage herself, which fits with the fact that from the beginning she was interested in quickly acquiring as many followers as possible. In this respect, the newer fan page also seems to be part of this strategy to suggest as much influence as possible in order to get "real" followers quickly.

What the examples reveal is that, overall, the algorithmic technologies behind Instagram can directly undermine trust in the platforms' infrastructures. On the one hand, there is a loss of trust in the algorithms themselves, as shown by the first case of @alltagsgold, who suddenly felt that her posts were only reaching a fraction of her followers and who therefore asked her community if they were even seeing her posts anymore. The simplest explanation for this, which the users developed together in the comments under the post, was ultimately an all-determining algorithm that was imagined in a humanisation gesture and thus just "sometimes does what it wants". On the other hand, the initial doubts of other users could be seen in these comments, as they cautiously suggested that @alltagsgold may have cheated a bit with the followers and like numbers of her account.

Regardless of whether this was actually the case, a structural problem of social media based on algorithmic organising principles can be addressed beyond this observation. As the example of the user @anna_ix_ has also shown, this has a lot to do with an undermining of social value on the part of the users, who can now even prove the authenticity of influencers' statements themselves by using various software tools.

Unlike Facebook's Project Zelda, however, this is a loss of trust fuelled primarily by the platforms' algorithmic organising principles and the resulting invisibilities among users. While Facebook itself had argued during testing the zeldas that the project would have negatively influenced the organisation of the feed (then still called UFI), it is now the algorithmic feed itself that undermines the social value of the platforms. As has been shown, this leads to an affective attunement of mistrust that not only negatively affects the social logics of the platforms, but can also reduce the overall attractiveness of the social media platform for users because it is no longer primarily about negotiating sociality, but about maximising visibility. This apparently manifests itself not only in a migration to other social media such as Snapchat or TikTok, but also explains the regular and perfectly choreographed bot deletions on the part of Instagram. These are intended to counteract precisely such a loss of trust and strengthen social value.

On a structural level and from a more theoretical viewpoint, it can be seen here that when ranking algorithms are interposed between the social negotiation processes of users, this is tantamount to a shift toward economic value production on and for the platforms. That is the case because these algorithms are primarily programmed according to the economic interests of platform corporations. This leads users to seek tactics to gain more visibility on the platforms, such as resorting to automated follow-unfollow tools or buying likes and followers. However, this also results in users no longer being able to distinguish clearly between other users and supposed social bots or automated accounts. At the account level, it is therefore no longer so easy for users to see whether and to what extent a real person is behind an account. Not least, this is the case because their behaviours are aligned in many respects by automated follow-unfollow tools and users leave their accounts to automation for certain periods of time. Through these tools, the user accounts become human-bot assemblages, in a sense. As a result, the described affective attunement arouses mistrust among users, who in turn develop verification strategies, whether in the form of sceptical questions or with the help of tools for analysing accounts.

However, this shows frictions that are very similar to those of Facebook's Project Zelda. The crucial difference is that, in the case of the zeldas, the economic logic would have been strengthened only through user practices and without algorithmic mediation, while within the like-feed systems the algorithmic organising principles lie at the core of the friction between social and economic values, in favour of the latter. This is indicated at the frontend of the interfaces by the cross-platform alignment in the semantic meaning of likes. As has been shown, uncertainty increases on both sides: on the side of the users, who in addition to a general mistrust are sometimes no longer able to clearly distinguish between automated accounts and humans and therefore use certain tools. And on the side of the platforms, which now have to constantly rebalance the relationship between economic value production and social value through widely announced deletions of alleged social bots or new platform guidelines that highlight "authenticity".

Conclusion

The examples and descriptions of Project Zelda and the two influencers in this article have demonstrated that there are multiple sources of friction between social and economic logics, and that these have been inherent to platforms at least since the introduction of the like button and algorithmic feeds. As shown in the first part using the example of Project Zelda, the social value of the platform with the super likes would probably have been undermined by the disambiguation of user reactions and a potentially associated logic of outbidding, similar to the potlatch. Interestingly, this disambiguation returned a few years later with the semantic closure in the form of a cross-platform alignment of the like button with the little heart icon and an underlying algorithmisation. It could therefore be said that the more semantically closed a platform unit is, the higher the proportion of economic logic in it.

Nevertheless, it is important to point out once again that although algorithmisation plays a central role, it is not solely responsible for the predominant spread of economic logics. That would be too simplistic and just another techno-determinist narrative. Rather, and this is why the comparison to Project Zelda is so important, the same motivation of a more accurate data representation of users underlies the cross-platform introduction of algorithmic feeds and the unification policy of likes. In both cases, the goal is apparently a disambiguation of single-user reactions to get a real-world image of the users that is as accurate as possible.

However, as the influencer examples in the second part reveal, this also leads to an affective attunement, which is fuelled by the friction between social and economic value production and is reflected at the user level in a loss of trust in platforms and other users due to an economy of (in)visibility. This is precisely what marks another friction analysed in the text between supposedly "authentic" and "fake" user behaviour, which manifests itself concretely in practices of (self-)evaluation and (self-)justification, as the examples of the influencers @alltagsgold and @anna_ix_ have demonstrated. This problematic dichotomy between "authentic" and "fake" user behaviour is in turn reproduced by the platforms themselves, which attempt to balance out the friction between distrust and "authenticity" that arises among users and establish a narrative of neutrality on this basis.

Ultimately, this can also be seen as an attempt to avoid structural criticism by specifically denouncing the misbehaviour of individual users through the platform's guidelines. For future social media research, this also illustrates how important it is to adopt a cross-platform perspective that does not postulate structural determinisms, nor does it get lost in ever more detailed descriptions of individual cases. The concept of friction can be an adequate tool for such analyses, as it can be made productive both on an (infra-)structural level, as demonstrated in this article using the example of Project Zelda, and on a user level, as the second example of influencers' justification practices has shown.

List of References

Arrington, M. (2007): "Facebook Testing Virtual Gifts" (8 February 2007). Retrieved from: https://techcrunch.com/2007/02/07/facebook-testing-virtual-gifts/.

Bosworth, A. (2014): "What's the history of the Awesome Button (that eventually became the Like Button) on Facebook?" (16 October 2014). Retrieved from: https://www.quora.com/Whats-the-history-of-the-Awesome-Button-that-eventually-became-the-Like-button-on-Facebook.

Bucher, T. (2018) : If...Then. Algorithmic Power and Politics, Oxford: Oxford University Press.

Clark, D. B. (2015): "The Bot Bubble. How click farms have inflated social media currency" (21 April 2015). Retrieved from: https://newrepublic.com/article/121551/bot-bubble-click-farms-have-inflated-social-media-currency.

Constine, J. (2018): "How Instagram's algorithm works" (01 June 2018). Retrieved from: https://techcrunch.com/2018/06/01/how-instagram-feed-works/.

Constine, J. (2019): "Instagram tests hiding Like counts globally" (14 November 2019). Retrieved from: https://techcrunch.com/2019/11/14/instagram-private-like-counts/

Gerlitz, C./Helmond, A. (2013): "The like economy: Social buttons and the data-intensive web". New Media & Society 15 (8), pp. 1348-1365.

Gerlitz, C./Herma, L./Kyrimi, C.G. (2015): "The disambiguation of social buttons". Pop-Zeitschrift (16 November 2015). Retrieved from: https://pop-zeitschrift.de/2015/11/16/social-media-november/.

Gevinson, T. (2019): "What Would I Be Without Instagram? An Investigation". The Cut (16 September 2019). Retrieved from: https://www.thecut.com/2019/09/who-would-tavi-gevinson-be-without-instagram.html.

Gillespie, T. (2018): Custodians of the Internet: platforms, content moderation, and the hidden deciscions that shape social media, New Haven: Yale University Press.

Grosser, B. (2014): "What Do Metrics Want? How Quantification Prescribes Social Interaction on Facebook". Computational Culture 4, 9. Retrieved from: http://computationalculture.net/what-do-metrics-want/.

Gummadi, R. (2018): "Instagram Graph API Launches and Instagram API Platform Deprecation". Facebook Developers Blog (30 January 2018). Retrieved from: https://developers.facebook.com/blog/post/2018/01/30/instagram-graph-api-updates/

Hamberger, K. (2012): "Potlatsch und Verwandtschaft". In: P. Berz/M. Kubaczek/E. Laquièze-Waniek/D. Unterholzener (eds.), Spielregeln. 25 Aufstellungen. Eine Festschrift für Wolfgang Pirchner. Zurich and Berlin: diaphanes, pp. 131-140.

Haugen, F. (2023): The Power of One: How I Found the Strength to Tell the Truth and Why I Blew the Whistle on Facebook. New York: Little, Brown and Company.

Hénaff, M. (2010): The Price of Truth. Gift, Money and Philosophy. Stanford: Stanford University Press.

Hund, E. (2023): The Influencer Industry: The Quest for Authenticity on Social Media. Princeton, Oxford: Princeton University Press.

Jenkins, H./Ford, S./Green, J. (2013): Spreadable Media: Creating, Value and Meaning in a Networked Culture. New York: New York University Press.

Kincaid, J. (2010): "Facebook To Close Its Virtual Giftshop August 1st" (9 July 2010). Retrieved from: https://techcrunch.com/2010/07/08/facebook-gifts-closing/.

Kirkpatrick, D. (2010): The Facebook Effect. The Inside Story of the Company That is Connecting the World. New York: Simon & Schuster.

Kosinski, M./Stillwell, D./Graepel T. (2013): "Private traits and attributes are predictable from digital records of human behaviour". Proc Natl Acad Sci USA 110 (15), pp. 5802-5805.

Kozinets, R. V (2009): Netnography. Doing Ethnographic Research Online. London: Sage.

Kumar, A. (2015): "Hearts on Twitter, Twitter Blog" (3 November 2015). Retrieved from: https://blog.twitter.com/en_us/a/2015/hearts-on-twitter.html.

Leaver, T./Highfield, T./Abidin, C. (2020): Instagram: Visual Social Media Cultures. Cambridge/Medford: Polity.

Malinowski, B. (2005 [1922]): Argonauts of the Western Pacific: An Account of Native Enterprise and Adventure in the Archipelagoes of Melanesian New Guinea. London: Routledge.

Mauss, M. (2002 [1954]): The Gift. The form and reason for exchange in archaic societies. London/New York: Routledge.

Mauss, M. (2007[1967]): Manual of Ethnography. NewYork/Oxford: Durkheim Press/Berghahn Books.

Meier, F./Elsweiler, D./Wilson, M (2014): "More Than Liking and Bookmarking? Towards Understanding Twitter Favouriting Behavior". Proceedings of the International AAAI Conference on Weblogs and Social Media 8 (1), pp. 346-355.

Miller, D. (2011): Tales from Facebook. Cambridge/Malden: Polity Press.

Mosseri, A. (2021): "Shedding More Light on How Instagram Works". Instagram Blog (8 June 2021). Retrieved from: https://about.instagram.com/blog/announcements/shedding-more-light-on-how-instagram-works.

Parkinson, H. J. (2015): "Twitter is replacing favourites with likes—but does anyone heart it?" (3 November 2015). Retrieved from: https://www.theguardian.com/technology/2015/nov/03/twitter-replacing-favourites-with-likes-does-anyone-heart.

Paßmann, J. (2018): Die soziale Logik des Likes. Eine Twitter-Ethnografie. Frankfurt/NewYork: Campus.

Paßmann, J./Schubert, C. (2020): "Liking as taste making: Social media practices as generators of aesthetic valuation and distinction". New Media & Society 23 (10), pp. 2947-2963.

Petre, C./Duffy, B. E./Hund, E. (2019): "'Gaming the System': Platform Paternalism and the Politics of Algorithmic Visibility". Social Media + Society 5 (4), pp. 1-12.

Quadflieg, D. (2019): Vom Geist der Sache. Zur Kritik der Verdinglichung, Frankfurt/New York: Campus.

Rheingold, H.(1993): The Virtual Community: Homestanding On the Electronic Frontier. 1st Edition. Reading: Basic Books.

Roberts, S. T. (2019): Behind the Screen: Content Moderation in the Shadows of Social Media. New Haven: Yale University Press.

Rus, A. (2008): "Gift vs. commodity debate revisited. Anthropological Notebooks 14 (1), pp. 81-102.

Schröter, J. (2020): "Digitale Medien und Methoden. Zur Medienarchäologie der digitalen Medien". Zeitschrift für Medienwissenschaft, ZfM Online, Open Media Studies Blog, 10 July 2020. Retrieved from: https://zfmedienwissenschaft.de/online/open-media-studies-blog/digitale-medien-und-methoden-6-schroeter

Schulz, C. (2023a): "A New Algorithmic Imaginary". Media, Culture & Society 45 (3), pp. 646-655.

Schulz, C. (2023b): Infrastrukturen der Anerkennung. Eine Theorie sozialer Medienplattformen. Frankfurt/New York: Campus.

Slaby, J. (2017): "More Than a Feeling: Affect as Radical Situatedness". Midwest Studies in Philosophy, XLI, pp. 7-25.

Sumpter, D. (2018): "Why the Facebook data available to Cambridge Analytica could not be used to target personalities in the US Presidential election". Medium Blog (17 June 2018). Retrieved from: https://soccermatics.medium.com/why-the-facebook-data-available-to-cambridge-analytica-could-not-be-used-to-target-personalities-in-2904fa0571bd.

Sumner, E.M./Ruge-Jones, L./Alcorn, D. (2018): "A Functional Approach to the Facebook Like Button: An Exploration of Meaning, Interpersonal Functionality, and Potential Alternative Response Buttons". New Media & Society 20 (4), pp. 1451-1469.

Tsing, A. L. (2013): "Sorting out Commodities: How Capitalist Value Is Made Through Gifts." HAU: Journal of Ethnography Theory 3 (1), pp. 21-43.

Tsing, A. L. (2015): The Mushroom at the End of the World. On the Possibility of Life in Capitalist Ruins. Princeton/Oxford: Princeton University Press.

Whitnah, T.(2013a): "What does Facebook refer to as 'UFI' and what is the acronym for? Is this the like/comment section or the photo details? Is this term used internally?" (17 April 2013). Retrieved from : https://www.quora.com/What-does-Facebook-refer-to-as-UFI-and-what-is-the-acronym-for-Is-this-the-like-comment-section-or-the-photo-details-Is-this-term-used-internally/answer/Tom-Whitnah.

Whitnah, T. (2013b): "What was 'Project Zelda' within Facebook?" (14 August 2013). Retrieved from: https://www.quora.com/What-was-Project-Zelda-within-Facebook.

Quantifying Peer Review

Incentivising and Coordinating Academic Work
through Digital Currencies

Sebastian Koth, Anne K. Krüger, Sascha Friesike

Abstract

The academic peer review system is widely criticised for its inefficiency, ineffectiveness, conservatism, bias, and for failing to adequately recognize reviewers. In this article, we examine a recent attempt to reform this system by means of an alternative design of peer review based on quantitative methods. We draw on the case of the science platform project ResearchHub and its introduction of a digital currency as a remedy to these much debated deficit, exploring how this currency is weaved into peer review and how this attempt at quantification impacts the crucial element of science governance. Analysing the case, we find auctions where researchers buy and sell review services, incentive architectures that are supposed to foster specific forms of review work, accounting practices that organise the review process, and the economic coordination of crowd reviewing. We discuss the implications of our findings and highlight the commodification of review work, the algorithmic designability of the review process, the responsibilisation of the individual researcher, and the fragmentation of review communication. We argue that this attempt at quantification introduces a market mode of governing science, according to which research quality assessment and hence research resource distribution must rely on economic calculability. It turns out that this attempt to reduce frictions in the peer review process gives rise to new kinds of problems. We conclude by linking our argument to the broader trend of platforming science, emphasising the particular challenges digital currencies pose for organising academic work.

Keywords

platforming science, digital currency, peer review design

DOI 10.14361/dcs-2023-0205

DCS | Digital Culture and Society | Vol. 9, Issue 2 | © transcript 2025

Introduction

How should we assess quality in science? Hardly any topic in the context of science studies has been more controversial. Discussions of this topic revolve around two main debates. First, there is the debate on metrics and how they are supposed to enable quality assurance in science (Elkana et al. 1978; Lucas 2006; Wilsdon et al. 2015; Espeland/Sauder 2016). Metrics are based on quantitative measurements that capture activities of researchers and scientific organisations by counting things like citations, publications, acquired funding, or, more recently, social media activity such as mentions, likes, or downloads. These metrics are inevitably met with objections, however, about their actual usefulness and long-term impact on science, specifically on its organisation, culture, and work (Hammarfelt et al. 2016; de Rijcke et al. 2016; Sugimoto et al. 2017; Pardo-Guerra 2022). Several suggestions have been made to mitigate their weaknesses, for example, by exalting the number of metrics to increase precision (Priem et al. 2010) or monitoring and policing metrics with experts-in-the-loop (Hicks et al. 2015; Ràfols 2019), or withdrawing from metrics altogether (Stack 2021).

Second, there is the debate on peer review and how it is supposed to provide quality assurance in science. Typically defined as a process in which academic experts assess the validity, novelty, and prospective impact of research (Tennant et al. 2017), peer review has faced much criticism for numerous flaws, including the lack of recognition for reviewers, extended delays from submission to publication, and various biases such as gender, research discipline, reviewer selection, and publishing decisions (Smith 2006; Ware 2008, 2011; Lee et al. 2013; Flaherty 2017; Hesselmann et al. 2021). In an attempt to remedy these deficits and to reform peer review, various experiments have been launched such as "post-publication peer review", "open peer review", and reviewer recognition services (Tennant et al. 2017: 7). Another approach, which has been receiving increasing attention, aims at integrating quantitative methods such as ratings into qualitative reviews. Services like Publons enable reviewers to rate the quality and significance of the papers they reviewed on a ten-point scale (ibid.: 24). Similarly, ScienceOpen encourages reviewers to assess the quality of papers regarding importance, validity, and comprehensibility, using a five-point scale (ibid.: 23). Drawing on platforms like Stack Exchange or Overflow, where software developers use a reputation system to capture the quality of interactions, preprint platforms like PhysicsOverflow and MathOverflow allow comments and reviews that are rated for originality and accuracy (ibid.: 25). Most recently, the science platform ResearchHub proposed an even more fundamental measure, introducing a digital currency to quantify peer review.

While there is ample literature on the impact of quantitative assessment through metrics and qualitative assessment through peer review, there is surprisingly little on the emerging trend of quantifying peer review. Building on a case study of ResearchHub, we will explore in this article how quantitative methods are weaved into qualitative research assessment and how this attempt of quantification impacts this crucial scientific practice. In the following, we first delineate our theoretical perspective on peer review, highlighting how peer review is an instrument in governing science that distributes research resources by recognising and assigning research quality; hence, alternative peer review designs may be seen as proposals for alternative modes of science governance. We then describe the case of the science platform project ResearchHub as a recent attempt to address perceived deficits in peer review by introducing a digital currency. Building on qualitative interviews, self-descriptions of ResearchHub based on social media content, and observations made on the platform, we investigate ResearchHub's proposed peer-review design through the lens of the perceived deficits it aims to solve. Analysing the case, we find auctions where researchers buy and sell review services, incentive architectures that are supposed to foster specific forms of review work, accounting practices organising the review process, and economic coordination of crowd reviewing. We will discuss the implications of our findings and point out how objects and actions of scientific quality assessment are captured and rendered adaptable to market processes. Furthermore, we will emphasise that deepening quantification to resolve problems in peer review and the organisation of science gives rise to new problems. We argue that quantifying peer review introduces a market mode of governing science, entailing a shift from the democratically inspired scientific ethos to the principle of economic calculability. We conclude by linking the argument with the broader development of platforming science, pointing out that digital currency technology represents a new type of platformisation that fundamentally challenges the organisation of academic work.

Peer Review: Deficits, Alternative Designs, and Shifting Modes of Governing Science

While many scholars trace the origin of academic peer review to the 17th century and the formation of national academies in Europe (Kronick 1990), some argue that it gained its role and importance in the 1970s with calls challenging the massively expanded scientific funding by governments in the course of the Cold War. This led scientists and their supporters to institute standards of expert refereeing, so-called "peer review", to ensure the credibility of science and regulate the boundary between science and society more generally (Guston 2000; Baldwin 2018). In peer review research, which emerged alongside this public criticism of science and its governance, peer review is typically defined as the process of scientific experts assessing research for its validity, novelty, and potential impact (Tennant et al. 2017).

In its over 40-year history, peer review research accumulated a long list of deficits such as poor reliability and validity, inefficiency, ineffectiveness, lack of transparency, bias, conservatism, and corruption (Eve et al. 2021: 8). This has led to a range of conceptual and practical suggestions for improving the peer review process. In "post-publication peer review" designs, for instance, researchers draw on the management of open source software projects and make the review object publicly available. Review work is distributed to many reviewers, turning publishing into an "evolving dialogue" and review into "co-authorship" (Ghosh et al. 2012; Tennant et al. 2017). Platforms such as F1000Research, Preprints.org, or RIO draw on such ideas. Another set of alternative designs can be found under the banner of "open peer review", where, for instance, identities of authors and reviewers are disclosed, review reports are made publicly available, everyone is invited to participate in reviewing, and direct interaction between the involved parties is encouraged (Ross-Hellauer 2017). ScienceOpen and eLife accommodate such designs.

The much-debated deficits of peer review have also led to experiments that integrate quantitative methods into peer review. Numerous attempts have been made to quantify peer review, for instance, by rating the quality of papers and reviews in accordance with a numerical scale; one of the most far-reaching attempts is to introduce a currency. The first practical effort to do so was the Academic Karma project that started in 2014 (and ended in 2019), allowing academics to exchange karma points for providing and receiving review work. In fact, using a currency like Academic Karma to improve peer review has been proposed time and again (Havrilesky 1975; Riyanto/Yetkiner 2002; Prüfer/Zetland 2010; Fox/Petchey 2010; Srinivasan/Morgenstern 2021; for critique, cf. de Mesnard 2014). The idea finally gained traction with the rise of digital currencies and new technologies to organise value flow (Brunnermeier et al. 2019; Swartz 2020; Westermeier 2020; Scott 2022; O'Dwyer 2023). Launched in 2019, the science platform project ResearchHub implements the digital currency ResearchCoin into peer review. It does so not only by enabling researchers to compensate each other for peer review work, but by integrating the currency into the peer review process itself with the aim of addressing broader deficiencies within the peer review system.

All these ongoing attempts to reform and improve peer review are motivated by the prevalent and paradoxical view that peer review is the "gold standard" of scientific quality control and, at the same, it is "broken" (Tennant/Ross-Hellauer 2020). Some argue that this results from too narrowly focussing the peer review process with its immediate outcomes and underestimating the importance of theorising peer review (Hug 2022). Indeed, reshaping the peer review process affects more than just how quality is assessed. Peer review must be recognised especially for its role in the production of scientific knowledge more broadly. Understanding peer review, and consequently its ongoing technological and organisational transformation, requires acknowledging it as both a process of quality assessment and an instrument for governing science by distributing research resources (Reinhart/Schendzielorz 2024). Accordingly, peer review is not only a process relying on expert judgement to assess the quality of research, but a mechanism for the allocation of limited resources such as publication space, academic positions and funding. The processes and methods used to assess research quality thus influence resource allocation and, ultimately, shape how scientific knowledge is produced and by whom. Alternative peer review designs need to be understood as proposals for alternative modes of governing science.

Traditionally, peer review is modelled on the democratically inspired scientific ethos proposed, for instance, in Robert Merton's seminal "Note on Science and Technology in a Democratic Order" (1942; cf. 1938; for other suggestions, cf. Mitroff 1974; for critique, cf. Mulkay 1976). According to Merton, institutionalised procedures in science should align with "universalism, communism, organized skepticism, and disinterestedness" and thus involve voluntary and selfless action, impersonal criteria, and decisions grounded in the epistemic requirements of the scientific community. Other scholars have since argued that, in order to protect and support science, it is necessary to anchor academic procedures like peer review in a commons structure (Hagstrom 1982; Vermeir 2013). Alternative peer review designs challenge these traditional conceptions. Building on the perspective that different peer review processes reflect different modes of governing science, this article explores how proposals to reorganise peer review through quantification may be seen as attempts to shift the governance of science.

The Case of ResearchHub

ResearchHub provides a platform for researchers to post articles, preprints, or paper drafts, and initiate discussions, ask questions, or request specific comments and full reviews. ResearchHub aims to "accelerate the pace of scientific research" (ResearchHub 2020: 1) by introducing ResearchCoin, a digital currency based on distributed ledger technology. It was founded in 2019 by Patrick Joyce, a dropout medical PhD student, and Brian Armstrong, a software engineer turned start-up entrepreneur and notably co-founder and CEO of Coinbase, currently one of the biggest cryptocurrency exchanges. Facing the "old school incentive structure that was grandfathered, ending up producing all these unintended behaviours among the scientific community" (RH Multi Media 13), both founders were convinced that science needed to be reformed in its core activities. Inspired by open-source code repositories such as GitHub, a platform for software development that allows multiparty collaboration, they considered building something similar for researchers and launched the ResearchHub project. In early 2023, they were able to raise another round of funding to expand the platform to "reach more scientists worldwide" (Armstrong/Joyce 2023). Drawing on the idea that "science should operate more like open-source software" (RH Multi Media 13), they aim to translate what they regard as the advantages of software development practice into academic work.

The development of the ResearchHub project is linked to the technology and innovation trend web3 that offers infrastructural and organisational designs based on distributed ledger technology and peer-to-peer protocols. ResearchHub corresponds to the web3 innovation paradigm as it seeks not only to support a given domain (science) with technology, but to carve out a new platform territory where the domain can be reorganised from the ground up (Sadowski/Beegle 2023; Allen/Potts 2023). The idea of implementing distributed ledger technology in the domain of science gained attention around 2016; today it is a thriving innovation ecosystem (cf. Bartling 2019; Ducrée et al. 2021; Wang et al. 2022). The ResearchHub project builds on the idea of preprint servers like arXiv and academic social network sites like ResearchGate and adds to it the digital currency Research-Coin. ResearchCoins can be bought and sold on digital currency exchanges against other cryptocurrencies or fiat currencies such as USD by digital currency wallet holders, i.e. individual researchers or organisations. It is important to note that ResearchCoin can be independently acquired and used by everyone. Since it is not owned by someone who directly exerts control over its use (though issues like supply and issuance are subject to particular decision-making), organisations like universities or research funding bodies can also make use of it and create application interfaces to enable specific functionalities that serve organisational goals. Accordingly, ResearchHub can be seen as an application that tests and showcases the usefulness of the currency to organise academic work, aiming to integrate incentivisation and coordination mechanisms as a basis to improve peer review. In short, digital currencies like ResearchCoin enable a new type of platformisation. We will return to this important point in the conclusion.

Data and Methods

ResearchHub is still in the making and the use of digital currencies on social platforms is a very recent development. In this light, the aim of our explorative case study was to identify and delineate key aspects of quantifying peer review, and to investigate the implications of this trend for governing scientific knowledge production. We collected a variety of data in order to approach this question from two different angles.

First, we collected ResearchHub's descriptions of itself, focusing especially on its motivation to engage in reorganising peer review. We conducted sixteen semi-structured interviews with an adaptable questionnaire and a set of core questions regarding the workings of ResearchHub, the perceived deficits in academic publishing and reviewing, and the potential of distributed ledger technology and digital currencies for reorganising academic work. Four informants were directly involved in the ResearchHub project; all four are researchers who use the platform themselves. The other twelve informants were involved in similar projects in the broader start-up ecosystem centred around digital technology innovation in science organisation. We selected these informants according to their expertise in the field, especially regarding alternative academic publishing and reviewing practices based on web3. The interviews lasted between 60 and 90 minutes. We recorded ten interviews and transcribed them manually; during the remaining six interviews, we took notes and re-approached the informants when there were new questions or developments. Furthermore, we collected podcast episodes in which core members of ResearchHub talk about the project, and public information produced by ResearchHub such as press releases, white paper, blog and social media posts, and conference talks. This material provided information about how ResearchHub perceives today's scientific system, its shortcomings regarding peer review, how it deems to improve it, and how it distinguishes itself from other projects. Due to ResearchHub's open innovation character, we were able to closely monitor current and past developments on the project's Discord Server where developers and users meet, share news, plan, and discuss; moreover, publicly available weekly community calls allowed us to follow discussions over a long period of time.

Second, we collected data on the design features of the ResearchHub platform, observing functionalities enabled by the currency. We focused on configurations in which researchers are encouraged to participate in review activities. These activities involved interactions between peer researchers using the currency and interactions between researchers and the platform via the currency. Furthermore, we looked for configurations in which the researchers' review activity is coordinated through the currency-enabled functionalities of the platform, especially regarding communication during and around the actual peer review process. We took notes about how artefacts such as options, menus, graphics, notifications, tags, profiles, and buttons are placed and linked with the digital currency. Here, we focused on how the use of the currency is integrated into peer review through these artefacts and contextualised with specific information such as rankings, balance sheets, and statistics. We accumulated a broad and detailed description of currency-related platform features.

In the first set of data, we examined how ResearchHub problematises the current peer review system by conducting an inductive qualitative content analysis using MAXQDA (Kuckartz/Rädiker 2019). Starting with exploratory open coding, we went through the data to find preliminary categories and sort the data abundance with regard to the shortcomings of the scientific system. In the second step, we revised these categories and focused on deficits in peer reviewing. We clustered the resulting categories to generate groups of perceived deficits, showing what ResearchHub focuses on in its attempt to improve peer review.

For the second set of data, we relied on feature analysis (Hasinoff/Bivens 2021) as well as the walkthrough method (Light et al. 2018). These methods allowed us to examine digital platforms as sites of sociocultural and economic transformations and to inquire into how solutions for perceived problems are inscribed in technology. They helped us explore how technological affordances accommodate distinct problems perceived by their designers and to analyse the cultural norms and assumptions that are implicitly suggested to the users. We grouped the features regarding the types of action they enable (e.g. "tipping" a comment) and added their intended use (e.g. acknowledging someone or signalling importance) and involved parties (e.g. a peer researcher or researcher crowds). These groups encompass mechanisms, conditions, and expected outcomes of currency-related features. Linking these groups to the categories we obtained in analysing the first dataset, we were able to read the currency-enabled solutions through the perceived deficits in peer review.

This two-stage approach allowed us to study the differences between this new model of peer review and traditional peer review; in particular, it reveals how the use of quantitative methods reorganises peer review in terms of markets. In the following, we will present our findings by relating the perceived deficits and the proposed solutions along incentivisation and coordination as the crucial mechanisms in peer review that ResearchHub aims to change. First, we will look at the debates on reviewer shortage and inadequate reviewer recognition and describe how ResearchHub envisions incentivising peer review activity through a monetary reward system. We then turn to the debates around the delay and slowness of the peer review process from submission to publication, as well as biases in the selection of reviewers. We will show how the digital currency is expected to enhance matchmaking between authors and reviewers and improve coordination.

Incentivising and Coordinating Peer Review with a Digital Currency

Recognise, Reward, Incentivise

A central point in the current debates on the deficits of academic peer review revolves around the lack of recognition for review work, which is commonly seen as a cause of the "reviewer shortage" (DeLisi 2022; Flaherty 2022). Accordingly, it is argued that assessment bodies, institutions, funders, as well as publishers and journals, which effectively outsource peer review work to individual researchers who receive no compensation for their contribution, do not recognise peer review adequately as an important academic activity in need of compensation. Instead, they consider peer review a duty based on the principle of voluntary mutual exchange in academic collaboration—a duty that researchers ought to voluntarily fulfil. Studies indicate that most researchers believe that peer review is currently inadequately recognized and valued, and would be willing to dedicate more time to peer review if it were formally acknowledged for promotion, funding, and other forms of assessment (Warne, 2016; Nicholson/Alperin 2016). Commercial publishers and their journals rely heavily on voluntary work of researchers and developed recognition mechanisms, for instance, acknowledging reviewers once a year in special sections of their journals, giving free subscriptions or discounts on article processing charges, awarding annual prices, or featuring a list of their top reviewers (Tennant et al. 2017: 13). Furthermore, platforms such as Publons, F1000Research, ScienceOpen, and ReviewerCredits provide means to recognise peer review activity, for instance, enabling reviewers to receive due credit for their work in forms of peer review reports that have open licences and Crossref DOIs. Despite these attempts to grant reviewers more recognition for their work, the problem of "reviewer shortage" continues in every research discipline.

Incentivising each other for Review Work

ResearchHub approaches this deficit by developing a monetary reward system. In a podcast interview, the co-founder Patrick Joyce elaborated this idea by arguing that

"financial incentive would help greatly to rewire some of these behaviours where all of a sudden rather than paying to publish you get paid to publish and rather than volunteering your time for peer review you are compensated for doing so in a way that also helps build your résumé" (RH Multi Media 13).

The idea of economic incentives differs fundamentally from the traditional approach to peer review, which relies on the voluntary exchange of knowledge—a feature that the academic publishing industry has exploited. Yet ResearchHub does not want to become an academic publisher that pays reviewers for their work. Accordingly, ResearchHub does not distribute ResearchCoin (RSC) directly to individuals but builds on the idea that self-organised interaction based on a monetary reward system will improve peer review engagement. Incentivisation is thought to happen first and foremost between researchers. The digital currency is considered to be a device for researchers to enable the calculation of the value of reviewing, to signal interest and demand, and ultimately to reward each other's work. A researcher can, for instance, upload a paper on ResearchHub and call for reviews by adding a certain amount of RSC to encourage other researchers to engage in review work. Potential reviewers will evaluate the request based on the required time and skills to accomplish the task and subsequently make an offer; the final decision on which reviewer will be awarded the tender rests with the party requesting the review, which may choose to engage in further negotiation.

The idea of incentivising each other for review work through a currency transforms peer review into a service negotiated in auctions, where researchers bid for a scarce resource. Accordingly, the ResearchHub platform is designed as a "job marketplace where anyone can learn and demonstrate their value" (ibid.). Bidding for peer review as a scarce resource on a marketplace is thought to introduce competition into this originally non-competitive practice. While peer review traditionally does not incur costs, quantifying peer review and making its costs calculable and visible through a currency creates a competitive environment where obtaining assessment is contingent upon the capacity and willingness to offer adequate pay. Now, access to quality evaluation, which is key to acquiring further research resources, itself requires resources.

Incentivising Review Activity through the Platform

ResearchHub addresses the much-debated recognition deficit in peer review not only by providing currency-enabled auctions where researchers incentivise each other for review work. It also implements the currency to enable an incentive architecture on the platform:

"[I]f people like your content and upvote your content you are getting rewarded with some ResearchCoins. Same applies with the comments. So if you leave an insightful comment that people like via upvotes you are receiving ResearchCoins" (Notes Meeting 44).

Engaging with one another and performing evaluations is rewarded through the platform environment. This can involve all kinds of interactions. For instance, formulating key takeaways of a paper posted by someone else yields one RSC, while improving the quality of a summary through editing earns five RSC. Furthermore, users are encouraged to promote integrity and quality by flagging posts that are potential spam or copyright violations (ResearchHub 2020: 3). The type of activity that earns RSC and the specific amount awarded are determined by so-called "reward algorithms", which "will become more encompassing and complex as interactions on the platform occur" (ibid.). Instead of researchers individually calculating and allocating rewards for review collaboration, incentivisation is calculated by these algorithms which seek to affect and motivate researchers using the platform. Focused on rewarding specific actions, automated incentivisation is supposed to recognise "whether you're bringing value to the platform" (Notes Meeting 46). Aiming to emphasise particular valuation actions over others, the incentive architecture affects the behaviour of researchers and their decisions.

Since ResearchHub provides the collaborative features common to academic social media sites, the incentive architecture can be implemented in various ways. Co-founder Patrick Joyce highlights that the structure could be geared towards incentivising many different kinds of behaviour and that "there are a lot of different directions this [incentivisation] could go in the future" (RH Multi Media 13). This involves "study[ing] how incentives cause different behaviours among academics" in order to "create rewards that incentivise the best behaviours" (ibid.). Enabling "tokenomic structures" that "make science as a whole better" (ibid.), digital currencies bring about incentive architectures that can be monitored, evaluated, and adapted. For instance, activities on ResearchHub are currently rewarded through the algorithms regardless of the actual standing of the researcher; but since 2023, ResearchHub has also sought to acknowledge researchers' reputation so that their activity and contribution can be valued accordingly.

The idea of incentivising peer review work on the platform through automated reward systems involves transforming this traditionally individual-based and discipline-specific practice. Implementing a currency to reinforce those patterns of behaviour that generate desirable collaboration dynamics renders peer review practice an object of intervention. Accordingly, scientific quality control is aligned with quality standards that are deemed appropriate to those who design these systems.

Search, Match, Coordinate

Other much-debated deficits revolve around the coordination of the peer review process. This involves, for instance, the inefficiency of peer review rooted in the long delay from submission to publication, which is said to withhold research findings for subsequent research, ultimately leading to an overall slowdown of scientific productivity (Research Information Network 2008). Furthermore, peer review is said to be burdened with biases regarding, for instance, gender, research discipline, institutional affiliation, language, and the preference to publish positive results over negative ones (Ioannidis 1998; Budden et al. 2008; Fanelli 2010; García et al. 2016; Mlinarić et al. 2017). Various experiments have been launched in recent years to mitigate these factors and improve the speed of the procedure and the matchmaking between the different parties during the review process. Notable examples are the Copernicus journal system and eLife series where external readers can participate in the assessment of scientific manuscripts (Tennant et al. 2017: 11). Such approaches are usually referred to by the umbrella term "open peer review", encompassing various strategies that aim to address these deficits by enabling, for instance, openness in terms of reviewer and reviewee identities and review reports, and encouraging a broader participation in the peer review process (Ross-Hellauer 2017).

Coordinating by Accounting Academic and Economic Value

The debates around inefficiency and biases in peer review are also addressed by ResearchHub and its currency-enabled auction feature. This feature is not only supposed to increase review activity; it is also thought to enhance the coordination of peer review work. The basic idea is that auctions can effectively allocate collaboration resources among the involved parties, leading to increased transparency, greater efficiency, and improved selection processes.

Negotiating through auctions, review seekers and providers must first appraise the academic value in monetary terms. On the one hand, researchers seeking reviews will have to calculate an offer based on questions regarding, for instance, the size of the pool of potential reviewers and the timeline. They also have to take their own standing into account such as their position, reputation, and institutional affiliation. Furthermore, they have to consider the scientific context, for instance, the research field, the methods and theories applied, and whether it needs expertise from different research disciplines. Researchers must take all of these items into consideration in proposing an offer which can attract adequate reviewers. Reviewers, on the other hand, have to estimate whether they are eligible to provide a review. They have to assess factors such as their standing and whether they are knowledgeable and sufficiently renowned in the respective research field and sufficiently skilled and experienced in reviewing. Therefore, researchers need to identify and determine the decisive elements of the collaboration in financial terms. In other words, they have to ask themselves: "How much USD would I be willing to spend or receive for a service?" (Notes Meeting 46).

Researchers individually organising the supply and demand of peer review in auctions can be effectively coordinated only if they are capable of assessing academic reputation and expertise and translating it into economic value. This entails especially the calculation of their own academic worth and that of potential collaborators in monetary terms. This individual calculative task does not exist in traditional peer review, where coordination is aligned with the review object. In contrast with traditional peer review, coordination through a digital currency is not based solely on the academic value of the review object; instead, it is researchers and their academic or economic interests that are decisive for the peer review process. In translating academic worth into economic worth (and vice versa), researchers must compare and calculate their own value and the value of others to arrive at a favourable "deal". Now the peer review process relies on the individual researcher and accounting practices that calculate coordination.

Coordinating Review Communication

Implementing a currency and new coordination mechanisms in peer review does not only bring about accounting practices that enable individual researchers to calculate their academic value and those of others to assess quality; it also involves changing the coordination of review communication. On ResearchHub, this is achieved in two ways.

First, in contrast to traditional peer review, which involves evaluating an entire review object like a research paper, on ResearchHub review tasks can be subdivided into smaller parts. This is thought to allow one to specify what should be reviewed and for which amount of RSC, thereby improving matchmaking between review seekers and review providers. Making review tasks more granular and customisable to needs and budget ought to facilitate a quicker peer review process, reduce workload, and allow for a more precise calculation of the review price. Increasing the calculability of supply and demand of peer review work in order to improve coordination fundamentally changes peer review communica-tion. Although ResearchHub's interface allows one to choose between predefined review categories—for instance, "methods", "results", or "discussion"—review seekers and providers are free to specify the kind of review they request or offer. For review seekers, this opens up various options for review. They can ask for reviews of specific parts of the paper, for instance, whether the method section is comprehensible enough to allow for replication, whether the paper covers relevant references on the topic, or whether the argumentation overlooks important points.

They can also call for specific expertise or for particular researchers. On the other hand, breaking down review communication into smaller parts is supposed to enable review providers to identify the specific scientific expertise required for the task and to select more precisely the review request they want to engage regarding remuneration. As a ResearchHub developer puts it, "you do not have to understand everything, you just have to understand what is relevant to your expertise to be able to deliver a review" (Notes Meeting 43).

Second, as review work is distributed among a larger pool of researchers, economic signals are incorporated into the review communication process to coordinate this "researcher crowd". While traditional peer review involves dedicated peer researchers, on ResearchHub peer review becomes a collective effort. Research-Hub's interface, modelled after Reddit-style forums, allows researchers to publicly post and request reviews for their research content, while also providing diverse forms of interaction with the content to enable economic coordination. Researchers can "tip" content, granting RSCs for contributions like posted papers or outstanding answers to a question or review request. Thus, researchers can appreciate particular content, increase its visibility on the platform to attract other researchers who might critically assess its scientific value. Furthermore, researchers can upvote or downvote content, comments, or entire threads based on criteria such as quality or relevance. This voting system, where high-ranked posts and threads are presented at the top and lower-ranked at the bottom, relies on the law of large numbers to discover valuable contributions. As a developer at ResearchHub points out, rather than relying on the selection of contributions through journal editors and reviewers, this system "gets hundreds of people to give their own judgement" which can be "more valuable than getting just one opinion from one person" (Notes Meeting 44). This voting system is not only supposed to promote and enable the discovery of valuable contributions; it is also thought to determine how financial resources for "expert reviews" should be allocated. Co-founder of ResearchHub Patrick Joyce explains the idea as follows:

"A certain portion of the upvotes would be dedicated to a peer-review bounty, so maybe if a paper earned a hundred upvotes and there is a hundred RSC available to it, five percent automatically stack up within this growing bounty for peer reviewers as more people find this paper important. The idea here is that you can try and help to use financial incentives to direct people's critical attention towards the papers that are receiving the most 'love' at a given moment" (RH Multi Media 14).

Accordingly, a shared paper on ResearchHub that garners upvotes receives a proportional amount of RSC (depending on the design of the algorithm), which is automatically invested in a call for reviews. As the reward increases with the number of upvotes, it becomes a relevant incentive for researchers to engage in review work. This means that the review process is no longer based solely on competence and judgement of experts. Instead, more weight in the review process is given to the "wisdom of the crowd", whose positive evaluation becomes increasingly important for obtaining review. Access to expert reviews thus depends on popularity and what the crowd deems valuable.

Discussion: Quantifying Peer Review and the Market Mode of Governing Science

In our case study, we found four crucial aspects that characterise the reorganisation of peer review through quantitative methods. In this section, we will discuss the commodification of review work through auctions, the algorithmic designability of the review process on the basis of incentive architectures, the responsibilisation of the individual researcher through accounting practices, and the fragmentation of review communication through economic coordination of crowd work. We argue that the implementation of quantitative methods fundamentally changes peer review, entailing a shift from governing science in terms of a democratically inspired scientific ethos to governing science in terms of markets and economic calculability. Moreover, we want to highlight that, if problems in the organisation of science—for instance, concerning peer review—are framed as frictions that can be eliminated by deepening quantification and thus calculability, then new kinds of problems arise. These are an indication of the limits of this approach.

Commodification of Review Work

Implementing a digital currency for researchers to incentivise each other to engage in review work means that the peer review process is organised through auctions where receiving peer review is conditioned on the ability to pay for it. Traditionally free of charge and based on the idea of voluntary knowledge exchange, peer review is now a commercial service that comes with a price. In this respect, quantification of peer review amounts to its commodification. Once peer review has turned into a commercial service, the motivation to perform it shifts from professional commitment to financial benefit, which entails a change in how researchers access quality control. Researchers with greater financial resources can afford more and better reviews, which in turn has consequences for the distribution of further resources. Peer review has traditionally been provided at no cost. Equal access to high-quality peer review is thought to ensure an unbiased assessment and allocation of resources such as publication space, funding, and academic positions. Charging for peer review skews this mechanism: one must have resources in order to access quality assessment, and having access to quality assessment, in turn, increases the likelihood of gaining access to greater resources.

Algorithmic Designability of the Review Process

The incentive architectures at ResearchHub are supposed to encourage researchers to engage with the platform and perform specific review tasks; they also demonstrate how quantitative methods can be used to redesign the peer review process. Accordingly, peer review is divided into a set of distinct, separately performed actions, similar to itemised communication practices on social network sites where features like "sharing" or "liking" emulate social activity. An individual "review action" can be assigned quantitative value. Depending on its perceived importance or effort, the valorised action reflects its role and rank compared to other actions within the framework of the particular peer review design; flagging flaws in the dataset of a paper, for instance, earns more than answering a request for comments on the method section of the paper. Once actions have been captured and rendered calculable, review work within such architectures can be analysed and incentive algorithms can be adapted to meet particular goals. Quantification through incentive architectures, where cognition and behaviour are "nudged" to produce favourable outcomes, turns peer review into an algorithmically designable process. While traditionally organised by scientific communities according to disciplinary norms and routines that entail the epistemic and evaluative plurality of academic peer review, the algorithmic design of peer review is determined by the platform operators. Currently ResearchHub's incentive architecture is based mainly on designs that reflect its vision of scientific work and organisation. It is conceivable, however, that ResearchHub will expand its open innovation approach to platform organisation, encouraging researchers and their communities to regulate platform work.

Responsibilisation of the Individual Researcher

Traditionally, the peer review process is managed by researchers such as journal editors who identify and mobilise peer researchers to provide evaluation appropriate to the particular characteristics, e.g. research discipline and topic, of the review object. By contrast, currency-based peer review coordination involves individual researchers calculating the type of review work they need in terms of quantitative value. Accordingly, researchers must manage themselves within the peer review process. In this respect, quantification of peer review refers to the introduction of accounting practices leading to shifted responsibilities. Researchers do not only need to manage themselves regarding their expertise and knowledge of the field; they must also estimate, calculate, and translate their status and achievements and those of others into monetary terms in order to facilitate matchmaking in the peer review process. Unlike traditional peer review, which relies on impersonal criteria and the requirements of the review object, this new form of review that coordinates reviewers and tasks based on status and financial incentives could jeopardise the impartiality essential for evaluating scientific knowledge and distributing resources.

Fragmentation of Review Communication

The implementation of a digital currency into the peer review process reinforces fragmentation of review communication. According to the traditional model of peer review, researchers are supposed to evaluate particular objects such as papers; by contrast, in the currency-enhanced model of peer review proposed by ResearchHub, review work is distributed to many researchers who independently engage with those aspects of the review object that match their expertise and monetary expectations. To enable researchers to better estimate their contributions and assess their performance in the peer review process, review communication is broken down into a set of objects and interactions. Fragmented review communication is supposed to help identify the value of different components of review work and is thought to improve the resource allocation in the peer review process. Coordinating crowd review through a digital currency entails subdividing communication in order to improve calculability, avoid frictions in resource coordination and thus improve process outcomes. But transforming review communication in this manner has potential downsides that raise new problems. It may lead to biases by favouring certain aspects through greater financial rewards, neglecting crucial but less lucrative elements of the review process. Where there is a lack of financial incentive, gaps may result and critical aspects may be overlooked. Furthermore, the emphasis on smaller tasks may discourage reviewers from engaging in the more comprehensive analysis often required for a holistic assessment of complex and highly specific scientific matter. Relying on a monetary system to source and coordinate the "wisdom of the crowd" may thus lead to quality assessments that lack the rigour and depth of traditional peer review. Moreover, such granular review markets might initiate a "Matthew Effect", according to which differences are amplified over time, rewarding certain researchers with more attention and monetary advantages while others fall behind.

Taken together, these four aspects demonstrate that attempts to quantify peer review to address its deficits introduces a market mode of governing science, according to which quality assessment and resource distribution in science must rely on economic calculability. In quantified peer review, objects and actions of scientific quality assessment are captured and rendered adaptable to market processes. Managing access to resources by recognising and assigning quality on the basis of economic calculability, ResearchHub proposes a form of science governance according to which market-like organised platforms disclose and disseminate information to support or even substitute decisions about the advancement of science. Yet, as we have attempted to point out, this approach to solving social coordination problems and eliminating frictions in peer review, by mobilising markets through advanced technology, risks generating new problems. Integrating routines, practices, and social interactions of academic work into market-like platforms prompts questions about how such platforms are designed and which normative assumptions are embedded within them, especially regarding the role of information and decision options incompatible with market processes and outcomes.

Conclusion: Platforming Science and the Calculation of Research Quality and Resource Distribution

In this article, we set out to investigate a recent attempt to remedy deficits of the academic peer review system through the introduction of quantitative methods. Our point of departure was the claim that alternative designs of peer review need to be understood as proposals for modifying science governance. We studied the case of ResearchHub and its implementation of a digital currency into qualitative research assessment. In light of our analysis, we argued that quantifying peer review introduces a market mode of governing science. Accordingly, in order to operate appropriately, research resource distribution by means of research quality assessment must no longer rely solely on a democratic ethos but also, and in particular, on economic calculability.

This has important implications for the digital transformation of science, especially for the perennial proliferation of science platforms, absorbing scientists, science managers, and entrepreneurs because of their ability to fundamentally change academic work and institutions. In this regard, it is important to recognise that digital currency technology such as ResearchCoin enables a new type of platformisation (Caliskan 2020; Scott 2022). The main feature of this type of platformisation is that the use of digital currencies is not limited to specific applications or organisations; they are not owned by a single entity that exerts direct control. Although issues like supply, issuance, and updates to the underlying protocol are subject to decision-making and questions of power, anyone may build and organise on top of them. Since digital currencies rely solely on digital currency exchanges that offer access to currency tokens, they can be independently acquired and used by everyone, allowing for the creation of application interfaces to enable specific functionalities through the currency. Accordingly, ResearchHub is just one of many sites where ResearchCoin can be implemented to organise academic work. Scientific communities, universities, or research funding bodies, for instance, could design applications themselves and use this particular digital currency (or create and use their own) to establish an incentivisation and coordination system aligning actions with organisational goals. The specific characteristics of such a system would be determined by the application designers.

This contrasts with an important line of argumentation in the research literature on the digital transformation of science, emphasising that platforms privately owned by academic publishers, edtech, and bigtech firms drive a market-based transformation of science, whereas public and local initiatives may preclude such developments (Hammarfelt et al. 2016; Plantin et al. 2018; Delfanti 2021; Pooley 2022; Goldenfein/Griffin 2022; da Silva Neto/Chiarini, 2022; Fecher et al. 2024;

Williamson 2024). However, as we tried to show with our investigation, market logic and the principle of economic calculability extend beyond closed forms of ownership, the prevailing pursuit of profit, and unaccountable control over infrastructure. Rather, they emerge by design, meaning from the specific ways in which scientific practices and organisation are problematised and how digital technology solutions are accordingly implemented. In the case of peer review, the absence of an agreed-upon theory of peer review and the reliance on a deficit model for changing procedures seems to welcome every alternative. This raises the crucial question: If the powerful quantification technology of digital currencies is here to stay, then how can it be properly applied? Because digital currencies are particularly well-suited to public and local initiatives, we must carefully consider how problems are framed and continuously reflect what kind of scientific system we want to achieve when relying on such technology to organise scientific knowledge production.

We emphasise this because of the numerous problematisations driving the digital transformation of science. There is, for instance, the call to overcome the "journal-centric" paradigm and to restructure the functions of scholarly communication and employ advanced technology in archiving, registration, dissemination, and certification (Priem and Hemminger 2012). Indeed, it is not uncommon for anyone aiming to change science for the better—including scientists, science managers, policy makers, and entrepreneurs—to point out deficiencies or even declare that there is a "crisis of science". The successful and influential metascience movement, for instance, emerged with the "reproducibility crisis". It brings together open science activism and methodologists from various fields such as psychology, economics, and medical science, and seeks to diagnose and solve problems in scientific practice by relying on quantification and experimentation (Peterson/Panofsky 2023). But the wish to translate scientific practice into quantified units for comparison, evaluation, and ultimately manipulation for improvement is not something unique to science reform movements like metascience. Platforming science embodies this approach at scale. Providing the basis to create environments more adaptable to the needs of science, of its stakeholders, and of societal transformation more broadly, platforms and their ability to reshape domain-specific valuation regimes and connect a vast array of functions and actors are key to reconfiguring the norms and institutions that underpin the traditional organisation of science (Plantin et al. 2018; Baudry et al. 2022; for critique cf. Mirowski 2018).

The currency-enabled platformisation approach that ResearchHub proposes is particularly well adapted to serving this purpose and addressing the much-discussed discrepancy between the current and the potential organisational configuration of science. For instance, the platform's use of digital currency facilitates the seamless integration of a general funding mechanism. According to ResearchHub's white paper, ResearchCoin can serve as a "novel vehicle to fund academic research" and be used to "incentivise research outputs in specific fields". Project funding was tested already in 2020, when a replication study was funded using ResearchCoin. Moreover, applications like the Jupyter notebook embedded in the platform—enabling researchers to share all kinds of research outputs in real-time, such as code, experiment protocols, and data—complements the funding feature. In a community call in 2021, a developer at ResearchHub explains that researchers putting their work in progress on the platform can easily apply for funding, indicating that this will "disrupt the whole research flow" (RH Multi Media 3). As we pointed out above, the currency-enabled platformisation approach does not only aim to address deficiencies in particular academic procedures such as peer review. Providing the basis for deepening quantification, it facilitates the further integration and rearrangement of the research cycle, establishing a comprehensive "science market" in which economic calculations determine which research succeeds and which does not.

List of References

Allen, D. W. E./Potts, J. (2023): "Web3 Toolkits: A User Innovation Theory of Crypto Development." Journal of Open Innovation: Technology, Market, and Complexity, 9(2), pp. 1–8. https://doi.org/10.1016/j.joitmc.2023.100050

Armstrong, B./Joyce, P. (2023, June 15): ResearchHub Raises $5m to Help Scientists Monetize Their Research. https://doi.org/10.55277/ResearchHub. vb2h5jvp

Baldwin, M. (2018): "Scientific Autonomy, Public Accountability, and the Rise of "Peer Review" in the Cold War United States." Isis, 109(3), pp. 538–558. https://doi.org/10.1086/700070

Bartling, S. (2019): "Blockchain for Science and Knowledge Creation." In: R. Haring (ed.), Gesundheit digital: Perspektiven zur Digitalisierung im Gesundheitswesen. Springer, pp. 159–180. https://doi.org/10.1007/978-3-662-57611-3_10

Baudry, J./Tancoigne, É./Strasser, B. J. (2022): "Turning Crowds into Communities: The Collectives of Online Citizen Science." Social Studies of Science, 52(3), pp. 399–424. https://doi.org/10.1177/03063127211058791

Brunnermeier, M./James, H./Landau, J.-P. (2019): The Digitalization of Money (w26300). National Bureau of Economic Research. https://doi.org/10.3386/w26300

Budden, A./Tregenza, T./Aarssen, L./Koricheva, J./Leimu, R./Lortie, C. (2008): "Double-blind Review Favours Increased Representation of Female Authors." Trends in Ecology & Evolution, 23(1), pp. 4–6. https://doi.org/10.1016/j.tree.2007.07.008

Caliskan, K. (2020): "Platform Works as Stack Economization: Cryptocurrency Markets and Exchanges in Perspective." Sociologica, 14(3), pp. 115–142. https://doi.org/10.6092/issn.1971-8853/11746

Da Silva Neto, V. J./Chiarini, T. (2022): "The Platformization of Science: Towards a Scientific Digital Platform Taxonomy." Minerva, *61*(2), pp. 1–29. https://doi.org/10.1007/s11024-022-09477-6

de Rijcke, S. D./Wouters, P. F./Rushforth, A. D./Franssen, T. P./Hammarfelt, B. (2016): "Evaluation Practices and Effects of Indicator Use—A Literature Review." Research Evaluation, 25(2), pp. 161–169. https://doi.org/10.1093/reseval/rvv038

Delfanti, A. (2021): "The Financial Market of Ideas: A Theory of Academic Social Media." Social Studies of Science, 51(2),pp.   259–276. https://doi.org/10.1177/0306312720966649

DeLisi, L. E. (2022): Editorial: "Where Have All the Reviewers Gone?: Is the Peer Review Concept in Crisis?" Psychiatry Research, 310, 114454. https://doi.org/10.1016/j.psychres.2022.114454

de Mesnard, L. (2014): "On the Marketization of the Academic Review Process." SSRN Electronic Journal. https://doi.org/10.2139/ssrn.2503346

Ducrée, J./Etzrodt, M./Bartling, S./Walshe, R./Harrington, T./Wittek, N./Posth, S./Wittek, K./Ionita, A./Prinz, W./Kogias, D./Paixão, T./Peterfi, I./Lawton, J. (2021): "Unchaining Collective Intelligence for Science, Research, and Technology Development by Blockchain-Boosted Community Participation." Frontiers in Blockchain, 0. https://doi.org/10.3389/fbloc.2021.631648

Elkana, Y./Lederberg, J./Merton, R. K./Thackray, A./Zuckerman, H. (eds.) (1978): Toward a Metric of Science: The Advent of Science Indicators. Wiley.

Espeland, W. N./Sauder, M. (2016): Engines of Anxiety: Academic Rankings, Reputation, and Accountability. Russell Sage Foundation.

Eve, M. P./Neylon, C./O'Donnell, D. P./Moore, S./Gadie, R./Odeniyi, V./Parvin, S. (2021): Reading Peer Review. Cambridge University Press. https://doi.org/10.1017/9781108783521

Fanelli, D. (2010): "Do Pressures to Publish Increase Scientists' Bias? An Empirical Support from US States Data." PLoS ONE, 5(4), e10271. https://doi.org/10.1371/journal.pone.0010271

Fecher, B./Kunz, R./Sokolovska, N./Wrzesinski, M. (2024): "Platformisation of Science: Conceptual Foundations and Critical Perspectives for the Science System." LIBER Quarterly: The Journal of the Association of European Research Libraries, 34(1), Article 1. https://doi.org/10.53377/lq.16693

Flaherty, C. (2017): "Peer Review's Give-and-Take." Inside Higher Ed. https://www.insidehighered.com/news/2017/10/24/maybe-there-isnt-peer-review-crisis-least-terms-quantity

Flaherty, C. (2022): "The Peer-Review Crisis." Inside Higher Ed. https://www.insidehighered.com/news/2022/06/13/peer-review-crisis-creates-problems-journals-and-scholars

Fox, J./Petchey, O. L. (2010): "Pubcreds: Fixing the Peer Review Process by 'Privatizing' the Reviewer Commons." The Bulletin of the Ecological Society of America, 91(3), pp. 325–333. https://doi.org/10.1890/0012-9623-91.3.325

García, J.A./Rodriguez-Sánchez, R./Fdez-Valdivia, J. (2016): "Authors and Reviewers Who Suffer from Confirmatory Bias." Scientometrics, 109(2), pp. 1377–1395. https://doi.org/10.1007/s11192-016-2079-y

Ghosh, S. S./Klein, A./Avants, B./Millman, K. J. (2012): "Learning from Open Source Software Projects to Improve Scientific Review." Frontiers in Computational Neuroscience, 6. https://doi.org/10.3389/fncom.2012.00018

Goldenfein, J./Griffin, D. (2022): "Google Scholar—Platforming the Scholarly Economy." Internet Policy Review, 11(3), pp. 1–34. https://policyreview.info/articles/analysis/google-scholar-platforming-scholarly-economy

Guston, D. H. (2000): Between Politics and Science. Cambridge: Cambridge University Press.

Hagstrom, W. O. (1982): "Gift Giving as an Organizing Principle in Science." In: Barnes, B./Edge, D. (eds.), Science in context: Readings in the sociology of science. Open Univ. Press, pp. 21–34.

Hammarfelt, B./de Rijcke, S./Rushforth, A.D. (2016): "Quantified Academic Selves: The Gamification of Research Through Social Networking Services." Information Research. 21(2). https://www.informationr.net/ir/21-2/SM1.html

Hasinoff, A./Bivens, R. (2021): "Feature Analysis: A Method for Analyzing the Role of Ideology in App Design." Journal of Digital Social Research, 3(2), pp. 89–113. https://doi.org/10.33621/jdsr.v3i2.56

Havrilesky, T.M. (1975): "Towards a More Competitive Market for Scholarly Output." In: Frontiers of economics. Blacksburg: University Publications, pp. 61–69.

Hesselmann, F./Schendzielorz, C./Krüger, A. K. (2021): "Sichtbarkeitskonstellationen im Journal Peer Review—Konsequenzen von In/Transparenz in wissenschaftlichen Bewertungsverfahren." In: O. Berli/S. Nicolae/H. Schäfer (eds.), Bewertungskulturen. Springer Fachmedien Wiesbaden, pp. 71–92. https://doi.org/10.1007/978-3-658-33409-3_4

Hicks, D./Wouters, P./Waltman, L./de Rijcke, S./Rafols, I. (2015): "Bibliometrics: The Leiden Manifesto for Research Metrics." Nature, 520(7548), pp. 429–431. https://doi.org/10.1038/520429a

Hug, S. E. (2022): "Towards Theorizing Peer Review." Quantitative Science Studies, 3(3), pp. 815–831. https://doi.org/10.1162/qss_a_00195

Ioannidis, J. P. A. (1998): "Effect of the Statistical Significance of Results on the Time to Completion and Publication of Randomized Efficacy Trials." JAMA: The Journal of the American Medical Association, 279(4), pp. 281–286. https://doi.org/10.1001/jama.279.4.281

Kronick, D. A. (1990): "Peer Review in 18th-Century Scientific Journalism." JAMA: The Journal of the American Medical Association, 263(10), pp. 1321–1322. https://doi.org/10.1001/jama.1990.03440100021002

Kuckartz, U./Rädiker, S. (2019): Analyzing Qualitative Data with MAXQDA: Text, Audio, and Video. Springer International Publishing. https://doi.org/10.1007/978-3-030-15671-8

Lee, C. J./Sugimoto, C. R./Zhang, G./Cronin, B. (2013): "Bias in Peer Review." Journal of the American Society for Information Science and Technology, 64(1), pp. 2–17. https://doi.org/10.1002/asi.22784

Light, B./Burgess, J./Duguay, S. (2018): "The Walkthrough Method: An Approach to the Study of Apps." New Media & Society, 20(3), pp. 881–900. https://doi.org/10.1177/1461444816675438

Lucas, L. (2006): The Research Game in Academic Life. Open Univ. Pr.

Merton, R. K. (1938): "Science and the Social Order." Philosophy of Science, 5(3), pp. 321–337.

Merton, R. K. (1942): "Science and Technology in a Democratic Order." Journal of Legal and Political Sociology, 1, pp. 115–126. Republished in Merton, R. K. (1973): The Sociology of Science. Theoretical and Empirical Investigations, pp. 267–278.

Mirowski, P. (2018): "The Future(s) of Open Science." Social Studies of Science, 48(2), pp. 171–203. https://doi.org/10.1177/0306312718772086

Mitroff, I. I. (1974): "Norms and Counter-Norms in a Select Group of the Apollo Moon Scientists: A Case Study of the Ambivalence of Scientists." American Sociological Review, 39(4), pp. 579–595. https://doi.org/10.2307/2094423

Mlinarić, A./Horvat, M./Šupak Smolčić, V. (2017): "Dealing with the Positive Publication Bias: Why You Should Really Publish Your Negative Results." Biochemia Medica, 27(3), 030201. https://doi.org/10.11613/BM.2017.030201

Mulkay, M. J. (1976): "Norms and Ideology in Science." Social Science Information, 15(4–5), pp. 637–656. https://doi.org/10.1177/053901847601500406

Nicholson, J./Alperin, J. P. (2016): "A Brief Survey on Peer Review in Scholarly Communication." The Winnower, pp. 1–8.

O'Dwyer, R. (2023): Tokens: The Future of Money in the Age of the Platform. Verso.

Pardo-Guerra, J. P. (2022): The Quantified Scholar: How Research Evaluations Transformed the British Social Sciences. Columbia University Press.

Peterson, D./Panofsky, A. (2023): "Metascience as a Scientific Social Movement." Minerva, 61(2), pp. 147–174. https://doi.org/10.1007/s11024-023-09490-3

Plantin, J.-C./Lagoze, C./Edwards, P. N. (2018): "Re-integrating Scholarly Infrastructure: The Ambiguous Role of Data Sharing Platforms." Big Data & Society, 5(1). https://doi.org/10.1177/2053951718756683

Pooley, J. (2022): "Surveillance Publishing." Elephant in the Lab https://doi.org/10.5281/zenodo.6384605

Priem, J./Hemminger, B. (2012): "Decoupling the Scholarly Journal." Frontiers in Computational Neuroscience, 6. https://www.frontiersin.org/articles/10.3389/fncom.2012.00019

Priem, J./Taraborelli, D./Groth, P./Neylon, C. (2010): altmetrics: A manifesto. http://altmetrics.org/manifesto/

Prüfer, J./Zetland, D. (2010): "An Auction Market for Journal Articles." Public Choice, 145(3/4), pp. 379–403.

Przybylski, L. (2021): Hybrid Ethnography: Online, Offline, and in Between. SAGE.

Ràfols, I. (2019): "S&T Indicators in the Wild: Contextualization and Participation for Responsible Metrics." Research Evaluation, 28(1), pp. 7–22. https://doi.org/10.1093/reseval/rvy030

Reinhart, M./Schendzielorz, C. (2024): "Peer-Review Procedures as Practice, Decision, and Governance—The Road to Theories of Peer Review." Science and Public Policy, scad089. https://doi.org/10.1093/scipol/scad089

Research Information Network. (2008): Activities, Costs and Funding Flows in the Scholarly Communications System in the UK.

ResearchHub. (2020): The ResearchCoin Whitepaper—ResearchCoin: A Cryptographic Incentive Designed to Accelerate the Pace of Scientific Research. ResearchHub. https://www.researchhub.com/

Riyanto, Y. E./Yetkiner, I. H. (2002): "A Market Mechanism for Scientific Communication: A Proposal." Kyklos, 55(4), pp. 563–567. https://doi.org/10.1111/1467-6435.00202

Ross-Hellauer, T. (2017): "What is Open Peer Review? A Systematic Review." F1000Research, 6, 588. https://doi.org/10.12688/f1000research.11369.2

Sadowski, J./Beegle, K. (2023): "Expansive and Extractive Networks of Web3." Big Data & Society, 10(1). https://doi.org/10.1177/20539517231159629

Scott, B. (2022): Cloudmoney: Cash, Cards, Crypto and the War for Our Wallets. The Bodley Head.

Smith, R. (2006): "Peer Review: A Flawed Process at the Heart of Science and Journals." Journal of the Royal Society of Medicine, 99(4), pp. 178–182. https://doi.org/10.1177/014107680609900414

Srinivasan, S./Morgenstern, J. (2021): "Auctions and Prediction Markets for Scientific Peer Review" (arXiv:2109.00923). arXiv. http://arxiv.org/abs/2109.00923

Stack, M. (ed.). (2021): Global University Rankings and the Politics of Knowledge. University of Toronto Press.

Sugimoto, C. R./Work, S./Larivière, V./Haustein, S. (2017): "Scholarly Use of Social Media and Altmetrics: A Review of the Literature." Journal of the Association for Information Science and Technology, 68(9), pp. 2037–2062. https://doi.org/10.1002/asi.23833

Swartz, L. (2020): New Money: How Payment Became Social Media. Yale University Press. https://doi.org/10.2307/j.ctv10sm94k

Tennant, J. P./Dugan, J. M./Graziotin, D./Jacques, D. C./Waldner, F./Mietchen, D./Elkhatib, Y./Collister, L. B./Pikas, C. ... Colomb, J. (2017). "A Multi-Disciplinary Perspective on Emergent and Future Innovations in Peer Review." F1000Research. https://doi.org/10.12688/f1000research.12037.3

Vermeir, K. (2013): "Scientific Research: Commodities or Commons?" Science & Education, 22(10), pp. 2485–2510. https://doi.org/10.1007/s11191-012-9524-y

Wang, F.-Y./Ding, W./Wang, X./Garibaldi, J./Teng, S./Imre, R./Olaverri-Monreal, C. (2022). "The DAO to DeSci: AI for Free, Fair, and Responsibility Sensitive

Sciences." IEEE Intelligent Systems, 37(2), pp. 16–22. https://doi.org/10.1109/MIS.2022.3167070

Ware, M. (2008): "Peer Review: Benefits, Perceptions and Alternatives." Publishing Research Consortium.

Ware, M. (2011): "Peer Review: Recent Experience and Future Directions." New Review of Information Networking, 16(1), pp. 23–53. https://doi.org/10.1080/13614576.2011.566812

Warne, V. (2016): "Rewarding Reviewers—Sense or Sensibility? A Wiley study explained." Learned Publishing, 29(1), pp. 41–50. https://doi.org/10.1002/leap.1002

Westermeier, C. (2020): "Money is Data—the Platformization of Financial Transactions." Information, Communication & Society, 23(14), pp. 2047–2063. https://doi.org/10.1080/1369118X.2020.1770833

Williamson, B. (2024): "Re-Infrastructuring Higher Education." Dialogues on Digital Society, 0(0). https://doi.org/10.1177/29768640241251666

Wilsdon, J. (2015): The Metric Tide: Independent Review of the Role of Metrics in Research Assessment and Management. SAGE Publications Ltd. https://doi.org/10.4135/9781473978782

Dogs and Data

The Conflicting Values of Self-Representation in Social Media

Felix Raczkowski

Abstract

The paper proposes to consider fakes on social media platforms as phenomena that arise from conflicts between different modes of (self)representation. A media-historical discourse analysis traces the changes in self-representation from the early commercial internet in the 1990s to the contemporary era of social media platforms, with special attention to the shift occurring as part of the Web 2.0 paradigm of data-extraction as a business model. This analysis is linked with social media research to argue that the advent of Web 2.0 platform capitalism shapes the discourse on fakes by complementing the practices of self-representation and the discursive criteria they are judged by with the automated capturing of user data. Web 2.0 and platform capitalism thus give rise to a second, economically viable layer by which individual users appear as "real" or "authentic", this time by corporate instead of community standards. The paper closes by examining user's reactions to these developments, which indicate another shift in the discourse on fakes on social media platforms.

Keywords

Fake, Identity, Social Media, Capture, Profile

During the process of acquiring Twitter in spring of 2022, Elon Musk put the acquisition on hold, citing his doubt in the data provided by Twitter regarding the percentage of "fake accounts" on the platform. Musk alleged that the actual percentage of fakes on Twitter are higher than the platform's official estimates, thereby diminishing its stock value and rendering Musk's offer too high (Roumeliotis/Dang 2022). Musk's doubts regarding Twitter's value are just the most recent prominent example of fakes significantly diminishing the perceived value of social networks and social media platforms, with Facebook and Instagram similarly making headlines in trade publications for the amount of fake profiles on their platforms in the past (Rushe 2012).[1] Fakes and fake profiles are never

---

1   Due to the historical argument developed here, I will refer to Facebook and Instagram as distinct platforms, disregarding the rebranding as Meta that took place in 2021.

DOI 10.14361/dcs-2023-0206

DCS | Digital Culture and Society | Vol. 9, Issue 2 | © transcript 2025

specifically defined in these debates—they can refer to automated profiles with minimal user involvement or to deviant user practices violating a platform's terms of service. The fake has come to be a vague concept and an umbrella term in digital cultures, its wide array of meanings encompassing, among other things, forgeries, hoaxes, propaganda, misinformation or dishonesty. This semantic scope ties fakes to the frictions shaping digital cultures: They are regarded as threats not only to business models (like in the case of Musk and Twitter), but also national security or democracy. This paper proposes to regard fakes in contemporary social networks as symptoms highlighting frictions that result from conflicts among users and between them and platforms, while also making apparent the overarching economic and technological shifts (trans)forming the internet since the 1990s. A historical discourse analysis will be conducted to outline the different meanings of fake in the context of self-representation on the internet since the commercial availability of the World Wide Web in 1990, connecting these transformations to paradigm shifts in the web's commercialisation and contextualising them with current social media research. The scope of the research presented in this paper is limited to a few examples corresponding to different phases or periods of the web's development—because of this, services or concepts like personal websites or blogs are not discussed here. This emphasis on "periodization" (20–27), albeit on a smaller scale compared to Alexander Galloway's (2004) argument, foregrounds shifts, breaks, and transformations, which is also where fakes become apparent. Through this historical argument, my account offers a perspective on fakes that differs from the research mostly focused on the identification of fakes in social networks or on countermeasures against their impact, instead understanding them as indicators of overarching technological and economical transformations in digital cultures. The concept of friction associated with fakes here is employed as a modification of Michel Foucault's (1982) oft-quoted assessment that criticism means "to render the too-easy gestures difficult" (34); it is understood here as a source of difficulty for the sometimes "too-easy gestures" of commodified self-representation and automated data-extraction (e.g. social networking profiles), as we will see below. This is not to be confused with the paper understanding fakes as intentional practices of resistance by (groups of) users against what José van Dijck, referring to Facebook, has described as a paradigm of "frictionless sharing" (van Dijck 2013: 65). While some practices of faking discussed in this paper could also be interpreted this way, the paper aims to contribute to understanding fakes as complications and frictions that arise out of (not against) dominant practices of online self-representation and the various services and platforms enabling (or enforcing) them.

What are fakes in social networks? The term is broad and open to interpretation, to the point where it can serve as both an adjective and a noun, referring to a quality attributed to content and profiles on social networks as well as a particular type of content circulating through these networks. A Facebook profile that exhibits no discernible relation to the person using it might be described as fake in the sense that it is not conforming to the expected way of using the site, while a news story reporting the pope's endorsement of Donald Trump in the 2016 election circulating on Facebook may be called a fake because it is referring to an event that never happened (Evon 2016). It may be possible to argue that both cases are fakes because of a (perceived) discrepancy between what they present or perform and what other users expect from the social network or regard as the truth. However, this perspective turns each fake into an individual problem depending on subjective experiences and expectations of users. Instead, I suggest to follow Martin Doll's critical discourse analysis in viewing fakes as specific problems or challenges for what Michel Foucault would refer to as "regimes of truth" (Foucault 1980: 131), meaning the various discursive "mechanisms and instances" by which a given society produces 'truth'. Setting the parameters for truth in this way also determines what is regarded as not true, as a deception, a lie or a fake. Doll argues that fakes are "discourse-critical" (Doll 2015: 75, [trans. by author]) phenomena in that they appropriate the discursive markers for truth to appear true for a limited time. Compared to other forms of deception, fakes to Doll always assume that they will be revealed and recognized as fake, which enables them to critique the reigning regime of truth. To return to my initial example, a fake Twitter/X profile impersonating a well-known politician (e.g. Garrity 2023) by using a name and profile picture alluding to the real-life person could be understood as a critical intervention into the discursive mechanics by which truth is produced on the platform after it is unveiled as a fake.

However, contrary to Doll, who completed his research on fakes in 2012 mainly studying historical fakes in science and journalism as well as the effects their unveiling had on the respective regimes of truth validating them, I'm interested in the recent discourse on fakes in digital cultures that first took shape during the presidential campaigns for the United States election in 2016 as well as the Brexit referendum in the United Kingdom in the same year. Here the fake emerged as a problem in digital cultures, reaching from geopolitics and elections to individual interactions with unknown profiles on social networks. In the terms of a discourse analysis following Foucault that is interested in the regimes of truth of any given society like outlined above, the challenge posed by these fakes amounts to the question of what truth is in digital cultures. What are the discursive mechanisms, processes, and institutions that determine truth in digital cultures, on internet forums, and on social networking sites? I propose to trace this question through the changing and evolving notions of what counts as a fake, as an attempt at deception or as dishonesty on the internet since 1990. I will do so by looking at three distinct examples during different phases of the commercial web's develop-ment and outlining the differences between them. The frictions resulting from fakes and the conflicts they enable might not always be discourse-critical like in the cases studied by Doll, but they demonstrate the way truth is produced on the internet through the reactions they provoke. I am limiting my analysis to the commercial world wide web because even though there is reason to assume that fakes were present in computer culture before that and some of the processes of producing truth that I will be discussing may have emerged during that earlier period, my research focus is on the changes brought on through the commercialisation of the Internet, particularly the Web 2.0 period beginning in the early 2000s. The argument presented here is also necessarily incomplete because it is not possible to discuss all relevant platforms that have become sites of fakes—for example, services primarily focused on video content such as YouTube and TikTok are not addressed. The examples chosen nevertheless are indicative of the transformations that I aim to trace.

On the Internet, Nobody Knows You're a Dog— Identity and Deception in the 1990s

During the early days of the commercial internet, the question of what is and is not considered fake online was not nearly as prevalent as it is today. On the contrary, many practices that are framed as fakes and faking today were among the great promises of utopian 'cyberspace' discourse that began in the 1980s and continued throughout the 1990s: You can be anyone you want on the internet. This promise is most poignantly encapsuled in the famous *New Yorker* cartoon from 1993 that remains the most reproduced and widely distributed cartoon in the magazine's history: Two dogs are sitting in front of a typical early 1990s personal computer, with the dog directly in front of the machine telling the other: "On the internet, nobody knows you're a dog" (Steiner 1993). Peter Steiner's cartoon quickly achieved the status of what could be described as an early internet meme, with the phrase, if not the illustration, still circulating today. The cartoon is also, as we will see, regularly cited in internet research on self-representation, where it is apparent that it is open to a wide range of interpretations. The cartoon can both be read as a promise of anonymous, explorative and playful self-representation as well as a warning of potentially harmful deception and of the uncertain and non-committal nature of interactions and relationships on the internet. I propose to understand the differences between the interpretations of Steiner's cartoon as a discursive effect of the conflicts arising from contradictory practices of self-representation on the internet.

"On the Internet, nobody knows you're a dog."

Figure 1: On the Internet, nobody knows you're a dog

Sherry Turkle's widely received book *Life on the Screen* sits firmly among the early internet research discussing the utopian potential of networked computing as a means of communication. To her, Steiners cartoon "captures the potential for MUDs as laboratories for experimenting with one's identity" (Turkle 1995: 12). The *Multi User Dungeons* studied by Turkle through interviews with their users are akin to multi-player text-adventures[2] and invite their users to playfully invent and perform characters in the game-worlds. To Turkle, these practices allow for the exploration of the postmodern "identity as multiplicity" (178). In MUDs, users are able to cycle through many selves (Turkle: 178) in a mostly frictionless manner, partly due to the clearly fictional theme of many MUDs, which frequently feature narrative framing from fantasy- or science-fiction settings. Additionally, most MUDs are non-profit offerings that do not require their users to set up permanent accounts, it is instead possible to connect through guest logins, which further enables the play with many different characters (or selves). However, as Turkle

---

2   Multi User Dungeons or Multi User Domains (MUD) are text-based services hosted on (and accessible through) networked computers that usually develop elaborate fictional worlds in which the users or players participate through characters they create (write) for themselves. Most MUDs do share characteristics with (early) digital games like items, Non-Player-Characters or progression systems.

and other early scholars of MUDs observe (cf. Ito 1994), they nevertheless serve as online environments in which stable communities of regular users emerge, which leads to expectations regarding user behaviour and regular practices of play and self-representation. Turkle's interviews never touch upon the potential for conflict emerging from the differences between these expectations and actual user behaviour, which may be due to the utopian cyberspace discourse in the early 1990s (see Rheingold 1993, Barlow 2001) that tended to de-emphasise problems and challenges.[3] Only two short passages in Life on the Screen describe practices and cases that show some similarities to today's discussions around fakes on social networking sites. In the first case, Turkle briefly recounts how she runs into a character named Dr. Sherry during her ethnographic exploration of MUDs, which turns out to be the creation of two college students gathering data for a paper they are writing on MUDs (Turkle 1995:15–16).

The second case is discussed in more detail by Turkle and had already attained "near-legendary status" (Turkle 1995: 228) by the time of Turkle's writing in 1995. The "case of the electronic lover" (Turkle 1995: 228) refers to an incident that allegedly took place in the 1980s, but that is highly visible in the early 1990s discourse on cyberspace, mostly as a warning against deception (cf. van Gelder 1985; Rheingold 1993: 164–165; Branscomb 1995: 1664–1665). The "electronic lover" as described by van Gelder (1985) concerns an allegedly disabled woman, Joan, regularly using a CompuServe chat in the 1980s, befriending and becoming emotionally involved with other women using the chat. After more and more of her friends try to contact or meet Joan in "real-life", it becomes clear that a male, non-disabled psychiatrist named Alex is the user behind Joan. In typical diction of cyberspace visionaries, Howard Rheingold uses his reference to the anecdote for a call to "formulate norms and spread them around" (Rheingold 1993: 166), while Anne Wells Branscomb discusses the legal ramifications of anonymity on the Internet and brings up the "electronic lover" as a complicated case highlighting the difference between "undesirable" and "appropriate" uses of anonymity (Branscomb 1995: 1665). Turkle herself refers to both the irritation among the chat community that a man gained access to women's spaces as well as criticism regarding the use of "Joan" as a character for "virtual sex" (Turkle 1995: 223), something that Turkle links to prostitution (230). In all four accounts, the character of Joan as played, performed or impersonated by Alex is understood as a form of deception: Rheingold and Turkle outright use the term, while Branscomb speaks of Alex as an "impostor" (Branscomb 1995: 1665).

The solitary, "near-legendary" (Turkle 1995: 228) anecdote thus serves as a cautionary tale in early internet discourse, its reception offering examples of the frictions that arise whenever the perceived differences between one's self-repre-

---

3   Thomas Foster provides a review of anthologies that are critical of these utopian visions for cyberspace (Foster 1999).

sentation online and the way one presents in 'real-life' are judged as too great by other users or external observers like journalists or researchers. This seems particularly likely when the "cross-expression" (Hall 1996: 151) across gender binaries is concerned, although it is for this very reason that the cyberfeminist Allucquére Rosanne Stone, writing in 1993, presents a more nuanced perspective on the same story. Stone works through the ambivalence of presenting different "personae" (79) in different contexts, thereby either conforming to or defying expectations. To Stone, there is no hierarchical difference between these personae on the internet, where different rules apply: "A few [interviewees in Stones' research] sympathized with the women Julie[4] had taken in, and understood that it takes time to realize, through experience, that social rules do not necessarily map across the interface between the physical and virtual worlds. But all of them had understood from the beginning that the nets presaged radical changes in social conventions, some of which would go unnoticed" (Stone 1993: 80). The technological conditions of these radical changes in the 1990s explicitly concern what Stone refers to as "the limited bandwidth mode of the net" (79) and what Turkle understands as the ability to "write our online personae into existence" (Turkle 1995: 263): social interaction on the internet of the early 1990s is near exclusively written. And with the exception of the "electronic lover", neither deception nor fake are terms that are used to describe deviations from the implicit norms of self-representation. In turn, this analysis of the discourse in the first half of the 1990s also reveals that truth is produced solely in writing during that period, like Turkle and Stone suggest—a coherent and continuous mode of self-representation will be regarded as true over time (see also Hall 1996: 159). The only exception to this is early strategies of voice verification in Bulletin Board Systems, where entry into specifically curated and moderated safe spaces (e.g. women-only groups) depends on a phone call with the administrator (cf. Driscoll 2022: 150). Here the limited bandwidth asserted by Stone is broadened through a transmedia verification process that can demand another layer of gender performance—truth depends on a change of medium.

Trolls and Fakesters

By the late 1990s and the early 2000s, the utopian promises of cyberspace regarding the possibility to explore different identities are met with more scepticism. Fakes and deception are starting to play a more relevant role in the discourse, and they first appear as mass phenomena in social networks in the early 2000s. In 1999 Judith Donath offers a less favourable interpretation of Steiner's cartoon than Turkle:

---

4   Stone uses different names for the characters and people in the anecdote. Instead of Joan and Alex, it is Julie and Sanford.

"The Net is a great leveler: no one knows if you are male or female, boss or underling, gray-haired or adolescent; 'on the Internet, nobody knows you're a dog.' This is not to your advantage if in the real world you hold some authority: no one can see that you are a respected professional at work in your office, not a teenager logging in from a bedroom" (Donath 1999: 38).

The internet's ability to hide differences in social status, age or gender is no longer taken as a chance for a new form of social relations, but it instead poses a risk to expertise and authority in online discussions. Donath explores several strategies to "anchor the virtual person to the real-world person" (38), all of which are aimed at the production of written truth. The signature for E-Mails or forum posts is singled out as a way to showcase one's credentials and affiliations (38–42), while E-Mail domains offer a technological hint towards their user's background (e.g. university domains) even though Donath admits that neither is safe from manipulation or deception (42). What was discussed through singular cases in the early 1990s now is subsumed under a collective noun, as Donath mentions trolls as users primarily interested in disrupting discussions and provoking other users. Unlike later scholarship on trolling that connects trolls to specific websites and platforms (cf. Phillips 2015) while also emphasising the troll's dependence on emotional responses, Donath operates with a far narrower understanding of what trolling is about: "Trolling is a game about identity deception, albeit one that is played without the consent of most of the players. The troll attempts to pass as a legitimate participant, sharing the group's common interests and concerns; the newsgroup members, if they are cognizant of trolls and other identity deceptions, attempt to both distinguish real from trolling postings and, upon judging a poster to be a troll, make the offending poster leave the group" (1999: 43). Donath perceives trolls as deceptive both with regard to their interest in the debates they try to disrupt as well as concerning the position from which they contribute to the debates, which necessitates the deciphering of what Donath calls "identity cues", so those technological or written markers that allow users to judge each other's self-representation. I propose to understand this reference to deception as well as the earlier uses of the term in the debates around the "electronic lover" as discursive precursors to later discussions about fakes.

In the late 1990s and early 2000s, Donath's research is accompanied by other contributions that either advocate for closer links between users and their online self-representation (cf. Punday 2000 for a similar argument regarding MUDs) or that explicitly criticise the early 1990s utopian cyberspace discourse for its view on the internet as an egalitarian space enabling identity exploration, like Lisa Nakamura studying "identity tourism" (2002: 40–44) in MUDs and chatrooms. The consequence-free identity exploration promised by Turkle no longer appears as an ideal enabled by technology, instead trolls derail discussions, deviant players harass others in MUDs and identity tourists perpetuate racist stereotypes by drawing upon the broadest possible clichés to roleplay the 'Other'. While the fake is not yet a term that appears frequently in these debates, the problems identified by the authors are already similar to today's discussions on the dangers of social media, in which fakes play a pivotal role.

The fake first becomes visible as a challenge to the values of 'true' self-representation on social networks in the early 2000s on Friendster. While not the first social networking site, Friendster is the most popular one from 2002 to 2004 and it became the first social network that was studied by researchers interested in identity performance (Marwick 2005; boyd/Heer 2006) or social organisation (boyd 2004; boyd 2006), while also being retroactively studied as a case for the decline and disintegration of social networks after its closure in 2011 (Garcia/Mavrodiev/Schweitzer 2013; Seki/Nakamura 2017). During the height of its popularity, Friendster is the site of a struggle between different values that erupts between a small, but vocal subset of its user-base and the company's leadership, especially its founder Jonathan Abrams. The "Fakester Revolution" (Angwin 2009: 50–58) is concerned with the question of whether or not Friendster's users should be allowed to maintain profiles with little to no relation to their 'real-life' self-representation. While Abrams understands his website as a service that highlights social relations that already exist before and beyond the internet, the self-proclaimed Fakesters insist on their right to be anyone or anything they want on the service, from celebrities to religious figures, animals, products or abstract concepts. Abrams' arguments, laid out in an interview with Lessley Anderson, are grounded in then-contemporary concerns regarding intellectual property violations on the internet while also demonstrating that the data-harvesting of Web 2.0 has not yet become the dominant business model of social networking sites:

"Abrams says he always knew Friendster would be 'more than just a dating site,' but he doesn't share the fakesters' vision of what it should be. Fakesters, he claims, expose him to possible lawsuits by companies like Disney, whose characters or images get co-opted by fakesters. He also thinks the fictional profiles screw up the networking effect. 'The whole point of Friendster is that you're connected to somebody through mutual friends, not by virtue of the fact that you both like Reese's Peanut Butter Cups,' he says (Anderson 2003).

Gathering data on its user's affinity for, among other things, peanut butter will become an important part of the revenue stream of Facebook and later social networks, but for Abrams, only social relations between 'real' people are of interest for his service. The Fakesters, on the other hand, articulate their demands in a manifesto that recalls the utopian promises of cyberspace. Authored by a user under the pseudonym of "Roy Batty", the replicant leader from *Blade Runner*, it calls for the far-reaching freedom of constantly shifting identities:

"Who we are is whom we choose to be at any given moment, depending on personality, whim, temperament, or subjective need. No other person or organization can abridge that right, as shape-shifting is inherent to human consciousness, and allows us to thrive and survive under greatly differing circumstances by becoming different people as need or desire arises. By assuming the mantle of the Other, it allows us, paradoxixcally[sic!], to complete ourselves. Every day is Halloween" (Batty 2003).

Consequently, one of the main claims of the "Fakester Manifesto" is that "Identity is provisional" (Batty 2003) and as such subjected to constant and continuous change that, for the Fakesters, can also result in Friendster profiles for God (Angwin 2009: 54). The "Fakester Revolution" plays out in a similar fashion to later social network movements, with many of the strategies employed similar to what Donath or Whitney Phillips might describe as trolling. Particularly Abrams himself is targeted, with a lot of Friendster profiles copying or modifying his own (Anderson 2003). Likely because of Friendster's quick decline in popularity after 2004, the "Fakester Revolution" is rarely discussed in research, but it remains an important event when studying the history of fakes on social networks. I argue that the Fakesters occupy a liminal space in the discourse on fakes by bridging the identity experimentation of the 1990s on the one hand and the rigid limits imposed on self-representation in social networks following the success of Facebook from 2006 on the other. Fakes are no longer singular cases of potentially harmful deception like in the 1990s, and they have not yet become the large-scale risk as which they are portrayed in the 2010s. Faking is partly play- and harmful on Friendster and the frictions it causes are (at least in hindsight when studying a long-defunct social network) not mainly between users, but between users and a specific corporate vision or a business interest held by the service's owners. In addition, Friendster does not yet have a (technical) solution for what speaking or asserting truth on the service means; there is no official policy on the acceptable range of self-representations in Friendster profiles and no verification process. This means that the truth of any Friendster profile is determined by its network of friends on the service and, again, the coherence of its performance over time.

Facebook, Capture, and Truth Through Data

Friendster is initially surpassed by Myspace in the number of users on the service, which according to Julia Angwin (2009: 60–61) is at least partially due to the flexibility Myspace offers its users in designing and customising their sites on the network. The dominant paradigm of self-representation on social networks, however, is shaped by Facebook from 2006 onwards. It is again a single anecdote or story that is very visible in the discourse surrounding self-representation and identity on Facebook. In his 2010 book on the inception and development of Facebook, the journalist David Kirkpatrick quotes Mark Zuckerberg from a 2009 interview:

"Zuckerberg designed Facebook that way. 'You have one identity', he says emphatically three times in a single minute during a 2009 interview. He recalls that in Facebook's early days some argued that the service ought to offer adult users both a work profile and a 'fun social profile'. Zuckerberg was always opposed to that. 'The days of you having a different image for your work friends or co-workers and for the other people you know are probably coming to an end pretty quickly', he says. He makes several arguments. 'Having two identities for yourself is an example of a lack of integrity', Zuckerberg says moralistically. But he also makes a case he sees as pragmatic—that 'the level of transparency the world has now won't support having two identities for a person'" (199).

The passage from Kirkpatrick's book is quoted frequently both in journalism as well as in academic writing and scholarship on Facebook (van Dijck 2013; Nunes 2016; Brusseau 2019). Some of these quotations mistakenly attribute the interview itself to Kirkpatrick (Bernard 2019: 25), whereas I have been unable to locate the source Kirkpatrick is quoting from. Not unlike the "electronic lover", what else Zuckerberg said and in which context the interview was conducted remains unclear, which turns Kirkpatrick's reference into an anecdote or a story that has several functions in the debates around identity on Facebook.[5] The most important one of these functions appears to position Zuckerberg's statement as evidence of a fundamental shift or change in the way that self-representation on the internet works and is enabled by websites and platforms. The apparent clarity in which Zuckerberg states his vision in Kirkpatrick's quote also contributes to its lasting popularity, even though it is necessary to point out that his idea of a unified and coherently articulated identity has never been an accurate description of the way Facebook is or was used. However, much like some of the other examples discussed in this paper, I argue that his quote is important because it outlines an ideal of how the internet or particular services should be used, regardless of whether or not this is the case. Zuckerberg's quote in Kirkpatrick's book thus fulfils a discursive function as much (if not more) as it can be interpreted as Facebook's company policy or mission statement: similar to Steiner's cartoon, it serves as a short hand for how (parts of) the internet are thought to work during a specific time and by a particular group. Indeed, Zuckerberg's vision for Facebook can be understood as a definitive denial of Steiner's dogs; it is no longer possible or desirable to leave people or platforms online guessing about who you are in 'real-life'. The example of the Fakesters discussed above shows that Zuckerberg's idea isn't new, even though it still signifies a shift in discourse through the moralistic frame in which he paints the experimentation with self-representation and identities as showing a lack of integrity, adding a dimension to the debate that was not present in the way Abrams tried to justify Friendster's rules. In the context

---

5   This is not to say the interview did not take place, in the same way as there is most likely an actual event as the source of the "electronic lover".

of the preceding analysis, I argue that Kirkpatrick's quote of Zuckerberg shows how he indirectly marks those ways of using Facebook as suspicious; they are no longer the ambivalent figures they were in the 1990s (as deceptions or trolls), but are clearly unwelcome, aberrant, and outdated practices. It is thus necessary to interrogate the discursive and economic transformation happening between Friendster and Facebook, to develop an understanding of how the idea of singular identities for every user came to be a central tenet for Facebook. Because of this the following paragraphs will supplement the discourse analysis conducted so far with a discussion of some of the concepts and ideas that underlie and inform the shift to Web 2.0 business models as well as the theoretical work that already connects said shift to questions of conflicts arising from differences in using the new platforms.

As I mentioned in passing when discussing Friendster, it is clear from Abrams' arguments in the Fakester debate that Friendster did not embrace the collection, use and sale of user data as part of its business model. However, following the Web 2.0 paradigm, it is becoming increasingly important for corporations to have access to unique sources for user data (O'Reilly 2005) which enable, among other things, targeted advertising. The Web 2.0 paradigm gave rise to a variety of new business models on the internet, most of them centered around user-generated content as well as user data. These developments have been widely criticised as violating user's privacy (cf. Zuboff 2019) or as extending capitalist exploitation to encompass all user activity on digital platforms (Heilmann 2015). Phillip Agre's 1994 concept of capture plays an important role in the debates around platform capitalism: originally envisioned as a complementary alternative to surveillance when discussing human-computer interaction in informatics, it has since been understood as a foundational concept for Web 2.0 data extraction (Chun 2016: 59–62; Mejias/Couldry 2019: 20; van Doorn/Badger 2020). Writing in 1994, Agre is concerned with the requirements for introducing computers to (industrial) workplaces and integrating them into the established workflow.

Instead of conceiving of computers in this context as surveillance technologies that somehow 'observe' workers, Agre argues that, coming from the established use of computer-based tracking technologies, it is necessary to understand the prerequisites for tracking in terms of computer science, namely the need for capturing human actions in a machine-readable manner (Agre 1994: 106–107). Capturing necessitates not only enabling computers to acquire specific data (from human actions), but also to represent or model these actions in the computer program, to be able to work with or act on them. Agre calls these models "grammars of action", based on their grounding in linguistic metaphors (107–113). Implementing these grammars of action in any system has several consequences, the most important of which is that human action must be reformulated around the grammar of action, so as to be machine-readable and capture-able. In Agre's example of the fast-food restaurant, this means that all the possible orders must be formulated as grammars of action, so that the restaurant's computer system can keep track of them. Both waiters and kitchen personnel then have to adhere to these grammars, enabling an efficient capturing of all relevant activities and transactions in the restaurant (Agre 1994: 103, 106, 117). The strength of Agre's approach as a complement to my analysis and one of the reasons for its lasting impact is that he already envisions the social and political dimensions of capture, which includes resistance against the implementation of capturing systems: "In particular, the work of imposing a capture system frequently involves conflict, as the affected parties organize resistance to it and its beneficiaries organize to overcome, dissolve, or circumvent this resistance" (1994: 121).

The large-scale capturing operations of social networks ostensibly are not facing much resistance by its users, which, according to Till Heilmann, may be due to the pleasurable and entertaining nature of the services offered by them (2015: 43). Instead of being confined to working environments, capturing is extended to leisure activities, with Facebook developing restrictive grammars of action around "friending" and "liking" other profiles, products, services, or brands (cf. Kaldrack, Röhle 2014). Using the platform means participating in its regime of capturing, which, as has been frequently documented (Fowler 2021) extends beyond the website or the social network of Facebook and captures user's behaviour on other digital platforms and services as well. The main node for these capturing operations remains the individual Facebook profile—of which, as becomes clear in Kirkpatrick's quote of Zuckerberg, each user is supposed to have only one. Andreas Bernard cites the same quote to argue that the Facebook profile marks the end of the "fantasies about a fluid and multiple self in boundless space" (2019: 24) that defined cyberspace discourse in the 1990s. According to him, the multiple identities that Zuckerberg denounces in Kirkpatrick's book pose a threat to Facebook's business model (Bernard 2019: 24–26). Following Agre, I argue that this threat works through interrupting, resisting, or introducing frictions into the capturing process. In this context, fakes can be considered practices of resistance against platform capitalism, which may be understood as discourse-critical according to Doll: Fakes expose and criticise the logic of capitalist data extraction through capture. Most social networks, most prominently Facebook, consequently seek to limit and control the practices of self-expression on their services, sometimes (as evidenced by Zuckerberg's position) by narrowing the range of accepted practices of self-representation or by attempting to connect users to their (single) profiles more closely.

However, the concept of capturing invites a different way of thinking about fakes, deception, and the frictions caused by them, as well as the discursive production of 'truth'. According to Grant Bollmer, social networks demand of their users to perform truth through data: "[...] the subject of social media is interpellated to perform truth through a full and total revelation of self as defined by the limits of network technology. This once again reduces both the human and the political to the circulation and flow of data over social media [...]" (2016: 157). He develops the concept of "nodal citizenship" to describe how only users that conform to these requirements and continuously produce, share and circulate data are granted "citizenship" in social networks in that they are regarded as "real", "true" or "authentic" users by their peers as well as the platforms, which also enables them to participate in the discourse in a different way (Bollmer 2016: 111–114). While the debates from the 1990s, as discussed above, clearly show truth on the internet as written, the era of social networks from Facebook onwards determines truth through data circulation.

This also means that everyone who does not participate in performing truth through data, who does not continuously share and circulate their personal data, is not only denied nodal citizenship, but also suspected of being a fake: "Failure to perform truth results in the branding of an individual as a liar, fake, or fraud, consequentially unworthy of inclusion within the social, unable to participate in the political" (Bollmer 2016: 156). Bollmer demonstrates this in his analysis of a well-known and widely discussed social network fake, the weblog and social media accounts of "Amina Arraf", ostensibly a young queer woman writing about her life in Damascus amidst the Syrian civil war and later revealed to be the creation of Tom MacMaster, an American student. MacMaster, Bollmer argues, perfectly spoke the truth of networks as Arraf, while still hiding behind her "fabricated identity" (Bollmer 2016: 168). In other words (and in accordance with Doll), Arraf is a successful fake because MacMaster adheres to the discursive criteria by which truth is produced in social media, namely openness and circulation of personal data, which leads to the character of Arraf being mistaken for a real person existing independently from social media profiles. While MacMaster was widely criticized after his fake was revealed, Bollmer cautions against criticizing him on the grounds of discursive, networked truth-production, which would depend on internalising those criteria, thereby extending the "regime of veridiction" (Bollmer 2016: 174) of social networks. Bollmer's approach offers a more nuanced understanding of the discursive mechanisms of truth-production in social networks: by emphasising the imperative of sharing, it becomes clear that the perception of truth among users of social networks depends on the circulation of personal data. This understanding of discursive truth differs from the one that informed the debates in the 1990s, where truth depended on coherently writing oneself, expressing one's personality and performing authenticity through writing. Nodal citizens, on the other hand, only exist in and through networks if they continuously provide personal data to other users (the 'nodes' to which they are linked on social networks), and, thereby, also to the platforms.

Capture, I want to argue with and against Bollmer, offers another form of truth on social networks altogether, in which the question of truth is decoupled from the discursive dimension of intentional self-representation and the judgement of other users. The passive, automatic data collection that happens through the usage of (not only) social networking sites can be considered independent from the content of individual profiles and the data users actively choose to circulate there, their "nodal citizenship" and validity depending on how other users judge their self-representation. Most of the data that is continuously captured is not part of a conscious project of self-representation, because it tracks a variety of user behaviours, from shopping to web searches. It influences advertising and search results and forms the model of the user that social networks and other Web 2.0 corporations are working with. Truth is neither written nor performed through actively shared data in this model, but it is the result of continuous capturing, ubiquitous tracking and data processing. In this way, capturing is more closely related to the "Quantified Self" (cf. Lupton 2016; Ruckenstein/Pantzar 2017) discourse and its promise of discovering (personal) truth through extensive data collection than it can be understood in the context of conscious and curated self-representation. As such, the resistance anticipated by Agre cannot take the form of playful, experimental, or deviant approaches to self-representation in social networks, because even the profile in which one claims to be a dog, to invert Steiner's vision, still captures user data that is made productive for the platform. Capturing knows no fakes—unless the users decide to intentionally use platforms and services in a way that supposedly does not correspond to their interests or regular usage practices. Instead, the practices of resistance reacting to capturing involve the attempt to evade capture altogether or to sabotage its implementation (Agre 1994: 121). Wendy Chun points out that "gaming the system" in the sense of unintended optimisation is also among the responses provoked by capturing (2016: 60–61). While all of these practices certainly introduce friction into the "economization of all interactions" (Chun 2016: 60) enabled by capturing in Web 2.0 platforms, they do not account for the status of fakes on these platforms.

Finsta and Personal Truth on the Social Web

The changing status of fakes and cases of deception related to self-representation on the internet raises questions regarding the discursive modes of truth-production on the internet and social networks more specifically. This has been demonstrated above, where I also draw on Agre's concept of capture to argue that the continuous capturing of user data constitutes a form of truth in social networks that can be considered as largely independent from the conscious efforts of self-representation. This means that with social networks in the Web 2.0 era, there is a dual logic to speaking or 'performing' individual truth. One is the discursive dimension that is briefly discussed by Doll and more extensively by Bollmer. This one continues the traditions of 'writing' truth on the internet from the 1990s, in addition to exacerbating the requirements for authenticity to also include other media like photography or video. Most users on these platforms expect a relationship between the profiles they encounter and the users maintaining said profiles. The refusal to self-represent according to these expectations introduces frictions that are frequently described as fakes (or as deception or, in case of Zuckerberg, as a lack of integrity). It is also this dimension that is accessible to discourse analysis, as has been shown in the first half of the paper. The second dimension to truth in social networks is the truth captured through individual user data that is automatically and continuously collected during the usage of Web 2.0 platforms and services. This one continues considerations in human computer interaction and organisational studies from the early 1990s and is made ubiquitous and profitable through the Web 2.0 paradigm. Most users on these platforms do not (and cannot) consciously manage all the data that is captured in this way. The refusal to have one's data captured or the attempts to 'game' the capturing system for one's benefit introduce frictions into these systems. Grasping this second dimension necessitates drawing upon theory to understand the way platform economies shape networked truth.

It can be assumed that there are some interrelations between these two dimensions. Capturing, for instance, can only be commercially successful if a large user base enjoys the platform (like Facebook) enough to spend time on there and use the services. The presence of profiles judged as fakes in an environment where users have come to expect a traceable relationship between profiles and their users can make that platform unattractive to use. The same is true if profiles come to regularly be associated with nonhuman actors such as bots, because the data captured from them holds no value for commercial purposes. Both Zuckerberg's interview cited by Kirkpatrick as well as Musk's reservations against fakes on Twitter before the acquisition can be understood in this context. On the one hand, capturing influences the individual user experience, not only through targeted advertising, but also by enhancing the visibility of profiles that are deemed successful according to the logics of capture. On the other hand, the dual modes of 'speaking truth' on social networks account for the well-documented (Margolin/Rahman 2020) reluctance of platforms to address disinformation (or Fake News), because this type of content regularly provokes reactions by users, which in turn aids the capturing process. Fakes, then, are frictions in the regimes of truth-production in social networks, but they only interfere in the capturing of user data indirectly.

A final point has to be made regarding how user's perceptions of what a fake is on social networks has changed and evolved since Facebook, especially with regard to capturing and the ways users deal with the demands of platforms. While fakes on Facebook follow the rules of discursive friction laid out by Doll and Bollmer, Instagram sees an inversion of these debates among users. Since around 2015 the term "Finsta", a portmanteau of fake and Instagram, emerges in web slang among the platform's users (Merriam-Webster), while gaining in popularity towards 2019 (Sherwood 2019). Finstas have since been mentioned in a US senate hearing and are defined in a *New York Times* article in 2021 as follows:

"'Fake' here does not refer to the account owner — finstas are real accounts run by real people, not bots — but instead distinguishes the private, and to some extent secret, account from the 'real' public-facing one. For instance, many celebrities with official verified

Instagram accounts are also believed to maintain secret private accounts for personal use; in such cases, the personal accounts would be referred to as finstas. Accounts with this unofficial designation are typically regarded as provinces of their owners' trusted friends — a group that may exclude family members" (Weaver/Issawi 2021).

The "fake Instagram" becomes the attempt to re-introduce privacy into an environment where it has become a contested concept (Johnson 2010) while also de-coupling the successful performance of self-following the logic of capture from a way of using the platform that puts less emphasis on metrics of success such as likes or shares. The Finsta practice has become the topic of research, most of which is concerned with the self-representation of teenagers and young adults on Instagram (Ross 2019; Dewar/Islam/Resor/Salehi 2019; Kang/Wei 2020). Through interviews with college students, Scott Ross is able to show how Instagram's users are acutely aware of how the platform works and which strategies regarding shot composition, aesthetics, tags or the timing of posts are likely to enhance their profile's visibility (2019: 7–9). What Ross calls "The Science of Instagram" and one of his interviewees refers to as her "pretty much strategic" (2019: 4) use of the platform can also be understood as an optimisation at the junction of what Chun calls "gaming the system" of capture and Bollmer's idea of nodal citizenship as a regime of veridiction on social networks. The way the platform is used no longer is 'just' about sharing enough personal details to be accepted as a valid user by others, but it increasingly becomes about optimising the process in which this sharing takes place, in accordance with the implicit requirements of capture. In turn, the users interviewed by Ross aspire to a way of using Instagram that allows them to show more different facets of themselves: "In their view, on Instagram one has to put forth an image that is aesthetically pleasing, funny, or interesting. *Finstas*, by contrast, allow users to be self-deprecating, goofy, or ugly. The taboos of Instagram can be traversed on *finsta*; by using a "fake" account, one could be more *real*" (Ross 2019: 3 [original emphasis]). In the context of tracing the changing notion of what is considered fake on the internet from the 1990s this development in the use of social networks makes apparent the consequences of the Web 2.0 economy and the logic of capture it relies on. Among Instagram users, fakes are not the profiles that are deemed too loosely (or not at all) connected to or representative of their users, but instead they are those profiles that only loosely (or not at all) submit to the logic of capturing and the metrics of popularity on the platform. The profiles that, as documented by Ross, sometimes are not even used to showcase photos or pictures at all; the profiles that do not aspire to be widely connected or to share lots of content. To their users, these profiles feel more real. In the context of the platform's logic of capturing, they can be considered fake, because they divert from the algorithmic metrics of success and introduce frictions into the discursive regimes of veridiction.[6] The regime of truth on social networks then has become fully intertwined with the media-technological conditions of their economies.

Conclusion

The paper has demonstrated the gradual shifts of what is considered fake on the internet between the 1990s and contemporary social networks. Understanding fake as a discursive term following Doll and Bollmer has enabled the analysis of both discussions among users and academics, such as Turkle or Stone as well as the economic and technological conditions of today's social media platforms. It has been shown that while fakes and deception were present among the earliest internet communities, the playful experimentation with identities and ways to self-represent online were perceived as a chance instead of a liability in the utopian cyberspace discourse of the 1990s. And even after this gradually changed in the later 1990s and early 2000s, the 'regimes of veridiction', the discursive rules for 'speaking truth' remained largely unchanged: truth was to be written in a continuous, coherent form of self-expression over time. This still allowed for playful aberrations that introduced frictions into early social networking sites as well as blogs. This changes when the business models developing from the Web 2.0 paradigm instantiate a different, technological regime of truth in social networks: capturing as the attempt to make human (inter)action on the internet machine readable and convert it to a source of data, which can then be capitalised upon. This introduces a second layer that is mostly inaccessible to users to the criteria through which truth in social networks is determined: platforms are able to develop an understanding of who their users are that is independent of the different modes of self-representation that are prevalent on networks like Facebook or Instagram. And only developing an understanding of the implicit rules of capture enables users to 'game the system' by using platforms like Instagram purely strategically, to maximise their metrics for success. This, in turn, changes the meaning of what is regarded as fake, because truth now appears to be tied to submitting to capturing—inefficient and personal social network profiles appear 'fake' in contrast to this.

Fakes, then, are probably not the danger to the business models of social media platforms they are sometimes made out to be. However, as discursive figures they are effective ways of tracing the transformations taking place in and through the communities, technologies, and economics of social networks. They figure both

---

6   Finstas do still capture their user's data, but the fairly limited way in which they are used according to the ethnographic research by Ross and others suggests that they do not invite participation to a degree that could be considered significant for capturing, at least not compared to their respective "rinsta" or Real Instagram counterparts.

in utopian as well as in dystopian perspectives on the (early) internet, while also being present as constant sources of friction on the social web. Through interrogating what is and is not labelled as fake on the internet at different points in time, it becomes possible to get a grasp on the different systems of values that shape how users, scholars, corporations, or institutions view the internet. This includes, but is not limited to, the discursive and technological means through which truth is produced on various services and platforms. Perhaps in there lies the potential to make fakes productive—not economically, but as a chance to develop a better understanding of digital cultures and their transformations.

Acknowledgements: The author wishes to thank the editors, both anonymous peer reviewers as well as Christine Hanke for their valuable comments on the first draft of this paper.

List of References

Agre, P.E. (1994): "Surveillance and Capture: Two Models of Privacy." The Information Society, 10(2), pp. 101–127.

Anderson, L. (2003): "Attack of the Smartasses." In: SFWeekly, 19 August. Retrieved from www.sfweekly.com/issues/2003-08-13/feature.html.

Angwin, J. (2009): Stealing MySpace: The Battle to Control the Most Popular Website in America. New York: Random House.

Barlow, J.P. (2001): "A Declaration of the Independence of Cyberspace". In: P. Ludlow (ed.), Crypto Anarchy, Cyberstates, and Pirate Utopias. Cambridge, MA/London: MIT Press, pp. 27–30.

Batty, R. (2003): "The Fakester Manifesto." danah boyd | apophenia, 30 July. Retrieved from https://www.zephoria.org/thoughts/archives/2003/08/17/the_fakester_manifesto.html.

Bernard, A. (2019): The Triumph of Profiling: The Self in Digital Culture. Cambridge: Polity Press.

Bollmer, G. (2016): Inhuman Networks: Social Media and the Archaeology of Connection. New York/London/Oxford/New Delhi: Bloomsbury.

boyd, d. (2006): "Friends, Friendsters, and Top 8: Writing Community into Being on Social Network Sites." First Monday, 11(12).

boyd, d./Heer, J. (2006): "Profiles as Conversation: Networked Identity Performance on Friendster." In: Proceedings of the 39th Annual Hawaii International Conference on System Sciences (HICSS'06), Kauai.

boyd, d. (2004): "Friendster and Publicly Articulated Social Networking." In: CHI '04 Extended Abstracts on Human Factors in Computing Systems. CHI 2004 Conference on Human Factors in Computing Systems, New York: Association for Computing Machinery (CHI EA '04), pp. 1279–1282.

Branscomb, A.W. (1995): "Anonymity, Autonomy, and Accountability: Challenges to the First Amendment in Cyberspaces." The Yale Law Journal, 104(7), pp. 1639–1679.

Brusseau, J. (2019): "Ethics of Identity in the Time of Big Data." First Monday, 24(5–6), pp. 00–11.

Chun, W.H.K. (2016): Updating to Remain the Same: Habitual New Media. Cambridge, MA,/London: The MIT Press.

Dewar, S. et al. (2019): "Finsta: Creating 'Fake' Spaces for Authentic Performance." In: Extended Abstracts of the 2019 CHI Conference on Human Factors in Computing Systems. New York, NY, USA: Association for Computing Machinery (CHI EA '19), pp. 1–6.

Doll, M. (2015): Fälschung und Fake: Zur Diskurskritischen Dimension des Täuschens. Berlin: Kadmos Verlag.

Donath, J.S. (2005): "Identity and Deception in the Virtual Community." In: P. Kollock/M.A. Smith (eds.), Communities in Cyberspace. London/New York: Routledge, pp. 27–57.

Driscoll, K. (2022): The Modem World: A Prehistory of Social Media. New Haven/London: Yale University Press.

Evon, D. (2016): "Did Pope Francis Shock World by Endorsing Donald Trump for President?" Snopes, 10 July. Retrieved from https://www.snopes.com/fact-check/pope-francis-donald-trump-endorsement/.

Finsta (no date). Retrieved from: https://www.merriam-webster.com/wordplay/what-does-finsta-mean-fake-instagram.

Foster, T. (1999): "The Rhetoric of Cyberspace: Ideology or Utopia?" Contemporary Literature, 40(1), pp. 144–160.

Foucault, M. (1980): Power/Knowledge: Selected Interviews and Other Writings, 1972-1977. C. Gordon (ed.). New York: Pantheon Books.

Foucault, M. (1982): "Is it Really Important to Think? An Interview Translated by Thomas Keenan." Philosophy & Social Criticism, 9(1), pp. 31–40.

Fowler, G.A. (2021): "There's No Escape from Facebook, Even if You Don't Use It." In: Washington Post, 24 September. Retrieved from https://www.washingtonpost.com/technology/2021/08/29/facebook-privacy-monopoly/.

Galloway, A. (2004): Protocol: How Control Exists after Decentralization. Cambridge, MA/London: MIT Press.

Garcia, D./Mavrodiev, P./Schweitzer, F. (2013): "Social Resilience in Online Communities: The Autopsy of Friendster." In: Proceedings of the first ACM Conference on Online Social Networks. New York: Association for Computing Machinery (COSN '13), pp. 39–50.

Garrity, K. (2023): "No, that isn't the real AOC you may have seen on Twitter." In: POLITICO, 30 May. Retrieved from https://www.politico.com/news/2023/05/30/fake-aoc-twitter-account-musk-00099319.

Hall, K. (1996): "Cyberfeminism." In: S.C. Herring (ed.), Computer-Mediated Communication. Amsterdam: John Benjamins Publishing Company, pp. 147–170.

Heilmann, T.A. (2015): "Datenarbeit im 'Capture'-Kapitalismus: Zur Ausweitung der Verwertungszone im Zeitalter informatischer Überwachung." Zeitschrift für Medienwissenschaft, 2/2015(13), pp. 35–48.

Ito, M. (1994): "Cybernetic Fantasies: Extensions of Selfhood In a Multi-User Dungeon." In: Annual Meeting of the American Anthropological Association, Atlanta, Georgia, pp. 1–14.

Johnson, B. (2010): "Privacy no longer a social norm, says Facebook founder." In: The Guardian, 11 January. Retrieved from https://www.theguardian.com/technology/2010/jan/11/facebook-privacy.

Kaldrack, I./Röhle, T. (2014): "Divide and Share: Taxonomies, Orders and Masses in Facebook's Open Graph." Computational Culture, 4.

Kang, J./Wei, L. (2020): "Let Me Be at My Funniest: Instagram Users' Motivations for Using Finsta (a.k.a., fake Instagram)." The Social Science Journal, 57(1), pp. 58–71.

Kirkpatrick, D. (2011): The Facebook Effect: The Inside Story of the Company That Is Connecting the World. New York: Simon & Schuster.

Lupton, D. (2016): The Quantified Self. Cambridge, UK: Polity.

Marwick, A.E. (2005): "'I'm a Lot More Interesting than a Friendster Profile': Identity Presentation, Authenticity and Power in Social Networking Services." In: Association for Internet Researchers 6.0, Chicago, pp. 1–26.

Mejias, U.A./Couldry, N. (2019): The Costs of Connection: How Data Is Colonizing Human Life and Appropriating It for Capitalism. Stanford: Stanford University Press.

Nakamura, L. (2002): Cybertypes: Race, Ethnicity, and Identity on the Internet. New York: Routledge.

Nunes, M. (2013): "Ecstatic Updates: Facebook, Identity, and the Fractal Subject." In: J.M. Wise/H. Koskela (eds.), New Visualities, New Technologies. Routledge, pp. 7–27.

O'Reilly, T. (2005): "What Is Web 2.0." O'Reilly, 30 September. Retrieved from https://www.oreilly.com/pub/a/web2/archive/what-is-web-20.html.

Phillips, W. (2015): This Is Why We Can't Have Nice Things: Mapping the Relationship between Online Trolling and Mainstream Culture. Cambridge, MA: MIT Press.

Punday, D. (2000): "The Narrative Construction of Cyberspace: Reading Neuromancer, Reading Cyberspace Debates." College English, 63(2), pp. 194–213.

Rahman, H./Margolin, S. (2020): "Why Are Social Media Platforms Still So Bad at Combating Misinformation?" Kellogg Insight, 3 August. Retrieved from https://insight.kellogg.northwestern.edu/article/social-media-platforms-combating-misinformation.

Rheingold, H. (1993): The Virtual Community: Homesteading on the Electronic Frontier. Reading, MA/New York: Addison Wesley.

Ross, S. (2019): "Being Real on Fake Instagram: Likes, Images, and Media Ideologies of Value." Journal of Linguistic Anthropology, 29(3), pp. 359–374.

Roumeliotis, G./Dang, S. (2022): "Musk Says $44 Billion Twitter Deal on Hold Over Fake Account Data" Reuters, 16 May. Retrieved from https://www.reuters.com/technology/musk-says-44-billion-twitter-deal-hold-2022-05-13/.

Ruckenstein, M./Pantzar, M. (2017): "Beyond the Quantified Self: Thematic exploration of a Dataistic Paradigm." New Media & Society, 19(3), pp. 401–418.

Rushe, D. (2012): "Facebook Share Price Slumps Below $20 Amid Fake Account Flap." In: The Guardian, 3 August. Retrieved from https://www.theguardian.com/technology/2012/aug/02/facebook-share-price-slumps-20-dollars.

Seki, K./Nakamura, M. (2017): "The Mechanism of Collapse of the Friendster Network: What Can We Learn from the Core Structure of Friendster?" Social Network Analysis and Mining, 7(1), pp. 1–21.

Sherwood, J. (2019): "Why Generation Z Are Choosing 'Finsta' over 'Insta'." In: BBC News, 27 September. Retrieved from https://www.bbc.com/news/blogs-trending-49852428.

Steiner, P. (1993): "On the Internet, Nobody Knows You're a Dog." The New Yorker, 5 July.

Stone, A.R. (1996): The War of Desire and Technology at the Close of the Mechanical Age. Cambridge, MA: MIT Press.

Turkle, S. (1995): Life on the Screen: Identity in the Age of the Internet. New York: Simon & Schuster Paperbacks.

van Dijck, J. (2013): "'You Have One Identity': Performing the Self on Facebook and LinkedIn." Media, Culture & Society, 35(2), pp. 199–215.

van Doorn, N./Badger, A. (2020): "Platform Capitalism's Hidden Abode: Producing Data Assets in the Gig Economy." Antipode, 52(5), pp. 1475–1495.

Van Gelder, L. (1985): "The Strange Case of the Electronic Lover." Ms. Magazine, October. Retrieved from: https://lindsyvangelder.com/sites/default/files/Plinkers.org%20-%20Electronic%20Lover.htm_.pdf.

Weaver, C. and Issawi, D. (2021) "'Finsta,' Explained." In: The New York Times, 30 September. Retrieved from https://www.nytimes.com/2021/09/30/style/finsta-instagram-accounts-senate.html.

Zuboff, S. (2019): The Age of Surveillance Capitalism: The Fight for a Human Future at the New Frontier of Power. New York: Public Affairs.

To Be Real or Not to Be

On the Discursive Friction of "Authenticity" Displayed by Instagram and its Design Alternative BeReal

Oliver Ruf, Aleksandra Vujadinovic

Abstract

This article explores the concept of discursive friction and its relationship to design alternatives for the concept of authenticity within the social media platforms Instagram and BeReal. First, we provide an insight into media studies research on the perception of authenticity in social media, which clarifies the users' perspective on the concept. Subsequently, we examine how Instagram and BeReal define and promote authenticity in their branding process. In doing so, we contrast Instagram's tendency for unrealistic and idealised self-portrayals, which has been criticised, with BeReal's ethos of uncontrollability and spontaneity. By analysing the product descriptions and guidelines of these two platforms, we discuss whether BeReal offers a significant design alternative to Instagram which corresponds to the user's understanding of authenticity. In particular, we focus on the specific affordances and conventions each platform provides. Despite the fact that BeReal is a product of the Silicon Valley, which may limit its capacity for radical change, this article demonstrates that examining design alternatives like BeReal can foster critical thinking. Following these considerations, we want to address the thesis that design alternatives as a commentary concentrate and materialise discursive frictions or—in other words—value conflicts that emerge when BeReal actively comments on Instagram's idea of authenticity in its branding process.

Keywords

social media studies, media aesthetics, platform studies, design theory, digital media culture

1. Introduction

In response to the pervasive use of social media platforms like Instagram, which have gained a reputation for being deceptive, the application BeReal has posed the question of what it means to be authentic or inauthentic on social media since its inception in 2020. "Fakeness" or "inauthentic behaviour" in this media discourse

DOI 10.14361/dcs-2023-0207

DCS | Digital Culture and Society | Vol. 9, Issue 2 | © transcript 2025

on authenticity is typically discussed in relation to spam and bots,[1] the possibility of purchasing followers, likes and comments,[2] as well as on the (Instagram)culture including the positivity bias and algorithms as a black box.[3] This article builds on recent research on these topics and on the concept of authenticity as a value of social media (Wang/Skovira 2017; Maares/Banjac/Hanusch 2020; Haimson et al. 2021; Kreiling/Meier/Reinecke 2022). It adopts a perspective that focuses on the fabrication and branding of authenticity on or rather *by and in between* the social media platforms Instagram and BeReal in relation to the imagination of authenticity by social media users. This process can be understood as an expression of a certain discursive friction within those media phenomena that negotiate what the adjective "social" here reflects anew. The term "discursive friction" employed in this article is derived from the concept of design objects "acting as rhetorical devices, artefacts or scenarios meant to prove a point or mobilise conflicting worldviews" (Lorusso 2023: 149). In light of the understanding of discourse as practices that systematically form the objects they address (cf. Foucault 1981: 74), it can be argued that conflicting worldviews on the topic of authenticity in social media are communicated in the branding process of the object—here BeReal—and simultaneously form an idea of it. Building on Carl von Clausewitz, Wolfgang Ernst argues that the concept of "friction" (German: 'Friktionen') refers to "the differences [...] between the strategic diagram and the actual hindrances occurring in its practical implementation" (Ernst 2023: 121). This understanding emerged in the context of an anthology on cybernetic thinking and its frictions, which posits that a "friction-focused inquiry signals a networked space of epistemic exchange where the operations taking place in its nodes are essential to trace the course of such transfer, and moreover to grasp the constitution, even the transformation, of the episteme thus exchanged" (Gómez-Venegas 2023: 8). With regard to our subject—BeReal's branding process and its idea of authenticity—the strategic diagram corresponds to to the design of the platform, which encompasses the design choices of the platform owner and the material implementation of these. Consequently, our concept of design encompasses not only the physical appearance and materiality of the product but also the statements and explanations

---

1   See for example "A pornbot stole my identity on Instagram. It took an agonizing month to get it deleted" (27 February 2023). Retrieved from: https://www.theguardian.com/lifeandstyle/2023/feb/28/a-pornbot-stole-my-identity-on-instagram-it-took-an-agonising-month-to-get-it-deleted; "How Fake Is Instagram?" (26 October 2021). Retrieved from https://lunio.ai/blog/paid-social/how-fake-is-instagram/.

2   See for example "Instagram: Why pacing for followers and likes is bad news for real fans" (23 July 2019). Retrieved from: https://www.bbc.com/news/newsbeat-48952123.

3   See for example "'There is no standard': investigations finds AI algorithms objectify women's bodies" (8 February 2023). Retrieved from: https://www.theguardian.com/technology/2023/feb/08/biased-ai-algorithms-racy-women-bodies.

made during the branding process and product description, which collectively contribute to the formation of the perceived object.

As BeReal is being perceived as an alternative to Instagram[4] or even an "Anti-Instagram"[5], we aim to elaborate on the idea that discursive frictions regarding the authenticity of Instagram are materialised through the design alternative BeReal. In order to clarify the relationship between the concept of a "design alternative" and the concept of "friction", it is necessary to refer back to our understanding of the design choices made by the platform owner. These choices can be understood as "design alternatives" that reference and criticise an existing and established artefact (in this case, Instagram) while simultaneously adopting a general logic of a system (in this case, social media). However, before doing so, it is necessary to define more precisely the relationship between the concept of a "design alternative" and the concept of "friction". It can be argued that friction is a key concept in design. As design is not "focusing on the state of things" but "how things ought to be" ("[a]nd of course they ought to be better", Lorusso 2023: 63), it can be said that design creates friction in the sense that it uncovers the "chaos" (ibid.: 17) that it presupposes. A design alternative, therefore, is the concretisation of a problem that needs to be solved, and at the same time, the solution to that problem—"a commentary":

Especially since the '90s, a novel idea of the role of design has gained momentum: the idea that design can be not just about objects or services hitting the market, but about object acting as rhetorical devices, artefacts or scenarios meant to prove a point or mobilise conflicting worldviews. Such design outputs should make people think about and discuss relevant issues, perhaps even making them change their point of view. These products (be they speculative devices or fiction films) don't belong to the everyday life of the users but are divorced from it: they act like a commentary. This is what Bruce and Stephanie Tharp broadly call 'discursive design'. (ibid.: 149)

Despite the fact that the vast majority of design alternatives are futile attempts to effect social change, they can nevertheless shed light on the underlying value conflicts in the sociotechnical space. This framework does not "reconcile with commodification" (Taylor 2022: 138) as the design alternative itself is a critical product. In order to gain a fuller understanding of how design alternatives function as critical products within the capitalist framework, however, it would be beneficial to revisit the existentialist notion of authenticity and reconsider its

4   See for example "Be Real: the New App Replacing Instagram and Snapchat" (23 April 2021). Retrieved from: https://mediummagazine.nl/be-real-the-new-app-replacing-instagram-and-snapchat/.

5   "BeReal: Ist das Anti-Instagram besser als das Original?" (4 April 2022). Retrieved from https://www.computerbild.de/artikel/cb-News-Internet-BeReal-Ist-das-Anti-Instagram-besser-als-das-Original-33262533.html.

relevance in this context. As Banet-Weiser (2012) proposed, the existentialist view of authenticity, which posits the simplistic and false dichotomy of "authentic vs. inauthentic" and "authentic vs. commercial" (ibid.: 5, 10, 13), as well as the Marxist view of the authentic as an immaterial space, respectively the authentic inner self in opposition to the outer performed self, should be rejected:

Social theorists and commentators from Rousseau to Marx to Thoreau have contemplated the space of the authentic as a space that is not material. This arrangement is mirrored within individuals: the authentic resides in the inner self (or, for Marx, the unalienated self); the outer self is merely an expression, a performance, and is often corrupted by material things (and more specifically, as Marx points out so eloquently, by capitalism). (ibid.: 10)

Building on Banet-Weiser, we define "authenticity" "as [a] cultural space defined by branding" as well "as a relationship between consumers and branders" (ibid.: 10). Authenticity, therefore "can be branded" (ibid.: 13) and "is itself a brand" (ibid.: 14). Consequently, we posit that authenticity is a complex value that is fabricated between producers and consumers of social media and its content. This theoretical background allows us to examine phenomena that are excluded from existentialist discourse (cf. Wortmann 2018: 209). However, while the current research focuses on the producer of authenticity as the "content creator", we want to discuss the imagination of authenticity declared by another actor: the platform owner. To do so, we will first provide an overview of the current research in media studies on the imagination of authenticity. Secondly, we will examine the ways in which BeReal and Instagram define authenticity and how they position themselves in relation to one another. In particular, we will focus on how authenticity is discussed in the process of announcing and branding the alternative BeReal. As Haimson et al. (2021: 13) observed, "[d]ifficulties arise when a multifaceted concept—authenticity—poses as a simple value". Our perspective aims to contribute another layer to the ongoing discussion on this topic. This layer, or rather our perspective derived from media culture studies, focuses on the entanglement of users' and platform owners' ideas of authenticity, as well as the materialisation of authenticity in the form of interface elements (conventions) or the design of the platforms in general (affordances). In this sense authenticity is a practice that occurs in "nature" as well as in "technology" that forms values and directs performances.

In accordance with our initial assumption that authenticity is a complex value that is fabricated between producers and consumers of social media and their content, our analysis is structured as follows: Using the method of discourse analysis, we elaborate on the imagination of authenticity announced by the two platforms. Our material consists of official statements about authenticity, which can be found on the platform owners' websites, and the platform's self-presentation in the app stores. On the one hand, we analyse material of an advertising nature that is typically placed on the home page or the description of the product in the app store. On the other hand, we analyse statements that are not immediately visible to the users and are typically found on the websites' guideline pages. In order to elaborate on the platform owners' scope of action in terms of authenticity, we will employ the approach of affordances. This approach is used to identify the practices enabled or restricted by the platforms regarding the creation and expression of authenticity based on their logic and structure. The concept has been adapted by numerous disciplines to align with their respective ontologies and epistemologies: for instance, by Levine in her publication *Forms. Whole, Rhythm, Hierarchy, Network* (2017) and by Helmond and Bucher in their paper on *The Affordances of Social Media Platforms* (2017). The concept was already reintroduced in 2008 by Zillien in her contribution on the concept of affordances in media sociology (cf. Zillien 2008: 163). These modified approaches are on one hand based on the work of Gibson, who conceptualised affordances as a relationship between the human and their environment (Gibson 1982), and on the other hand on the ideas of Norman, who examined the relationship between humans and everyday things (cf. Norman 2014: 24). In summary, there are three different approaches to choose from: 1. Gibson's end-user-centred approach, 2. Norman's designer-centred approach and 3. Bucher and Helmond's platform-sensitive approach that concentrates on "how platforms may afford different things to various types of users, including end-users, developers and advertisers" (30). In focusing on the perspective of platform owners and not considering the diverse end-users, we will adopt the designer-centred approach proposed by Norman. However, this approach can be further elucidated by taking into account the differentiation between high-level and low-level affordances proposed by Bucher and Helmond (2017). The high-level affordances of social network sites include "persistence, replicability, scalability, and searchability [...] visibility, editability, [...], and association" (ibid.: 12). These affordances address the "dynamics or conditions" (ibid.) enabled by media. In contrast, low-level affordances are set in connection with the "materiality of the medium, in specific features, buttons, screens and platforms" (ibid.). The authors posit that these technical features correspond to the furniture of the technical landscape (cf. ibid.), a reference to Norman's conceptualisation of the design of everyday things. However, Norman already denounced this understanding of affordances in 1999 in a critique: "When designing a graphical screen layout, designers greatly rely on conventional interpretations of the symbols and placement. Much of the discussion about the use of affordances is really addressing conventions, or what I call cultural constraints" (Norman 1999: 40). In this context, the concept of "low-level affordances", as defined by Bucher and Helmond, differs from the affordances as understood within Norman's designer-centred approach. Rather than affordances, these low-level affordances can be more accurately described as conventions. This distinction between affordances and conventions will be further explored in the subsequent discussion of existing research on social media users' perceptions of authenticity, our analysis, and the presentation of our findings.

2. Authenticity as a Value of Social Media

The findings presented in the following paragraphs are derived from research positions that analysed two distinct aspects of social media: the affordances of social media in relation to the possibility of authentic display and the question of what authenticity is, or rather, what is perceived as authentic by users and why. In order to gain multifaceted insight into the concept of authenticity as a value of social media, this brief literature review aims to depict different approaches and their ontologies. This insight serves as the basis for the analysis of the branding process of BeReal, with a view to identifying the ideas of authenticity that can be discerned within this process. To begin, we will first present a study that can be classified as existentialist, since it is based on the differentiation of inner and outer self (Wang/Skovira 2017). This will be followed by an introduction to a study that demonstrates what users perceive to be authentic and the reasons why they do not act in accordance with their ideas of authenticity (Haimson et al. 2021). Subsequently, the focus will turn to the visual aspects. The study by Maares, Banjac, and Hanusch (2020) on Instagram and the research by Kreiling, Meier, and Reinecke (2022) on the formats "story" and "post" are key concepts used in the BeReal's branding process to differentiate BeReal from Instagram. In contrast to Wang and Skovira (2017), the latter three positions perceive authenticity as a social construct rather than an innate value. This allows them to discuss the connection between ideas of authenticity and material artefacts, such as the formats "story" and "post".

Although we reject the existentialist conceptualisation of authenticity proposed by Wang and Skovira (2017), their theoretical model for studying relationships between authenticity and technology may prove to be a productive framework for examining the social media platforms' images and imaginations of authenticity. Their method is based on the "theory of quality" proposed by Dewey (1960) and the distinction between the man-made and the natural taken on by Pallud and Straub (2007), which connotes fakeness and simulation with technology—the man-made—contrasting it with the "natural" (cf. Wang/Skovira 2017: 1). The authors propose three dimensions of authenticity: the authentic self, the authentic being, and the authentic context. The *authentic self* is defined as "conscious of [its] location and stand in a particular situation" and is "living in a paradigmatic space and whose rationality in decisions and actions affects honest and true consequences in affording and constraining situations" (ibid.: 3). Consequently, the authentic self appears to be a reflective and relational self that considers the two forms also examined by Wortmann (2018): "Sich-zu-sich- und [...] Sich-zu-anderen-Verhalten" (214), signifying the accounting of a relation to one's self and others. The *authentic being* is concerned with living as an authentic self. In this context, authentic is defined as "to live in-between" (Wang/Skovira 2017: 3). This state is described as "a mirror, a bond, a merging, a together-ness of action-and-reaction that reflect and embody the mutualness" (ibid.). Additionally, the authentic being is described as an "innate given" or a "cognitive effort" (ibid.).

This implies that the self must move freely within the space with constraints (cf. ibid.). The final and most crucial dimension to be considered is the *authentic context*. It focuses on the environmental freedom of choice, or, as we argue, the affordances or conventions of the platform: "Everyday actions are choices made about the purpose of being-in-the-world among the many possibilities which our environing world presents to us" (ibid.: 4). An authentic self needs to be aware of these possibilities respectively the context it lives in, in order to count as authentic. Referencing Barrett's work *What is Existentialism?* (1964) the authors associate the absence of awareness of the context with an inauthentic life "especially in the presentational mode of social media" (Wang/Skovira 2017: 4). Social media as a context has the affordances of "immediacy and lack of real-time control" (ibid.). According to the authors, the content "is not filtered, edited, or regulated as that of traditional media has been" (ibid.) and lacks professionals like editors, balancers, and controllers (cf. ibid.). Marketing in connection to the affordances of social media is seen as a "side-effect" (ibid.) that stirs up questions about the quality of the presented content. Following Dewey's discussion of the Peircian theory of quality, Wang and Skovira distinguish three levels of quality: "Firstness of self-experience, Secondness of relationships, and Thirdness of symbolic representation" (ibid.: 6). (Social) media are situated on the third level according to Wang and Skovira, which withdraws the possibility of a true experience on social media: "If a large portion of one's daily life is spent in languages and/or in broadcasting texts and images, then one is reducing the percentage of truly living in life experiences. When one is living life through a screen, there is an opportunity cost. The cost is not being present when experiencing the moments that make life authentic." (ibid.) The authors adhere to the existentialist narrative that does not allow for an in-between perspective. We assume that the same perspective will be dominant in the negotiation of authenticity in the discourse surrounding Instagram and the alternative BeReal.

Another perspective taken on by Haimson et al. (2021) focuses on the perception of authenticity during prevalent life events. These include graduation from college, starting a new job, and the death of loved ones or recovery from addiction (cf. ibid.: 2). The authors discuss the following research questions: "How do people who have recently experienced life transitions view online authenticity?", "Do these people consider online authenticity to be achievable?", and "How does people's conception of online authenticity relate to their self-disclosure and self-presentation on social media during major life transitions?" (ibid.). As a result, the authors identify an authenticity paradox:

(1) Many consider authenticity an important construct to uphold in their personal lives and online presentations. (2) Many believe that authenticity requires sharing both positive and negative experiences with broad networks online. (3) Thus, though they do not always recognize it, online authenticity may be unachievable for many, particularly in relation to

difficult or stigmatized events (due to factors including positivity bias, impression manage-ment, and context collapse). (ibid.: 11)

The positivity bias appears to be a rule that discourages users from sharing negative content, despite their perception of it as crucial for authenticity (cf. ibid.: 10). Impression management through the curation of online content is also linked to the positivity bias and is performed regularly, which also contradicts the imagination of authentic behaviour on social media (cf. ibid.). Furthermore, the authors note that users tend to present different personas on different social media platforms, for example, Facebook and LinkedIn (cf. ibid.). The idea of the authenticity paradox highlights the impact of the platform's power over its users. Despite their awareness of biases and the logic of social media platforms respec-tively the context as described by Wang and Skovira (2017), they tend to act against their imagination of the concept of authenticity. It becomes evident that mere awareness is insufficient to alter usage practices. The implications for design, as proposed by the authors at the conclusion of the paper, are crucial for the develop-ment of design alternatives or redesigns. In the case of the authenticity paradox, the authors suggest that a superior user experience could be attained if the connection between users with similar experiences were enhanced. Furthermore, the imple-mentation of anonymous sharing is proposed as it would encourage individuals to share negative experiences. Conversely, the provision of users with the option of establishing multiple accounts would satisfy the requirement for the consistent display of different aspects of their identity. The implications that appear to be absent are proposed as a solution, nevertheless, as will be demonstrated in our analysis, they are often already a part of social media platforms that are in general perceived as inauthentic. Connecting Wang and Skovira's thoughts on context and the issue presented by Haimson et al., context is either deliberate but not effective or perceived as deliberate but not deliberate to full extent.

The research conducted by Maares, Banjac, and Hanusch (2020) focused on the labour of visual authenticity on social media. The study aimed to investigate how producers and audiences perceive authenticity on Instagram. Concluding on their literature review the paper proposes that authenticity, on the one hand, can be understood as a performance linking it to the editing process of the visual (cf. ibid.: 2) and on the other hand, as a "concept [that] is commonly used to evaluate the genuineness and originality of objects or individuals" (ibid.). Authenticity is once again perceived as a social construct that "has become the core narrative to overcome the perception of a mere profit-orientation across all fields of cultural production" (ibid.). This perception of the concept has its roots in cultural studies (cf. Ruf/Rupert-Kruse/Grabbe 2022), where it is conceptualised as a display effect or a discursive strategy relating it to "obfuscation" (Wortmann 2018: 208). The term "obfuscation" implies that someone is intentionally trying to deceive or mislead others by, for example, making information unnecessarily complex, unclear or even by not addressing important information at all. Therefore, obfuscation is linked to dishonesty and manipulation for example in the advertising industry. However, although the term "obfuscation" has negative connotations, the above-mentioned authors do not support the existentialist differentiation of authentic and commercial. The objective is to reconstruct the processes by which authenticity is constituted and attributed. In alignment with our thesis that the discourse, as well as the materialisation in the form of BeReal, rely heavily on the existentialist narrative, Maares et al. (2020) note that in social media culture, "'authenticity' encapsulates 'honesty without pretense' along with displaying one's 'hidden inner life'" (ibid.: 2). Furthermore, it is noted that "the Self and all its narrations are transformed into a commodity which can be consumed by the Other, to an extent that they satisfy the Other" (ibid.: 3; see also Mau 2019). Therefore, authenticity is validated through audience engagement (cf. Maares et al. 2020: 3) as a practice that relates to fabricating images and imaginations of authenticity in social media. Drawing on that, the authors describe authenticity labour as a careful performance that can translate sociocultural capital into economic capital (cf. ibid.). They locate the authenticity markers "consistency", "calibrated amateurism" and "transparency" (ibid.). Calibrated amateurism is then further elaborated as "absence of editing (amateurism); absence of posing (spontaneity); absence of overt overall composition (selected social sharing)" (ibid.: 4). The findings of this research (cf. ibid.: 6-7) indicate that producers use live videos as a means of creating content that is perceived as authentic. Additionally, the video format itself is perceived as a conduit for authenticity by consumers. In terms of content, consumers perceive non-staged content as authentic, whereas the overuse of editing tools is perceived as inauthentic. In particular, the use of Photoshop is linked to inauthenticity (cf. ibid.: 7). Furthermore, users welcome imperfection, as evidenced by the positivity bias observed on social media. With regard to the authenticity of photographs, consistency is perceived as authentic (cf. Ruf 2024b). While pictures do not have to be perfect, they must adhere to a specific style, such as a "cool urban touch" (Maares et al. 2020: 7). Consumers are totally aware that users invest time in editing and fabricating the "perfect" photo and report that they can identify if something is not real or has been edited too much. Nevertheless, the authors observe a discrepancy between the conscious and moral judgement and the "subconscious inclination towards aesthetical pleasing images." (Ibid.: 8) Regarding collaborations and sponsorship, the consumers perceive these as authentic if they align with the inner self of the producers, if they are subtle and not excessive in quantity, and if the producers do not receive financial compensation for their actions (cf. ibid.: 8). In conclusion, the results demonstrate that there is a congruence between the authenticity of the producers and the audiences in three forms: a) presenting a "real" side of life; b) presenting an unedited self, preferably in videos; and c) being transparent about sponsorship content and collaborations. Central to our thoughts on authenticity as a brand, as well as a branded cultural space, is again the reference to the existentialist differentiation of inner and outer self that seems to be an underlying fundament of production and consumption practices. Furthermore, the described disparity between moral judgement and the subconscious, as well as the replacement of pictures by videos as markers of authenticity will be discussed in relation to the fabrication and branding of BeReal in opposition to Instagram.

Linking Maares, Banjac and Hanusch (2020) with Haimson et al. (2021), another study conducted by Kreiling, Meier and Reinecke (2022) discusses the labour of visual authenticity by comparing the affordances of the formats "story" and "post", especially on Instagram. Whilst other research results understand authenticity to be a constructed rather than an initial value, this position explores levels of subjective authenticity "that users experience when self-presenting via Stories versus Posts on Instagram." (ibid.: 2) With regard to their theoretical framework the authors focus on *state authenticity, which refers to subjectively feeling an alignment with oneself in the moment*" (ibid. [original emphasis]). They highlight that arguing based on overall social media affordances (e.g., persistence) would distort the research. A precise analysis of the affordances of the single features, the format of functions shows that "even within one SNS the affordances of individual features may differ." (ibid.: 4). Here the authors focus on the research gaps that occur by declaring social media as inauthentic in general. By ascribing the affordances of persistence, visibility, association and editability to the two formats, they conclude that stories are "a tool facilitating more authentic self-representation than Posts" (ibid.: 4) as they are "more reflective of their lives as a whole [...]", and as "lowered visibility may prevent users from self-censoring and fearing others' judgement through negative feedback" (Ibid.). With regard to this hypothesis, the authors identify three *drivers* of subjective authenticity in "stories" and "posts" of social media formats: expectation of response, privacy control, and spontaneity (cf. ibid.: 4-6). Consequently, they posit that "stories" result in lower response expectations, higher privacy control, and higher spontaneity (cf. ibid.: 7). This demonstrates that authenticity issues can be structural issues of mediality (cf. Wortmann 2018: 218), as the mediality and materiality have an impact on the perception of authenticity. In this context, Wortmann (2018) explains the relationship between authenticity and mediality for what he calls "philological authenticity" (ibid.: 212), where scripture as a medium requires a reconnection to the author that in contrast is not necessary for oral conversation (cf. ibid.). When these perspectives are brought together, it becomes evident that authenticity as a value of social media is primarily discussed in four ways: Firstly, as a relationship to one's self, to others, and to the context, respectively to the technical infrastructures and its values and laws, secondly, as a practice e. g. of performance or labour, thirdly, as a concept of evaluation, lastly, as a kind of narration in the context of branding and marketing. Moreover, the existentialist differentiation of the outer and inner self appears relevant in terms of branding, self-perception but also research. Moreover, the disparity or rather paradox between users' definitions of authenticity in social media in comparison to their actual practice has been noted. In summary, the concepts associated with authenticity are consistency, amateurism, transparency, the display of negativity, the need to show different factettes of the self as well as anonymity. It is now appropriate to discuss these imaginations, features, and functions that have been identified in existing research as promoting authenticity in a comparative analysis of Instagram and BeReal.

3. BeReal vs. Instagram: Redesigning Authenticity

The inauthenticity especially of the platform Instagram has been discussed from various perspectives. One such perspective is the political discourse about bots, which defines "authenticity" as "being human" in opposition to being something that consists of code.[6] In light of the consequences of the post-truth era and the emergence of the phenomena of "fake news" as an example of disinformation (cf. Shu et al. 2020), Instagram is compelled to address the issue of misleading followers when it comes to political events or economic interests of companies—both attempting to manipulate users to their own advantage and the users' disadvantage (cf. Ferrara 2020). Conversely, another dimension of the discourse concerns the concept of "buying authenticity". This implies that the valuation logic of the platform is linked to the concept of authenticity, which has resulted in the introduction of authenticity markers such as the "verified badge" or "meta verified", which have a specific materiality. In the following section, we will analyse the occurrence of these two dominant topics and explore how authenticity is constructed on Instagram versus BeReal, by discussing relevant product descriptions of the two platforms.

The verified badge is linked to the initial topic, as it is employed to "confirm that a notable account is the authentic presence for that person or brand, or entity"[7]. The term authenticity is thereby defined in a legal sense, meaning that the individual utilising the platform can be identified as such via an identity card. Prior to 13 August 2020,[8] the concept of authenticity on Instagram was understood to be based on the following three criteria "importance", "authority" or "subject matter expertise" (ibid.). These criteria encompass the following social values:

---

6   Cf. "Introducing New Authenticity Measures on Instagram" (13 August 2020). Retrieved from https://about.instagram.com/blog/announcements/introducing-new-authenticity-measures-on-instagram.

7   "Requirements to apply for a verified badge on Instagram". Retrieved from https://help.instagram.com/312685272613322.

8   See also the announcement for the new authenticity measure on Instagram: https://about.instagram.com/blog/announcements/introducing-new-authenticity-measures-on-instagram#:~:text=We%20want%20the%20content%20you,pattern%20of%20potential%20inauthentic%20behavior.

Authentic: Represent a real person, registered business or entity.

Unique: Represent the unique presence of the person or business. Only one account per person or business may be verified, with exceptions for language-specific accounts. We don't verify general interest accounts (e.g. @puppymemes).

Complete: Your account must be public and have a bio, profile photo and be active when you apply.

Notable: Your account must represent a well-known, highly searched for person, brand or entity. We review accounts that are featured in multiple news sources, and we don't consider paid or sponsored media content as sources for review.[9]

It would appear that the company has overlooked the social components. The verification of authenticity does not carry any additional weight beyond the following in the present:

- To be at least 18 years old.
- A public or private profile that's associated with your full name, aligns with naming standards and has a profile picture that includes your face.
- To meet minimum activity requirements, such as prior posting history.
- A valid photo ID that matches your profile name and profile picture.
- Two-factor authentication enabled on your profile.
- To follow our Terms of Use and Community Guidelines.[10]

In the context of cyber-criminality, this appears to be a reasonable rule, as the primary value of authenticity here is to hold users legally accountable. In contrast, Meta Verified "is a paid subscription for eligible profiles to establish their presence on Instagram and Facebook".[11] The service includes the verified badge, but also incorporates account protection, customer support, and exclusive features such as "exclusive stickers on Stories and Reels" (ibid.). Here, the social component becomes relevant once more. While Instagram attempts to alter the authenticity narrative from one imbued with values to one that is legally oriented, they situate and disguise social components within the paid area as a surplus that apparently serves individuality. However, the legal definition of authenticity is not limited to the verified badge alone. The Instagram community guidelines posit that the image of an "authentic and safe space for inspiration and expression"[12] is inextri-

9   "Requirements to apply for a verified badge on Instagram". Retrieved from https://help.instagram.com/312685272613322.

10   "Eligibility requirements for Meta Verified profiles on Instagram". Retrieved from https://help.instagram.com/2419286908233223?helpref=faq_content.

11   "About Meta Verified for Instagram profiles". Retrieved from https://help.instagram.com/738055111270671?helpref=faq_content.

12   Ibid.

cably linked with compliance with the law.[13] Furthermore, inauthentic content is defined as content "that you have copied or collected from the Internet that you don't have the right to post."[14] One value layer of Instagram authenticity is thus the imagination of authenticity as being true to one's self and to others in the sense of obeying the law.

In addition to the legal requirements, Instagram offers a number of features and functions that have been perceived as supporting the authentic representation of self by producers and consumers, or even as a design alternative. For instance, it is possible to have multiple accounts on Instagram.[15] The connection to the legal name is only relevant in terms of the verified badge or Meta verified, but not in terms of having multiple accounts respectively profiles. This implies that users may maintain distinct accounts that represent a single aspect of their identity while maintaining stylistic and content consistency across these different spheres.

In addition to the multitude of accounts and profiles,[16] Instagram addresses the issue of authenticity during prevalent life events. On the subpage "Being your authentic self on Instagram" of the page "staying safe" (see Help Center) Instagram refers to the difficulties of a transitioning process, for example, including the change of a legal name.[17] However, the identity in question is once again linked to ID-identifying items such as birth certificates, driving licenses, and official name change paperwork.[18] In general, Instagram states that names, gender identity, and personal pronouns are not required on the platform. This is in line with another concept related to authenticity: anonymity. This concept may be perceived as helpful in certain situations, such as when negative experiences are being displayed (cf. Haimson et al. 2021). Therefore, self-censoring due to the positivity bias can be prevented by using the offered possibility of multiple accounts. This multiplicity is still perceived as authentic if the individual is able to successfully change between profiles and play different personas (cf. Wortmann 2018: 215).

---

13   Cf. ibid.
14   "Community Guidelines". Retrieved from https://help.instagram.com/477434105621119.
15   Cf. "Adding Accounts". Retrieved from https://help.instagram.com/589697191199 472/?helpref=hc_fnav.
16   The terms "account" and "profile" are often used as synonyms in everyday language but also in research which neglects the different affordances these two concepts have developed over time and in relation to each other. While the "account" is a materialisation of the need for legal accounting of actions online, the "profile" is a place for creating an authentic self that can be fed into the valuation system of a platform.
17   Cf. help.instagram.com (g): "Being your authentic self on Instagram". Retrieved from https://help.instagram.com/401525221649141/?helpref=hc_fnav.
18   Cf. "Types of ID that Instagram accepts". Retrieved from https://help.instagram. com/271237319690904?helpref=faq_content.

In comparison to previous research, it is evident that the verified badge, which is commonly used as an authenticity marker on social media platforms, was not explicitly identified or discussed by the participants of the aforementioned studies on authenticity in social media. However, it is important to note that the platform owners themselves have consistently highlighted the significance of this badge as a marker of authenticity. In contrast, the concept of authenticity in previous studies was not directly linked with quantitative or material markers, such as badges, comments, or likes. In practice, those who produce and consume social media content tend to rely on qualitative concepts such as transparency and consistency to assess the authenticity of individuals or entities. However, maintaining consistency on Instagram is challenging, as there are numerous offers that promise "individuality" but, in practice, result in conformity and the creation of an "Instagram-Aesthetic". Moreover, the opportunity to engage in discourse and comparison with one another has led to a surge in demand for effective self-presentation and role-playing in the sphere of the digital public sphere (cf. ibid.: 213). The creation of multiple accounts and profiles may allow users to adopt different communication and design aesthetics (cf. Ruf 2024a; Ruf 2023). However, despite this, each profile remains embedded in the valuation system of the platform. This condition makes it challenging for users to act independently of the embedded expectations, as evidenced by Haimson et al. (2021) in relation to the authenticity paradox (see also Mau 2019). Consequently, in the social and legal context, authenticity is employed as a value that is used to differentiate or to "code" difference in a mathematical sense, with the objective of designing decision-making processes "objective" (cf. ibid.: 12 ff.; Wortmann 2018: 214). This differentiation is either achieved through the use of material markers or as a concept of evaluation. These differentiation practices can be identified as a secondary differentiation system that is necessary for reconnecting the medially conveyed to the non-medial, respectively the self (cf. Wortmann 2018: 221). In order to be considered authentic, it is necessary to be aware of the conventions that the platform provides and to adhere to them. Instagram monitors its users for behaviours that correspond to its understanding of authenticity. This legal understanding of authenticity is based on the concept of evidence rather than on what producers and consumers perceive as authenticity. In this case, the antonym to authenticity is "evidence" (cf. Wortmann 2018: 211). It is unnecessary to engage in discourse on the matter of authenticity if the evidence is clear.

While Instagram merely refers to the legal meaning of authenticity, BeReal addresses this concept in its community standards, which outline various criteria that users consider when determining whether an individual or object is authentic. Alexis Barreyat, who is one of the developers alongside Kevin Purreau, announced the launch of the platform on LinkedIn in 2020, stating that BeReal is "the First Uncontrollable Photo Sharing App."[19] Being "tired and annoyed with all

19 "Stoked to finally launch BeReal, the First Uncontrollable Photo Sharing App". Retrieved from https://www.linkedin.com/posts/alexisbarreyat_stoked-to-finally-

the bullshit on social media, [he] decided to launch [his] own" (ibid.). He demonstrates an understanding of authenticity by categorising likes, followers, advertisements, filters, and interactions with individuals who are not genuine friends as inauthentic (cf. ibid.). A further explanation of the values of BeReal can be found in the community standards:

BeReal is about discovery. We value authenticity, spontaneity, and kindness, and we are proud to offer a platform that empowers users like you to share a glimpse into your real life and discover that of your friends. We want BeReal to be a place where people can have fun and express themselves while feeling safe.
Our Community Standards are designed to help ensure that you, and all our users, use our services safely, and they must be taken seriously. They are part of our Terms of Service and our Privacy Policy (together the "User Agreement"). If you don't agree with any part of the User Agreement, including the Community Standards, then it might be that BeReal isn't for you.
The Community Standards are really just a collection of things that could be thought of as being respectful to other people. Basically, if you're doing something that you would not want other people to do to you on BeReal, then you're probably violating the Community Standards. But just in case you're not sure, here is a list: [...][20]

The concept of authenticity is linked to the real world, as well as spontaneity, kindness, and glimpses. However, the social aspect of authenticity, as defined by Instagram, has been erased. This definition is based on the legal definition of authenticity, which is unique, complete, notable, and authentic. BeReal, on the other hand, is attempting to reinstate the social aspect of authenticity, but without the valuation system that Instagram and other social media platforms have established. This marketing strategy positions BeReal in opposition to platforms that are known for violations of user privacy and acts therefore as a commentary on this topic. However, the legal dimension is also present in BeReal as well: the services can only be used by a "REAL human (because feelings matter)" (ibid.) and authentic in relation to content means—equally to Instagram—the prohibition of criminal behaviour like stealing content or disrespecting others (cf. ibid.). The platform's motto "Be kind. Be respectful. Be you. BeReal." (ibid.) displays its concept of authenticity. In the Google Play Store, this motto is further elaborated in the form of a "warning" in the section "About this app":

/!\ WARNING /!\
• BeReal won't make you waste time.
• BeReal is life, Real life, and this life is without filters.
• BeReal will challenge your creativity.

---

launch-bereal-the-first-activity-6633332857970532352-TMCx/.
20   "Terms" (25 April 2023). Retrieved from https://bereal.com/terms/.

- BeReal is your chance to show your friends who you really are, for once.
- BeReal can be addictive.
- BeReal might frustrate you.
- BeReal won't make you famous. If you want to become an influencer you can stay on TikTok and Instagram.
- BeReal doesn't care if you have millions of followers or if you're verified.
- BeReal may cause accidents, especially if you are riding bikes.
- BeReal is pronounced "BiRil", not bereale, or Bèreol.
- BeReal won't let you cheat, you can try and if you manage to do so, come work with us.
- BeReal doesn't send any of your private data to China.[21]

This initial warning "BeReal won't make you waste time" (ibid.) addresses and comments on the discourse surrounding the materiality and algorithmic logics of the Instagram feed or reels section, which are associated with the phenomenon of endless and mindless scrolling (cf. Purohit/Holzer 2021) or "doomscrolling", which refers to excessive consumption of negative information on social media (cf. Sharma et al. 2022). The phenomenon of mindless scrolling is perceived as having a negative impact on mental health, and efforts to reduce it are a common topic of discussion in both academic research and public discourse (cf. ibid.). This perception is based on the existentialist notion that individuals can engage in their "real life" activities without being constrained by the limitations of the digital realm (cf. Wang/Skovira 2017: 6; Purohit/Holzer 2021: 3). In terms of design, BeReal does not implement digital nudging design principles, which are defined as interventions in the decision-making process of users with the aim of achieving a specific behaviour (cf. Kammerl et al. 2023: 38). A nudge can be a feedback report on usage time, an app limit—both usually needs to be set in the smartphone settings—, or the possibility to unfollow or hide parts of the platform's content (cf. Purohit/Holzer 2021: 2). This latter option is already partly implemented in some social media platforms. In a more general sense, nudges can be divided into ten categories: default settings, simplifications, social norms, convenience and simplicity, disclosure of information, warnings, strategies of self-commitment, reminders, appeals to commitment, and information on the consequences of past behaviour (Kammerl et al. 2023: 39-40). In contrast to other applications that prompt users to interrupt ongoing processes, BeReal does not do so. Instead, it intervenes in what is called "real life" only for a single, unpredictable moment each day. This is done through a push notification that says, "Time to BeReal. 2 min left to capture a BeReal and see what your friends are up to!". During the process of recording all activities, including delayed recording and the number of recording attempts, are tracked and displayed together with the picture. While BeReal has

---

21   "BeReal. Your friends for real". Retrieved from https://play.google.com/store/apps/details?id=com.bereal.ft&hl=en_US.

opted not to implement the option of doomscrolling due to the absence of a feed, it employs a different form of nudging. The application itself serves as a nudge, interrupting users in the real world to encourage engagement through the act of taking a picture. Once the pictures have been recorded (BeReal utilises both the front and back camera simultaneously) and posted, the pictures of added friends become visible (see fig. 1). Consequently, BeReal is combining a reminder, "Time to BeReal", with a warning, "2 min left [...]", and addressing social capital, "and see what your friends are up to", to encourage action. While BeReal moves away from conventions such as the news and profile feed, likes, and filters occurring, it has identified an alternative method to engage its users and ensure a return on investment to their Silicon Valley investors. Despite a long-standing avoidance of advertisements and brand integrations, the platform resorted to these strategies due to insufficient user numbers and profitability.[22] To increase profitability, BeReal was sold to the gaming platform Voodoo in 2024, thereby integrating advertisements in between user-generated content.

Fig. 1: The landing page of the application BeReal displaying the "Post to view" feature. Screenshot © Aleksandra Vujadinovic.

---

22   "BeReal für 500 Millionen Euro verkauft: Jetzt ist Werbung da" (10 July 2024). Retrieved from https://onlinemarketing.de/social-media-marketing/ bereal-verkauft-jetzt-werbung.

Additionally, the concept of friends on BeReal contrasts with the concept of followers, which developed as a consequence of the evaluation practices of social media. The concept of "friends" in the context of BeReal is related to the phone numbers saved on a smartphone. Friendship is thus defined by the possession of sensitive data that indicates a close relationship. This contrast is further highlighted by the following warnings: "BeReal doesn't care if you have millions of followers or if you're verified"; "BeReal won't make you famous. If you want to become an influencer you can stay on TikTok and Instagram."[23] These statements serve as a commentary to the often criticised valorisation logic of social media that affords comparison and evaluation of performance via likes, comments, and follower count. Furthermore, it can be argued that this is an act of comparison and differentiation that is redefining the concept of friends, and at the same time, the imagination of authenticity in social media. Quantitative markers that are associated with authenticity by Instagram are irrelevant on BeReal, as the main affordance is the exchange of moments with friends and not the display of the self, identity-labour, and valorisation. Furthermore, the absence of a profile section as a space for identity labour is relevant here as the application does not provide a space where the often-desired consistent appearance and behaviour can be displayed and valorised. One can say that there is an area that can be identified as a mixture of the concepts "account" and "profile", as it makes the user legally accountable and provides space for the storage and display of content, but for oneself and in the absence of a valorisation system. The BeReal profile contains a profile picture, "Pins" which are visible to friends but cannot be valorised with likes or comments as well as "Memories": a section where past BeReals are collected and only displayed to oneself (see fig. 2).

The absence of the evaluation logic results in a different structure of the profile, or rather a deconstruction of what the profile is imagined as a format for profiling, self-representation and perceivable coherent structure (cf. Reckwitz 2020: 203-207). Unlike Instagram, BeReal's "profile" is not focused on displaying, comparing, and evaluating information, but serves as an archive of images created with the application. In the absence of a coherent representation of the self and the valuation logic of social media, the user is not at all accessible to an authenticity check in the social sense. The absence of a profile and the feed precludes the possibility of comparability as an affordance of BeReal. However, there is nevertheless a similar implementation to the feed that is called "Friends of Friends" (see fig. 3). This area, previously designated as "Discovery"[24] purported to facilitate the identification of contacts who are maintained through diverse communication channels that do not rely on a list of phone numbers (cf. Hurler 2023). The concept of "friends" has been expanded to include "friends of friends", and the implemen-

---

23   Ibid.

24   For more information on the Discovery feature see "Discovery". Retrieved from https://help.bereal.com/hc/de/articles/7531599991325-Discovery.

tation of the "RealChat"[25] is linked to "BeReal's Kafka-esque transformation into a Big Tech cockroach" (Hurler 2023). Already BeReal discovery had the affordance of global communication as it allowed users to discover BeReal from all over the world.

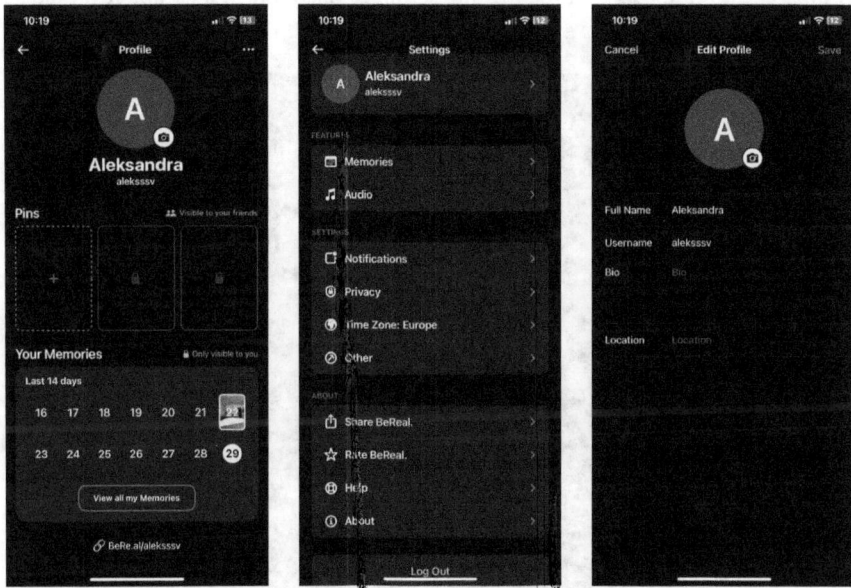

Fig. 2: *The profile area of the application BeReal (left) and the setting area connected to the profile area (middle and right). Screenshot © Aleksandra Vujadinovic.*

The key distinction between Instagram and BeReal is the inversion of the posting hierarchy. By posting, pictures on BeReal are *first* made visible to friends the user has fed into the app via phone numbers. Alternatively, they can make their posts visible globally via "discovery" respectively "friends of friends" (see fig. 3). In contrast, on Instagram, content is published globally as long as the account is set to public. Subsequently, the posts then are visible globally, which can be circumvented in terms of the story with the function "close friends" or in terms of the profile posts by setting the profile on "private". In conclusion, both platforms offer possibilities to limit visibility and interaction. However, the crucial difference is the absence of quantitative data (likes, comments, posts) being displayed to a community that provides information on performance, and visual enhancers like filters that contribute to the perceived inauthenticity of Instagram. However, BeReal is unable to fully manage communication without feedback. Instead of likes and comments, reactions on posts are performed through the fabrication of

---

25   For more information on RealChat feature see "RealChat". Retrieved from https://help.bereal.com/hc/de/articles/11280739918621-RealChat.

gamification features, such as "RealMojis".[26] This process involves the selection of an emoji and the subsequent imitation of the emoji by taking a selfie with appropriate facial expressions (see fig. 4). This gamification feature, which appears to facilitate personalised use of the platform, represents a strand of design methods, comparable to nudging and the infinite scroll. Consequently, it can be regarded as a strategy to enhance user engagement (cf. Interaction Design Foundation 2016).

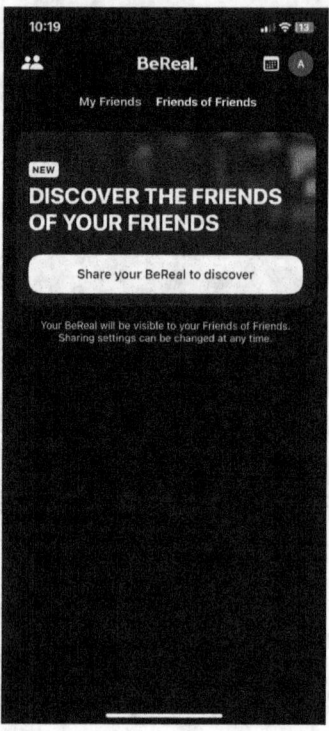

Fig. 3: The "Friends of Friends" area of the application BeReal. Screenshot ©️ Aleksandra Vujadinovic.

However, this gamification feature can also be understood as a means of reinforcing personal contact with one's own actions, thereby making them appear more authentic. Hence, BeReal, as a platform, provides information on the criteria that are crucial for constructing authenticity online. The platform designers employ these criteria in a radical sense, namely by abolishing everything that is linked to inauthenticity on Instagram, in order to create the brand "BeReal". In opposition to all forms of bias, including those associated with algorithms, quantitative data display, enhancers, and the lack of time control, the product description

---

26   For more information on RealMojis see "Real Mojis". Retrieved from https://help.bereal.com/hc/de/articles/7536240858653-RealMojis.

present authenticity as an unbiased and immediate concept.[27] This new aesthetic, which may be perceived as a revival of an older aesthetic relating to authenticity, is generated as a result of this opposition. Zeh (2023) identifies this aesthetic as a nostalgia for the early 2000s which contains sharing everyday pictures, information on the user's location, and an unaesthetic camera perspective that the author associates with "Boomers" and a double chin.[28] Once more, the comparison and differentiation performed by BeReal in the process of branding its application demonstrates that social media, which is understood to be inherently inauthentic, contains functions and features that support the authentic display according to the perceptions of social media users.

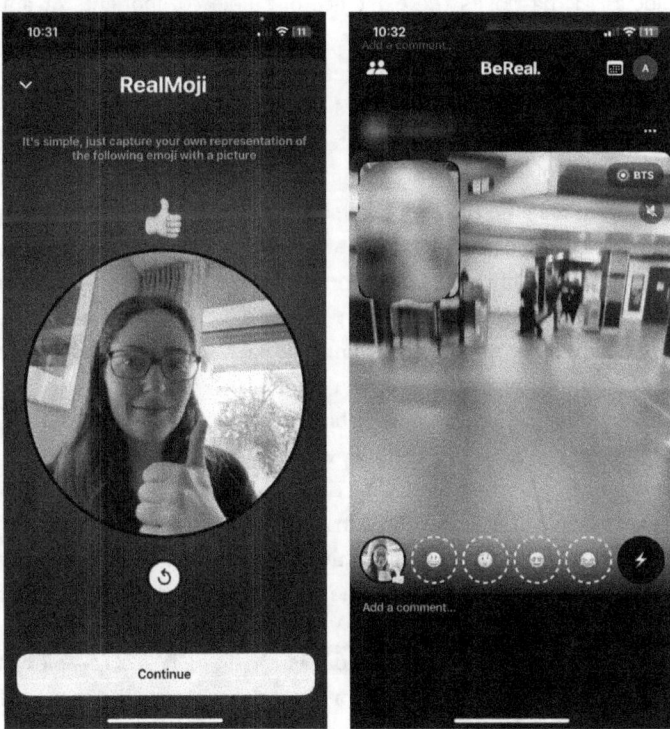

Fig. 4: A demonstration of the function "RealMoji". Screenshot © Aleksandra Vujadinovic.

---

27   Cf. "Wenn die Wirklichkeit bildförmig sein soll" (20 July 2023). Retrieved from https:// aktuelles.uni-frankfurt.de/unireport/wenn-die-wirklichkeit-bildfoermig-sein-soll/.

28   The question of whether there is a generational aspect to the perception and understanding of authenticity in social media represents an exciting research gap that requires further investigation.

4. Conclusion and Discussion

Previous research on the topic of authenticity in and of social media has demonstrated that authenticity from a user's perspective is something that can be created by some features, forms, and formats (e.g. live videos, stories) rather than by others. This is evidenced by an examination of the features, forms, and functions that the operators of BeReal have identified as authentic and thus implemented. The general logic of BeReal is to post what is understood as a "story" on other platforms. The application does not contain an area for displaying carefully curated and edited pictures and posts. Our elaboration on the concept of authenticity in social media posits the existence of stable components or authenticity markers, in contrast to the assumption that authenticity is ephemeral and that creators and audiences are perpetually seeking it, driving social media production (Taylor 2022: 133). In contrast to studies that rely on a "framework of performativity" (ibid.: 137), this paper demonstrates that authenticity in the case of BeReal is a cultural space defined by branding. This makes the relationship between consumers, branders, and the concept itself explicit.

The most valuable contribution of this paper is the description of how BeReal functions as a design alternative in the mode of commentary on authenticity issues on Instagram and similar social media platforms. For instance, we demonstrated that uncontrollability is equated with authenticity in the case of BeReal, which can be understood as a commentary on Instagram's control via algorithms and the biases it creates. BeReal positions itself as uncontrollable by taking nudging to another level: it interrupts in real life, whereas Instagram keeps users scrolling through advertisements and irrelevant content and away from real life. Furthermore, the absence of filters and the warning on the two-minute time frame for taking a picture attribute spontaneity to uncontrollability. Nevertheless, the notion of "real life" that stems mainly from the existentialist understanding of authenticity, may require further exploration in the future. The question of what constitutes "real life" and whether social media is a part of it is a complex one. Also, we demonstrated that, contrary to the product description, the notion of controllability seems to be a relevant concept, as BeReal also highlights the legal understanding of authenticity and the consequences of violating platform guidelines. Control is also exercised by using nudges and gamification that encourage the user to interact with the platform regularly. BeReal, in its own imagination, sees itself as the platform of authenticity. However, in comparison to the users, it has a different imagination of what creates the value. While users perceive consistency as authentic, enabling the recognition of a whole, BeReal declares that authenticity is understood as a glimpse, rather than a whole. This thought needs to be explored further in relation to the logic of social media in general. At this juncture, BeReal is not adapting to but rather criticising the notion of a "profile subject" or "performative authenticity", as identified by Reckwitz 2020[29] and others (e.g. Taylor 2022 or Serazio 2023), which is considered as a driving force behind the pervasive desire for a holistic display of the self online.[30] As these research approaches understand authenticity as something "performative", which may make one aware of the inner and outer forces that have an impact on the imagination of something as authentic, they miss a central point: that performativity is not exclusively a characteristic of the online sphere. Nevertheless, there are indications that alternatives like BeReal must adapt to the general logic of social media, including persistence, replicability, scalability, and searchability (cf. Boyd 2011: 46; see also Bucher/Helmond 2017) or programmability, popularity, connectivity, and datafication (cf. Van Dijck/Poell 2013), in order to survive, or more accurately, to keep their shareholder value. In the case of BeReal, there are several examples of design elements that could be considered as contributing to the platform's overall functionality. These include the nudge for persistence, the RealChat function for connectivity, and the feature "friends of friends" for searchability. However, it is important to note that these design elements, while beneficial, do not represent a fundamental shift in the design paradigm. It remains to be seen whether BeReal will remain a mere fad or evolve into a genuine alternative that can challenge Instagram as one of the most popular social networks, as indicated by the number of users (cf. Caliandro/ Graham 2020: 1). Regardless of its future trajectory, BeReal has the potential to unleash productive forces (cf. Schiesser 2004) by provoking discursive friction through discursive design. In more precise terms, the "Eigensinn" of Instagram is in conflict with the "Eigensinnigkeit" of the user, which ultimately results in the latter becoming a developer, as described by Alexis Barreyat in his quoted post on LinkedIn. The idea of "Eigensinn" and "Eigensinnigkeit" can be understood as a combination of stubbornness and originality in the case of BeReal. This unleashed not only creative or artistic productive forces but also economic ones. This is evidenced by the integration of the "Dual"-function[31] by Instagram and the

---

29 See chapter 'The Profile Subject: Competencies and Talents' and 'The Digital Subject: Performative Authenticity and Visibility'.

30 The profile subject is an entity that has emerged through the combination of cybernetic structures and culture. It is based on the ideas of the account and the profile: While the former categorises the profile subject in a digital file and thus makes it accountable and comparable, the latter is the place and drive of a project-like, modular performance respectively performative authenticity. By being integrated into the digital file of social media, the profile subject enters the valorisation market of the corresponding platform. At the same time, it has the privilege but is also subject to the compulsion to present itself (cf. Reckwitz 2020: 245).

31 For more information on the Dual-function see "Introducing New Ways to Collaborate and Create with Reels" (21 July 2022) Retrieved from https://about.instagram.com/blog/announcements/introducing-new-ways-to-collaborate-and-create-with-reels.

incorporation of BeReals spontaneity in the form of the tool "TikTok Now"[32] by TikTok (cf. Zeh 2023).

In conclusion, design alternatives may be considered to be "Material Media Theory", which discusses values in social media. In other words, BeReal, as a design alternative, represents an attempt to redesign "authenticity" as a social media value based on the practices of the initiation phase of media theory par excellence: primary intermediality. The core of this reflexive state is the comparison with existing media in terms of performance and social effect (cf. Leschke 2003: 35). When authenticity issues are understood as issues of mediality that arise in states of media change, alternatives like BeReal mark such a crucial point in the discourse. They incorporate the discursive frictions into an application logic and shape a specific materiality marking distinctions regarding different imaginations of authenticity in *and through* social media. It is worth noting that the process of what we might term "Comparative Design Approach" is currently visible to great effect in the cases of *X* and *Bluesky*, which becomes evident by looking at the public discourse on this topic.[33] Research into and with the notion of frictions as the core concept of design alternatives may therefore prove an enriching approach for further research on social media. Moreover, it can also serve as a tool for teaching, as the conceptualisation of design alternatives by students may, as we assume, initiate critical thinking. This approach can be employed to facilitate critical thinking among students during both the design and discussion process. While design sciences frequently lack access to theory (cf. Ruf 2021; Ruf 2015), this method enables the phase of primary intermediality to be effectively utilised as a means of reflection in the development of media.

List of References

Banet-Weiser, S. (2012): Authentic™ : The Politics of Ambivalence in a Brand Culture. New York/London: New York University Press.

Boyd, D. (2011): "Social Network Sites as Networked Publics: Affordances, Dynamics, and Implications". In: Papacharissi Z (ed.), A Networked self: Identity,

---

32   For more information on TikTok Now see "TikTok Now". Retrieved from https://play.google.com/store/apps/details?id=com.ss.android.ugc.now&hl=de&gl=US.

33   See for example "What Is Bluesky? Is It the Best X (Twitter) Alternative So Far?" (15 October 2023). Retrieved from https://www.makeuseof.com/what-is-bluesky-social-twitter-alternative/; "TechScape: Bluesky opens up to the world—but can anything really replace Twitter?" (13 February 2024). Retrieved from https://www.theguardian.com/technology/2024/feb/13/bluesky-twitter-jack-dorsey-social-network; "With Twitter gone and users unsure about X, is Bluesky the future? We try it out" (15 August 2023). Retrieved from https://www.euronews.com/next/2023/08/15/with-twitter-gone-and-users-unsure-about-x-is-bluesky-the-future-we-try-it-out.

Community, and Culture on Social Network Sites, New York: Routledge, pp. 39–58.

Bucher, T./Helmond A. (2017): "The Affordances of Social Media Platforms." In: J. Burgess/T. Poell/A. Marwick (eds.), The SAGE Handbook of Social Media. Preprint June 2016. London/New York: SAGE Publications Ltd, pp. 1–41.

Caliandro, A./Graham, J. (2020): "Studying Instagram Beyond Selfies." Social Media & Society, April-June: pp. 1–7.

Ernst, W. (2023): "On the Notion of Cybernetic Frictions and its Role in Radial Media Archaeology." In: D. Gómez-Venegas (ed.), Frictions: Inquiries into Cybernetic Thinking and Its Attempts towards Mate[real]ization, Lüneburg: meson press, pp. 119–132.

Foucault, M. (1981): Archäologie des Wissens. Frankfurt a.M.: Suhrkamp.

Gómez-Venegas, D. (2023): "Cybernetic Thinking and Its Frictions." In: D. Gómez-Venegas (ed.), Frictions: Inquiries into Cybernetic Thinking and Its Attempts towards Mate[real]ization, Lüneburg: meson press, pp. 7–18.

Gibson, J. J. (1982): Wahrnehmung und Umwelt: Der ökologische Ansatz in der visuellen Wahrnehmung. München: Urban & Schwarzenberg.

Gunkel, K. (2018): Der Instagram-Effekt: Wie ikonische Kommunikation in den Social Media unsere visuelle Kultur prägt. Bielefeld: transcript.

Haimson, O. L./Liu, T./Zhang, B. Z./Corvite, S. (2021): "The Online Authenticity Paradox: What Being 'Authentic' on Social Media Means, and Barriers to Achieving It." Proc. ACM Hum.-Comput. Interact. 5, CSCW2, pp. 423:1–423:18.

Interaction Design Foundation (2016): "What is Gamification (GF)?" (29 June 2016). Retrieved from https://www.interaction-design.org/literature/topics/gamification#gamification_in_user_experience_(ux)_design-1.

Kreiling, R./Meier, A. (2022): "Feeling Authentic on Social Media: Subjective Authenticity Across Instagram Stories and Posts." Social Media & Society, 8(1), pp. 1–13.

Leschke, R. (2003): Einführung in die Medientheorie. München: Wilhelm Fink.

Lorusso, S. (2023): What Design Can't Do: Essays on Design and Disillusion. Eindhoven: Set Margins'.

Maares, P./Banjac, S./Hanuscg, F. (2020): "The Labour of Visual Authenticity on Social Media: Exploring Producers' and Audiences' Perceptions on Instagram." Poetics, 84(2), pp. 1–10.

Mau, S. (2019): The Metric Society: On the Quantification of the Social. Transl. by S. Howe. Cambridge: Polity.

Norman, D. A. (1999): "Affordances, Conventions and Design." Interactions, (6)3, pp. 38–43.

Purohit, A. K./Holzer, A. (2021): Unhooked by Design: Scrolling Mindfully on Social Media by Automating Digital Nudges. AMCIS 2021 Proceedings (7), pp. 1–10.

Schiesser, G. (2004): "Arbeit am und mit EigenSinn. Medien | Kunst | Ausbildung, oder: Über den Eigensinn als künstlerische Produktivkraft." In: H.-P.

Schwarz (ed.): Produktionsweisen. Zürich: Hochschule für Gestaltung und Kunst, pp. 174–193.

Reckwitz, A. (2020): The Society of Singularities. Transl. by V. A. Pakis. Cambridge: Polity.

Ruf, O. (2015): "Diesseits des Ästhetischen. Designtheorie als Designwissenschaft." Öffnungszeiten—Papiere zur Designwissenschaft, 29, pp. 18–28.

Ruf, O. (2021): "What is Design Theory?" In: K. Purgar (ed.), The Palgrave Handbook of Image Studies, Cham: Palgrave Macmillan, pp. 779–798.

Ruf, O. (2023): "Technik(en) des Designs. Von der Philosophie der Medien zur Gestaltungsästhetik." In: M. Tamborini (ed.), Die Ästhetik der Technowissenschaften des 21. Jahrhunderts, Darmstadt: Wissenschaftliche Buchgesellschaft, pp. 119–133.

Ruf, O. (2024a): "Praktiken (digital-)ästhetischer Kommunikation. Eine Forschungsskizze." In: C. Axelsson/D. Blume/B. Volk (eds.), Bildung, Praxistransfer und Kooperation. Kompetenzentwicklung für die Hochschullehre in Netzwerken, Bielefeld: transcript, pp. 55–94.

Ruf, O. (2024b): "The Supplement of the Digital. Aesthetics and Communication." Studi di estetica LII.IV(1), pp. 5–19.

Ruf, O./Rupert-Kruse, P./Grabbe, Lars C. (2022): Medienkulturwissenschaft: Eine Einführung, Wiesbaden: Springer VS.

Serazio, M. (2024): The Authenticity Industries. Keeping It "Real" in Media, Culture, and Politics, Stanford: University Press.

Sharma, B./Susanna, S. L./Johnson, B. K. (2022): "The Dark at the End of the Tunnel: Doomscrolling on Social Media Newsfeeds." Technology, Mind, and Behavior, 3(1: Spring 2022), pp. 1–13.

Taylor, A. S. (2022): Authenticity as Performativity on Social Media. London: Palgrave Macmillan.

van Dijck, J./Poell, T. (2013): "Understanding Social Media Logic." Media and Communication, 1(1), pp. 2–14.

Wang, W./Skovira, R. J. (2017): "Authenticity and Social Media." Conference Paper, Twenty-third Americas Conference on Information Systems, Boston, pp. 1–10.

Wortmann, V. (2018): Authentizität als Wiedergänger. Die Konjunkturen eines ungeliebten Konzepts und ihre medialen Bedingungen. In: R. Fayet/R. Krähenbühl (eds.), Authentizität und Material. Konstellationen in der Kunst seit 1900. Zürich: SIK-ISEA, pp. 208–226.

Zeh, M. (2023): "Social-Media-Authentizität, ein weiterer Versuch." Pop. Kultur und Kritik, 22, pp. 10–13.

Zillien, N. (2008): "Die (Wieder-)Entdeckung der Medien. Das Affordanzkonzept in der Mediensoziologie." Sociologia Internationalis. Internationale Zeitschrift für Soziologie, Kommunikations- und Kulturforschung, 46(2), pp. 161–181.

Friction in the Materialities of Value
Relating Transparency, Algorithms and Credit Scoring

Miriam Fahimi and Katharina Kinder-Kurlanda

Abstract

Artificial Intelligence (AI) systems are classifying and predicting more and more areas of our lives, often in ways mysterious to us. As a result, there are growing demands for transparency to shed light on data and models, powerful companies, invisible labour, and energy resources. In this contribution, we challenge the idea that transparency can unequivocally be attained, and propose rethinking transparency as a relational notion: transparency does not unveil algorithms' mysteries but instead repositions algorithms in relation to material practices. Based on ethnographic research in a credit agency, we ask how existing practices changed for whom and for which reasons after transparency became a newly introduced value in the company. Grasping this change during moments of friction, we trace how the relations of transparency shifted from "closed" to "complete" to "aesthetic" to "credible", ultimately solidifying in a public scoring calculator. In the end, "credible" transparency did not become the desired panacea for opening the algorithmic black box. Yet, the journey it undertook revealed missing documents, unequal positions and hierarchies of expertise and access. When relations change, novel friction may be on the rise.

Keywords

Friction, Value Studies, Materialities, Transparency, Algorithms, Credit Scoring

Introduction

The mysterious state of AI seems to be gradually dissolving as the increasing demands for transparency manifest in novel regulations and standards (Ananny/Crawford 2018; European Commission 2022; 2024). In the wake of algorithmic transparency, credit agencies are taking steps to make their opaque credit scoring systems transparent to the data subjects affected by algorithmic classification (Aggarwal 2021; Bono/Croxson/Giles 2021; Mendes/Mattiuzzo 2022; Onay/Öztürk 2018). One prominent solution is the creation of so-called scoring calcula-

DOI 10.14361/dcs-2023-0208

DCS | Digital Culture and Society | Vol. 9, Issue 2 | © transcript 2025

tors, that allow data subjects to obtain an assessment of their personal credit score after responding to a series of questions.

CreditAI was one of the private companies that had recently released such a calculator as part of introducing transparency as a core value. Over the course of one and a half years, we studied the calculator's development ethnographically. Drawing from our empirical observations, we argue that a value does not exist in the abstract nor as a discursive account, but as a relational notion. From this perspective, transparency does not unravel opaque and mysterious algorithms, but positions and repositions them in relation to material practices. Some studies have already presented similar arguments. Neyland (2007) observed in reference to an IT system that transparency did not make IT accessible but merely re-oriented it. Ziewitz (2013) argues that multiple versions of transparency exist. He notes that while transparency is typically associated with clarity, enlightenment, insight, visibility, and open access, in practice, it just introduces an additional layer of accounts.

So far, less scientific attention has been paid to the moments when value in itself changes. Taking our empirical observations further, we trace what changed for whom and for which reasons after transparency became a newly introduced value in the company. These turbulent moments of change are what we conceptualise as *friction*. Friction, as we witnessed, can have productive, destructive and surprising effects for a value.

The paper is structured as follows: First, we condense how transparency is meant to be achieved in AI systems and identify four main dimensions. Second, we present three approaches that relate values with the material, and present our conceptualisation of friction as the turbulent moments when the relations of value change. After introducing our ethnographic case and CreditAI, we move to our field site. We trace three moments of friction when transparency changed—from closed, to complete, to aesthetic and to credible—each time changing relations between transparency, the scoring algorithm and their material practices. We conclude by discussing our empirical findings for understanding the material of value, and the consequences of friction for algorithmic transparency.

Achieving Transparency in AI Systems

How to "achieve" transparency has been a long-discussed issue (Heald 2006; Ball 2009), as well as subject to sociological critique, with scholars pointing out that the idea of plain facts merely needing to be "revealed" is overly simplistic and instrumental (Moore 2018; Neyland 2007). Notwithstanding these critical voices, transparency has become an important issue for assessing (new) technologies (Grunwald/Hillerbrand 2021), especially AI systems. The AI Act (2024) and other regulations (European Commission 2022) set out to introduce transparency obligations to enable people to understand and contest these systems (European

Union Agency for Fundamental Rights 2022; Goodman/Flaxman 2017). The recent regulatory updraft aligns with the general societal imperative of transparency, fostered by the idea of democratic control (Davis 2016; Waibel/Peetz/Meier 2021). Furthermore, civil rights organisations, consumer protection bodies, and the general public have been increasingly questioning private companies' opaque practices of storing, reordering, and monetising peoples' data (Ananny 2016; Ehsan et al. 2021; Wulff/Finnestrand 2023).

In the current AI narrative, transparency means to disclose four main dimensions. First, transparency should reveal which (personal) data is being used for which reasons (Angwin et al. 2018; Burrell 2016; Kitchin 2017). Second, transparency should challenge the powerful position of privatised and secret big tech businesses (Fuchs 2022; Joque 2022; Zuboff 2020). While the open source movement has long pointed out the necessity of democratising control over technology (Chopra/Dexter 2008), regulations and requirements for monitoring and auditing proprietary AI are still found to be insufficient or missing (Balayn/Gürses 2021; Seyfert 2022). Third, transparency should disclose all labour involved in the AI pipeline, particularly exploited work outsourced to the Global South (Abebe et al. 2020; Le Ludec/Cornet/Casilli 2023; Miceli/Schuessler/Yang 2020). Fourth, developing and using AI systems requires a substantial consumption of natural resources and energy flows that should be recorded (Crawford 2021).

One could thus conclude that transparency is achieved when AI systems are understandable and accountable on all four dimensions (Markus/Kors/Rijnbeek 2021; Ribeiro/Singh/Guestrin 2016; Robbins et al. 2021). Or one could conclude, the other way around, that transparency will never be attained as long as opaque AI systems are the premise for private companies (and other actors) to accumulate capital (Mau 2017; Rouvroy/Berns/Libbrecht 2013; Wark 2019; Zuboff 2020). These conclusions are tempting as they understand values as a discursive ideal that unequivocally can or cannot be attained. However, they overlook how transparency rather positions and repositions AI in relation to materialities and practices. Transparency relates algorithms with data, measurements, (big tech) corporations, standards, documentations, non-governmental organisations, labour, (EU) regulations, or natural resources. From this perspective, an interesting question then becomes what transparency is for whom, how, and when.

Relating Value and Conceptualising Friction

We find three approaches in science and technology studies (STS) that adopt a relational understanding of value. The *values by design* approach shows how designers deliberately tie values to technology (Ananny 2016; Friedman/Kahn/Borning 2002; Knobel/Bowker 2011; Verbeek 2006; Flanagan/Howe/Nissenbaum 2008). These scholars argue that some values such as efficiency, safety, and reliability are explicitly designed into technology, while designing societal values into technology is a more complex issue. Here, designers are perceived as being engaged not only with scientific and technical results but also with philosophical and societal questions, which are usually perceived as being outside of the boundaries of engineering expertise (Flanagan/Howe/Nissenbaum 2008). In *material semiotics*, a value can be delegated to the material, so that the material becomes an actant in its own right. For Latour[1] (1999; 1992) action is fundamentally a process of delegation that entails making others do things (and being made to do things as well) (Stanica 2016). A third stance argues that value is not only tied or delegated to the material but that value is material in itself. This *infrastructures of value* approach directs attention to the material relationality of value, arguing that values never exist independent of a material network (Lammer/Thiemann 2023). Here, a value is defined as the importance that actions (and their products) have for people as part of a larger whole. These larger wholes not only exist as the imagination of a person (Graeber 2001) but as material infrastructures.

Despite their slightly different conceptualisations of materiality, these approaches share the argument that values both shape and are shaped by a diverse set of practices, material networks and infrastructures (Mol 1999; Law/Urry 2004). However, what has not yet received much scientific attention are the ambiguous effects when a value in itself changes. By this research gap, we do not mean how one value is replaced by a different value, how its interpretation changes within the public discourse, or how values are negotiated between different social groups. Instead, we foreground the idea that a value relates to different material practices, contingent on what it intends to achieve and can thus exist as different versions.

We conceptualise the moments when existing relations of value change, as *friction*. Friction can be characterised by "turbulence" (Edwards et al. 2011) that creates thermal energy, and heat is known to produce unexpected effects. The ambiguities of friction makes it an intriguing analytical concept and metaphor for those concerned with the social studies of cultures (Tsing 2005), infrastructures (Jaton/Vinck 2016; Pelizza 2017), and numbers and data (Bates 2018; Edwards 2013; Edwards et al. 2011). Connecting this with the previous STS approaches on value, friction occurs *in* value not (only) *between* values. It is during friction that transparency shifts, adapts to other material practices, and changes what it wants to achieve.

---

1   Similarly, Bourdieu critically understood delegation as the process of transferring power and symbolic capital to political authorities, and as a form of expropriation (Bourdieu/Robinson 1985; Bourdieu/Wacquant 2013).

Studying CreditAI

Our account of friction is informed by a back-and-forth process between theory and ethnography research at CreditAI[2]. Ethnography involves immersing oneself into the field, active engagement, and the collection of thick descriptions to uncover novel patterns and meanings in the situations studied (Hess 2014; Atkinson et al. 2014; Spradley 1980; Goffman 2001). In this case, the lead author was afforded the opportunity to immerse herself in CreditAI through a joint research project involving both the lead and second authors, as well as several scientists from CreditAI. The empirical observations of the transparency initiative were initially sparked by an invitation by one of these scientists to attend one of the first meetings, and the coincidence that the initiative picked up speed just as the lead author began her field research on site.

Between 2021 and 2023, the lead author regularly participated in meetings of the transparency initiative, engaging in one-on-one discussions with its members and conducting ethnographic interviews. Additionally, she became actively involved in the user study of the initial prototype of the scoring calculator. The collected ethnographic material consists of detailed field notes, an ethnographic journal capturing reflections on observations and emotions during fieldwork, various documents, and transcripts from the ethnographic interviews, as well as records of bilateral discussions with around sixty employees (Knecht 2012). As we will now dive into our empirical observations, we intentionally shift the perspective to the viewpoint of the lead author.

Credit Scoring: From Absence to Closed Transparency

Credit agencies find transparency challenging, but this is not entirely their fault. After all, these agencies' very existence hinges on the absence of transparency, that is: opacity. The reluctance of other companies, financial institutions, telecommunications firms, and banks to share data with one another created a niche that credit agencies fill. Credit agencies act as intermediaries, where data from multiple companies can be consolidated to calculate a credit score, using a combination of their own and competitors' data (Hengel 2010). For instance, banks provide their customers' data to a credit agency in exchange for information on their customers' credit scores. Credit scores are algorithmic predictions of an individual's default risk calculated by a statistical comparison of the individual's data with the data of an "equivalent" risk group (Kiviat 2019). Thus, the concrete data, models, and weights, as well as the respective requirements a credit seeker

---

2   We changed the name of the company and people for anonymity reasons. All persons in this paper are intentionally not identifiable by gender.

must fulfill to obtain a credit, are not publicly known (Bridle 2018; Pasquale 2016; Rosamond 2016).

The presumed absence of transparency, or opacity, is not universal to a scoring algorithm (or AI systems in general). Instead, it is linked to the specific arrangement of credit agencies that include different technologies, organisational procedures and non-disclosure agreements (NDAs), authority of engineers over access to the algorithm, and relations beyond the credit scoring agency, such as close ties with the credit agency's clients. What is considered opaque is actually a specific version of transparency, one that positions the scoring algorithm within this "closed network" of relations. I call this "closed" transparency.

I was reminded of "closed transparency" each day. Everyone at CreditAI was required to a sign an NDA, a tangible reminder of the boundaries of transparency. Then, more importantly, I observed how laptops crashed when an external USB device was plugged in by an ignorant ethnographer, that e-mails were to be classified as confidential when they were sent to an e-mail address that didn't belong to CreditAI, and how warning messages popped up after attempts to send a written field note to an external university e-mail address.

"Closed" transparency also contained and constrained most of the employees' relations to the scoring algorithm. At the very beginning of my fieldwork and the transparency initiative, I was sitting with Quinn, the initiative's project manager, and talking about my ethnographic intentions at CreditAI. Over lunch, Quinn smiled at me and mentioned that my timing for researching algorithms was perfect. Becoming curious, I asked why this was the perfect time, considering CreditAI had been using algorithms for over twenty years. Quinn gave me another smile and explained that while automated scoring had indeed been in place for decades, it was only now that employees were allowed to be transparent about it among themselves. "You must understand, we have hardly ever discussed the scoring algorithm internally. A few colleagues know about it, but in the company, there was no conversation whatsoever about it", Quinn said. The "few colleagues" Quinn referred to were the engineers at CreditAI. They were responsible for developing the scoring algorithms and had privileged access to the actual calculations and models of these algorithms. I noticed what Quinn meant when I talked to employees outside of the engineering team: there was a remarkable absence of knowledge regarding the factors that would impact the score.

We will see next, how the introduction of transparency as a new value repositioned the scoring algorithm in the company. The algorithm became connected with (good and robust) explanations, engineering and non-engineering expertise, lay audiences, design requirements and risk management. During moments of friction, we trace different versions of transparency from "closed" to "complete" to "aesthetic" to "credible", each connected to different material practices.

Friction Between Closed and Complete Transparency

After widespread public concerns were raised about CreditAI's opaque credit scoring system (and after enduring these concerns for some time), CreditAI found itself in the position of needing to provide a solution to opacity. One prominent solution that other credit agencies had already implemented are scoring calculators that allow consumers to obtain an assessment of their personalised credit score after responding to a series of questions (FICO 2023; TransUnion 2023). A similar tool was now devised for CreditAI's scoring processes. Shortly after this decision was made by CreditAI's management team, ten employees from various departments were encouraged to form the "transparency initiative". The team comprised a diverse group of employees: four engineers, two computational researchers, one communication expert, two customer service representatives, and one legal expert. Additionally, other employees from different departments contributed intermittently throughout the initiative's various stages and phases. Developing the scoring calculator as a cross-divisional undertaking was a very welcomed and novel approach in the company.

To develop the question and answer options for the scoring calculator, one of the initial decisions made by the transparency team was to identify the most important variables and weights influencing a credit seeker's score. Given the numerous variables and feature combinations of the algorithm, it was not deemed possible to determine these factors manually. Instead, so-called explainability techniques were used, that comprised different statistical and machine learning methods to interpret (and debug) algorithms. For instance, the explainability technique SHAP identifies the most important variables that determines a persons' score, as Lou explained to me.

Lou was part of CreditAI's research department. Equipped with a PhD in computer science and trained in explainable AI, Lou was perfectly suited to identify and describe the most crucial variables of the scoring algorithm as a first step. The variables would then serve as the basis for formulating relevant questions, such as "How many credit cards do you own?". In a second step, Lou was supposed to semantically summarise the effects of a variable. For instance, for the variable "credit card", Lou was supposed to note down whether a credit card had a positive or negative impact on one's score, if there were distinctions based on the number of credit cards, and the reasons behind these variations. This second step was aimed to guide pre-given responses of the the the scoring calculators' questionnaire.

Despite having the required expertise, Lou struggled with the task. While the explainability techniques clearly showed that, for instance, having e.g. one credit card had a positive effect, while having e.g. five credit cards had a negative effect, Lou was not sure exactly why this was the case. During a team meeting with the research department, Lou thus sought assistance from their colleagues. Lou had hoped that, at the very least, their colleagues would understand why certain variables, such as one or five credit cards, made a difference. However, no one else was able to help. "I don't know, I assume, they use data discretisation [*a technique often used before training machine learning algorithms to transform continuous variables into discrete values*], and sometimes they base their decisions on their expert knowledge", Lou's team leader offered, accompanied by a shrug of uncertainty. For a better explanation, the team leader advised, Lou should better ask the engineers themselves.

It seemed that indeed, the engineers knew the reasons, as they had sometimes set explicit cut-offs for some variables. Furthermore, as we recall from "closed transparency", the engineers were the ones that had privileged access to data and models.

Unfortunately, Lou's quest remained unsuccessful. The engineers were not negligent toward Lou; rather, documenting or justifying decisions had not been necessary for their work before. In other words, "closed transparency" did not require the engineers to provide the necessary information that Lou required now.

Frustrated, Lou was already on the brink of giving up when an idea came to mind: Lou thought to use the very knowledge gap to explain the variables and variances intuitively—in fact, Lou had actually always considered themself a lay person to the scoring algorithm, as Lou mentioned to me. Despite having been working for CreditAI for some time, the transparency initiative marked Lou's first encounter with the actual data of the scoring algorithm. "That's why I decided to write down the explanations as I would instinctively explain them to myself", Lou told me.

From a lay person's understanding, having at least one credit card could be good as a credit card holder underwent scrutiny by the bank and identified as trustful. However, having five credit cards would significantly increase the likelihood of accumulating debt, or even raise suspicions of fraud. After writing down this and similar other explanations, Lou checked whether the explanations aligned with the outcomes of the explainability techniques. This was how, iteratively, Lou managed to note down (at least some) explanations of the variables and their variations.

Friction occurred between "closed" transparency and its own absent materialities (documentation and knowledge) on one hand, and the emerging demands for "complete" transparency on the other. And this time, friction proved to be productive. "Closed" transparency, where Lou was an outsider to the scoring processes, contributed to "complete" transparency, in which engineering and non-engineering knowledge were tied together. As we will demonstrate next, friction can also work rather destructively.

Friction Between Complete and Aesthetic Transparency

A problem with "complete" transparency quickly became apparent. The explanations became very long, wordy, and cumbersome; they were "tapeworm style", as Toni laughingly recalled over a coffee. Toni worked in the communications department and had been working for CreditAI for several years. Like Lou, however, this was Toni's first time dealing with the factors of the scoring algorithm. As the (only) communications expert in the transparency team, Toni was now tasked with improving the "tapeworm" explanations, which were deemed to be far from "user-friendly". Additionally, Toni was responsible for writing texts to appear alongside each question in the scoring calculator. These, too, had to be written in a "not too bureaucratic and simple enough language", as Toni described them.

Lacking any formal engineering education, Toni relied on the engineers to avoid providing incorrect explanations, so Toni thought. Toni told me how they spoke with the engineers over the phone nearly every day, often multiple times. In one of the early conversations, an engineer mentioned an unknown term all the time, "score card", until Toni realised it referred to what the engineers would call the scoring algorithm. Toni was intimidated and realised their lack of knowledge. "After that incident, I asked them even the tiniest questions", Toni recounted. Each time, Toni became aware of how complex the scoring processes actually were, now even more determined to find ways to explain them.

Despite Toni having invested considerable effort and time into carefully aligning their own and the engineers' different expertises, the feedback on Toni's first drafts was not as Toni expected. "People got really angry when I presented my drafts", Toni summarised disappointed after the meeting. By "people", Toni meant the engineers on the team, whose anger stemmed from their perception that Toni's user-friendly texts were too superficial and incomplete.

This intricate situation, caught between the still existing pursuit of "complete" transparency and the explanations being "completely incomprehensible" (as Toni put it), persisted for a couple of weeks. What both the engineers and Toni were unaware of during their disagreement was that the external design experts for the scoring calculator had imposed a word limit aimed to enhance the design of the scoring calculator. The shorter and clearer the explanations, the more visually appealing the design was (now, there was even room to incorporate comic drawings next to the explanations). Toni and the engineers only learnt of the design requirement at a later stage of the transparency initiative. Faced with the material constraints of the scoring calculator, Toni and the engineers had found a common enemy. For Toni, the enemy meant adapting the explanations once again, significantly shortening the texts while delivering as much "statistically accurate" information as possible. For the engineers, it meant surrendering to the material realities of the tool and accepting that the explanations had to be superficial out of necessity—visual design requirements were outside of their expertise anyway. In the end, the explanations were "no longer complete, but at least still correct", as Toni described the compromise they finally reached.

Toni and the engineers are two unequally positioned actors in the field, each seeing different purposes in transparency due to their respective work roles and expertises, each linked to different material practices. For the engineers, transparency was still attained through completeness and robust statistical information; for Toni, transparency was attained through comprehensibility, simplicity and user-friendliness. As Edwards and colleagues (2011) put it, "friction can arise when people from different social worlds struggle to establish common ground". To soothe friction, people from different social worlds "point to shared objects". Here, the shared object pointed to them as the materialities of the scoring calculator imposed a limitation. The "aesthetic" version of transparency related the scoring algorithm with both unequally positioned actors in the field, design and the materialities of the scoring calculator. Unlike previously, when one version of transparency was contingent on the other, this time, one version was replaced by the other.

Friction Between Aesthetic and Credible Transparency

Nico had only recently joined CreditAI. At the beginning, working for a company under public scrutiny for its lack of transparency felt ethically challenging for Nico. This is why Nico greatly appreciated their employer's efforts to become more transparent, as they shared with me during a train ride. Nico and I were both affiliated with the research department at CreditAI. Similar to Lou, Nico had a computational background and a PhD degree. Continuing our conversation, I began to touch upon a specific variable used in the scoring algorithm which had been a frequent topic of discussion within the transparency team regarding the best way to explain it. I wanted to know Nico's opinion about it. Suddenly, Nico's cheerful mood changed. Nico cast a glance around the train and whispered to me: "We should not speak too loudly about the score; you never know who might be listening." I was surprised for a moment—had not CreditAI intended to become transparent? Rather slowly, I realised my mistake. Transparency was still an ongoing process of negotiation, and no one yet knew what could or should be communicated publicly. A random eavesdropper on the train certainly did not belong to that audience yet.

So, who exactly was the audience? One year after the start of the initiative, and some months after my conversation with Nico on the train, a prototype of the calculator, i.e., questions, answers, and user-friendly scripts alongside each question, was finally completed. This prototype represented the version that the engineers and Toni had agreed on. Now, the transparency team decided to hire an external marketing agency to conduct a user trial of the prototype. The preparations for the trial led to heated discussions about organisational issues such as the set-up and the chronological order of the trials' different steps, and content-related topics such as the specific questions participants should answer. One of the most vividly discussed issues concerned the participants themselves, since the marketing agency had asked the team about the desired socio-economic demographics of the participants. Their request brought an important question to the surface: By whom would the calculator actually be used, and more importantly, for which reasons?

The answer to this question revolved around two contrasting figures. The first figure was *Jane Doe*, the "average consumer". Jane was expected to have only a "humble interest" in the calculator. Jane would mainly use the calculator to check whether her knowledge (and self-evaluation) of her score corresponded with the calculator's results. And this was deemed to be very important as Jane should gain trust in the calculator's results and in CreditAI as a trustworthy organisation. The other figure was *the hacker*. The hacker, as the transparency team suspected, could be working for a competing credit agency or a curious media institution. The hacker had other interests than Jane. The hacker would use a bot to find out (e.g., "scrape") calculations of the scoring algorithm.

The transparency team decided that what they actually needed was to determine whether the hacker would be able to discover anything when using the prototype scoring calculator. So, they tried to hack the calculator themselves. Nico was entrusted with this task and presented their results in the next meeting. To the surprise of the team, the unfortunate result was that most of the scoring algorithm's parameters used to build the calculator could be reconstructed. "Newspapers would publish that a hacker cracked our code", warned Sam, one of the engineers, and most people in the meeting agreed that this was the worst-case scenario. The "closed" versions of transparency had successfully prevented people from trying to "game the system", e.g. intentional changes in behaviour that one might make to improve or evade the algorithmic classification (Kear 2017; Poon 2014). There was no intention to alter this long-standing practice.

Now that the team knew the calculator could potentially be hacked, they were however confronted with a problem. From the perspective of Jane's needs, the calculator's results needed to be close to the actual score used by a bank to generate trust in the results (and in CreditAI). Yet, in order to not fulfil the needs of the hacker, the calculator's results should not be too close to the scoring algorithm that was used by the banks. Various members of the transparency team held differing viewpoints on what to do about this contradiction. The discussion circled from the option of releasing the calculator with the questions, answer options and explanations as originally planned ("aesthetic" transparency) to the option of removing some of the questions that had previously been identified as important variables. Yet, if questions were to be removed, there was concern that the scoring calculator would fall short of the expectations and demands expressed by vocal public actors demanding CreditAI to be transparent. It would also fall short of some of

Lou's work, crafting out all the important variables and their weights, and some of Toni's work in deleting some texts.

It was CreditAI's management who made the final decision. Ultimately, the management decided to remove some questions to make it more difficult for a potential scraping attempt. "You must know that the calculator is also a form of risk management", explained Sam, who had been directly communicating with the CEO, to the transparency team during their next meeting. Sam added that this would also offer the advantage of further simplifying the calculator, as answering some of the questions might have required consumers to peruse some of their existing contracts and documents for details. "It is an educational tool after all", Sam concluded.

A new version of what we term "credible" transparency connected the scoring algorithm to hackers, average users, reverse engineering, and trust in the results. This time, friction did not replace "aesthetic" transparency but rather updated it, moving away even further from "complete" transparency.

The end of the transparency initiative was marked by the release of the scoring calculator. What was now publicly accessible, was a gamified questionnaire that included eight questions, which represented parts of the main factors used in the calculations of the score. Each question was accompanied by a brief explanation of why certain factors influenced the score either negatively or positively. On the day of the calculator's release, numerous press representatives were invited on-site to test and review it. To the relief of the management, the media responded mainly positively, endorsing the company's move toward transparency. Amidst the press coverage and celebrations surrounding the calculator's launch, not everyone at CreditAI was pleased with how transparency ultimately unfolded. Thus, I found myself in the company of Nico and some other members of the transparency team, away from the festivities, sipping wine, and contemplating the purpose of it all. Indeed, what did transparency disclose?

Discussion: Materialities of Algorithmic Transparency

When studying opaque algorithmic decision-making in a credit agency, we did not only find opacity. Instead, we found four different versions of transparency that positioned and repositioned the scoring algorithm within different material relations. For the longest time, *closed transparency* demarcated the boundaries of information circulation and was reserved for engineers and banks, closely tied to NDAs and security measures. With the introduction of transparency as an explicit value in the company, *complete transparency* aimed to gather all possible engineering information to combine with non-engineering (lay) knowledge. While closed transparency and complete transparency were initially at odds, the latter ultimately proved to be productive for the former. When the materialities of the scoring calculator and the algorithm made it impossible to provide complete transparency, it was replaced by a compromise. *Aesthetic transparency* secondly aimed to deliver as much complete information as possible in a user-friendly and aesthetic manner. After transparency was successfully negotiated, a prototype version of the scoring calculator had been developed; friction occurred again when it was discovered that the prototype version of the scoring calculator could be reverse-engineered. The risk of being hacked prompted updates to aesthetic transparency, ultimately establishing *credible transparency*.

There is not much empirical research about the relations between value and its material practices, and how the materialities of value actually impede, allow, or contribute to a certain version of value. In our case, we saw all these processes at the same time: the materialities of the scoring algorithm *impeded* "complete" transparency as it was rendered unattainable. The design requirements of the scoring calculator *allowed* for a (temporal) agreement on "aesthetic" transparency. The possibility to reverse-engineer the scoring algorithm (and upholding trade secrecy) *contributed* to "credible" transparency. While the different versions of transparency evolved in a temporal order in this case, we believe they can also coexist simultaneously. For instance, "closed" transparency still partly exists as the development of the scoring calculator has not explicitly altered the bonds to banks and other clients as primary accessors to scoring.

We also saw that moments of friction in the materialities of value indicate ambiguous effects. In the case of Lou, we observed how friction between two versions of transparency became productive for one of the versions. In the case of Toni, however, we saw how friction had rather destructive effects, leading one form of transparency to be replaced by another. And in the case of Nico, we witnessed how two versions were aligned to soothe friction. Translating these insights into actionable guidance for designers, as social scholars of value (Nissenbaum 2001; Agre 1998; Knobel and Bowker 2011) advocate for, our takeaway is rather simple: designers of value do not always have full control over how a value takes form and ultimately manifests. We suggest that this lack of agency also extends to regulators of AI systems, as transparency (and standards) may be at odds with specific material practices within which transparency is meant to be achieved. What is more, while explainable AI appears to bridge the gap between complete, aesthetic, and credible versions of transparency, we need further empirical studies to understand if there are versions of transparency more commonly used or preferred than others.

Outlook

Transparency was not the initially anticipated panacea that opened up the algorithmic black box. While this story concludes with a rather diluted version of transparency, this is not to say that this version prevails (although dominant modes of production, and the profit-oriented logic of a private company may in most cases facilitate it). Yet, the journey it undertook, had changed other relations. Bringing our findings back to the practicalities of our field one last time, we conclude by underscoring that the transparency initiative for instance illuminated the inadequate documentation of decisions, and information primarily circling in a confined circle of engineers and banks. It also highlighted the varying levels of trust and access felt by differently situated actors within the company and underscored the authority of the engineers, gradually being contested. Remembering how our story ended with some people contemplating these newly revealed relations, novel moments of friction may already be on the rise.

List of References

Abebe, R./Barocas, S./Kleinberg, J./Levy, K./Raghavan, M./Robinson, D.G. (2020): "Roles for Computing in Social Change". In: Proceedings of the 2020 Conference on Fairness, Accountability, and Transparency. Barcelona, Spain: ACM, pp. 252–60. https://doi.org/10.1145/3351095.3372871.

Aggarwal, N. (2021): "The Norms of Algorithmic Credit Scoring". The Cambridge Law Journal, 80 (1), pp. 42–73. https://doi.org/10.1017/S0008197321000015.

Agre, P.E. (1998): "Toward a Critical Technical Practice: Lessons Learned in Trying to Reform AI". In: Social Science, Technical Systems, and Cooperative Work. Psychology Press.

Ananny, M. (2016): "Toward an Ethics of Algorithms. Convening, Observation, Probability, and Timeliness". Science, Technology, & Human Values, 41 (1), pp. 93–117. https://doi.org/10.1177/0162243915606523.

Ananny, M./Crawford, K. (2018): "Seeing without Knowing: Limitations of the Transparency Ideal and Its Application to Algorithmic Accountability". New Media & Society, 20 (3), pp. 973–89. https://doi.org/10.1177/1461444816676645.

Angwin, J./Larson, J./Mattu, S./Kirchner, L. (2018): "Machine Bias". Nieman Reports, 2018.

Atkinson, P./Coffey, A./Delamont, S./Lofland, J./Lofland, L. (eds.) (2014): Handbook of Ethnography. Reprinted. Los Angeles, London, New Delhi, Singapore, Washington DC: SAGE.

Balayn, A./Gürses, S. (2021): "Beyond Debiasing. Regulating AI and Its Inequalities". Brussels: European Digital Rights (EDRi). https://edri.org/wp-content/uploads/2021/09/EDRi_Beyond-Debiasing-Report_Online.pdf.

Ball, C. (2009): "What Is Transparency?" Public Integrity, 11 (4), pp. 293–308. https://doi.org/10.2753/PIN1099-9922110400.

Bates, J. (2018): "The Politics of Data Friction". Journal of Documentation, 74 (2), pp. 412–29. https://doi.org/10.1108/JD-05-2017-0080.

Bono, T./Croxson, K./Giles, A. (2021): "Algorithmic Fairness in Credit Scoring". Oxford Review of Economic Policy, 37 (3). pp. 585–617. https://doi.org/10.1093/oxrep/grab020.

Bourdieu, P./Robinson, K. (1985): "Delegation and Political Fetishism". Thesis Eleven, 10–11 (1), pp. 56–70. https://doi.org/10.1177/072551368501000105.

Bourdieu, P./Wacquant, L. (2013): "Symbolic Capital and Social Classes". Journal of Classical Sociology, 13 (2), pp. 292–302. https://doi.org/10.1177/1468795X12468736.

Bridle, J. (2018): New Dark Age: Technology, Knowledge and the End of the Future. London, Brooklyn, NY: Verso.

Burrell, J. (2016): "How the Machine 'Thinks': Understanding Opacity in Machine Learning Algorithms". Big Data & Society, 3 (1). https://doi.org/10.1177/2053951715622512.

Chopra, S./Dexter, S.D. (2008): Decoding Liberation: The Promise of Free and Open Source Software. Routledge Studies in New Media and Cyberculture 4. New York, London: Routledge, Taylor & Francis Group.

Crawford, K. (2021): Atlas of AI: Power, Politics, and the Planetary Costs of Artificial Intelligence. New Haven: Yale University Press.

Davis, G.F. (2016): The Vanishing American Corporation: Navigating the Hazards of a New Economy. First edition. Oakland, CA: Berrett-Koehler Publishers.

Edwards, P.N. (2013): A Vast Machine: Computer Models, Climate Data, and the Politics of Global Warming. First paperback edition. Infrastructures Series. Cambridge, Massachusetts, London, England: The MIT Press.

Edwards, P.N./Mayernik, M.S./Batcheller, A.L./Bowker, G.C./Borgman, C.L. (2011): "Science Friction: Data, Metadata, and Collaboration". Social Studies of Science, 41 (5), pp. 667–90.

Ehsan, U./Wintersberger, P./Liao, Q.V./Mara, M./Streit, M./Wachter, S./Riener, A./Riedl, M.O. (2021): "Operationalizing Human-Centered Perspectives in Explainable AI". In: Extended Abstracts of the 2021 CHI Conference on Human Factors in Computing Systems, pp. 1–6, 94. New York, NY, USA: Association for Computing Machinery. https://doi.org/10.1145/3411763.3441342.

European Commission. (2022): "AI Excellence: Ensuring That AI Works for People | Shaping Europe's Digital Future". https://digital-strategy.ec.europa.eu/en/policies/ai-people.

European Commission. (2024): "AI Act | Shaping Europe's Digital Future". 2 February 2024. https://digital-strategy.ec.europa.eu/en/policies/regulatory-framework-ai.

European Union Agency for Fundamental Rights (EU body or agency). (2022): Bias in Algorithms: Artificial Intelligence and Discrimination. LU: Publications Office of the European Union. https://data.europa.eu/doi/10.2811/25847.

FICO. (2023): "Free Credit Scores Estimator from myFICO". myFICO. http://www.myfico.com/fico-credit-score-range-estimator/.

Flanagan, M./Howe, D.C./Nissenbaum, H. (2008): "Embodying Values in Technology: Theory and Practice". In: J. van den Hoven/J. Weckert (eds.), Information Technology and Moral Philosophy. Cambridge Studies in Philosophy and

Public Policy. Cambridge: Cambridge University Press, pp. 322-53. https://doi.org/10.1017/CBO9780511498725.017.

Friedman, B./Kahn, P./Borning, A. (2002): "Value Sensitive Design: Theory and Methods". In: https://www.semanticscholar.org/paper/Value-Sensitive-Design%3A3A-Theory-and-Methods-Friedman-Kahn/54bfbe5a886807bf3b80cdd201a7140eaf26ad70.

Fuchs, C. (2022): Digital Capitalism: Media, Communication and Society, volume 3. Abingdon, Oxon, New York, NY: Routledge.

Goffman, E. (2001): Interaktion und Geschlecht H. Knoblauch/H. Kotthoff (eds.). 2. Aufl. Campus Studium. Frankfurt am Main: Campus.

Goodman, B./Flaxman, S. (2017): "European Union Regulations on Algorithmic Decision-Making and a 'Right to Explanation'." AI Magazine, 38 (3), pp. 50–57. https://doi.org/10.1609/aimag.v38i3.2741.

Graeber, D. (2001): Toward an Anthropological Theory of Value: The False Coin of Our Own Dreams. New York: Palgrave.

Grunwald, A./Hillerbrand, R. (eds.) (2021): Handbuch Technikethik. 2., Aktualisierte und erweiterte Auflage. Stuttgart: J.B. Metzler Verlag.

Heald, D. (2006): "Varieties of Transparency". In: C. Hood/D. Heald (eds.), Transparency: The Key to Better Governance? British Academy. https://doi.org/10.5871/bacad/9780197263839.003.0002.

Hengel, E. (2010): "Facilitating Access to Finance. Discussion Paper on Credit Information Sharing". OECD. https://www.oecd.org/global-relations/45370071.pdf.

Hess, D. (2014): "Ethnography and the Development of Science and Technology Studies". In: P. Atkinson/A. Coffey/S. Delamont/J. Lofland/L. Lofland (eds.), Handbook of Ethnography. Reprinted. Los Angeles, London, New Delhi, Singapore, Washington DC: SAGE, pp. 234-45.

Jaton, F./Vinck, D. (2016): "Unfolding Frictions in Database Projects". Revue d'anthropologie des connaissances, 10 (4), pp. a-m. https://doi.org/10.3917/rac.033.a.

Joque, J. (2022): Revolutionary Mathematics: Artificial Intelligence, Statistics and the Logic of Capitalism. London, New York: Verso.

Kitchin, R. (2017): "Thinking Critically About and Researching Algorithms". Information, Communication & Society, 20 (1), pp. 14–29. https://doi.org/10.1080/1369118X.2016.1154087.

Kiviat, B. (2019): "The Moral Limits of Predictive Practices: The Case of Credit-Based Insurance Scores". American Sociological Review, 84 (6), pp. 1134–58. https://doi.org/10.1177/0003122419884917.

Knecht, M. (2012): "Ethnographische Praxis Im Feld Der Wissenschafts-, Medizin- Und Technikanthropologie". In: S. Beck/J. Niewöhner/E. Sørensen (eds.), Science and Technology Studies. Eine Sozialanthropologische Einführung. VerKörperungen, MatteRealities, Band 17. Bielefeld: transcript, pp. 245–74.

Knobel, C./Bowker, G.C. (2011): "Values in Design". Communications of the ACM, 54 (7), pp. 26–28. https://doi.org/10.1145/1965724.1965735.

Lammer, C./Thiemann, A. (2023): "Introduction: Infrastructuring Value". Ethnos 89 (2), pp. 195–218. https://doi.org/10.1080/00141844.2023.2180063.

Latour, B. (1992): "Where Are the Missing Masses? The Sociology of a Few Mundane Artifacts". In: W.E. Bijker/J. Law (eds.), Shaping Technology, Building Society: Studies in Sociotechnical Change. Cambridge: MIT Press, pp. 225–58.

Latour, B. (1999): Pandora's Hope: Essays on the Reality of Science Studies. Harvard University Press.

Law, J./Urry, J. (2004): "Enacting the Social". Economy and Society, 33 (3), pp. 390–410. https://doi.org/10.1080/0308514042000225716.

Le Ludec, C./Cornet, M./Casilli, A.A. (2023): "The Problem with Annotation. Human Labour and Outsourcing between France and Madagascar". Big Data & Society, 10 (2). https://doi.org/10.1177/20539517231188723.

Markus, A.F./Kors, J.A./Rijnbeek, P.R. (2021): "The Role of Explainability in Creating Trustworthy Artificial Intelligence for Health Care. A Comprehensive Survey of the Terminology, Design Choices, and Evaluation Strategies". Journal of Biomedical Informatics, 113 (January):103655. https://doi.org/10.1016/j.jbi.2020.103655.

Mau, S. (2017): Das Metrische Wir: Über Die Quantifizierung Des Sozialen. Erste Auflage, Originalausgabe. Berlin: Suhrkamp.

Mendes, L.S./Mattiuzzo, M. (2022): "Algorithms and Discrimination: The Case of Credit Scoring in Brazil". In: M. Albers/I.W. Sarlet (eds.), Personality and Data Protection Rights on the Internet: Brazilian and German Approaches. Ius Gentium: Comparative Perspectives on Law and Justice. Cham: Springer International Publishing, pp. 407-43. https://doi.org/10.1007/978-3-030-90331-2_17.

Miceli, M./Schuessler, M./Yang, T. (2020): "Between Subjectivity and Imposition. Power Dynamics in Data Annotation for Computer Vision". Proceedings of the ACM on Human-Computer Interaction, 4 (CSCW2), pp. 1–25. https://doi.org/10.1145/3415186.

Mol, A. (1999): "Ontological Politics. A Word and Some Questions". The Sociological Review, 47 (S1), pp. 74–89. https://doi.org/10.1111/j.1467-954X.1999.tb03483.x.

Moore, S. (2018): "Towards a Sociology of Institutional Transparency: Openness, Deception, and the Problem of Public Trust". Sociology, 52 (2), pp. 416–30. https://doi.org/10.1177/0038038516686530.

Neyland, D. (2007): "Achieving Transparency: The Visible, Invisible, and Divisible in Academic Accountability Networks". Organization, 14 (4), pp. 499–516. https://doi.org/10.1177/1350508407078050.

Nissenbaum, H. (2001): "How Computer Systems Embody Values". Computer, 34 (3), pp. 120–119. https://doi.org/10.1109/2.910905.

Onay, C./Öztürk, E. (2018): "A Review of Credit Scoring Research in the Age of Big Data". Journal of Financial Regulation and Compliance, 26 (3), pp. 382–405. https://doi.org/10.1108/JFRC-06-2017-0054.

Pasquale, F. (2016): The Black Box Society: The Secret Algorithms That Control Money and Information. First Harvard University Press paperback edition. Cambridge, Massachusetts/London, England: Harvard University Press.

Pelizza, A. (2017): "Disciplining Change, Displacing Frictions: Two Structural Dimensions of Digital Circulation Across Land Registry Database Integration". TECNOSCIENZA: Italian Journal of Science & Technology Studies, 7 (2), pp. 35–60.

Ribeiro, M.T./Singh, S./Guestrin, C. (2016): "'Why Should I Trust You?': Explaining the Predictions of Any Classifier". In: Proceedings of the 22nd ACM SIGKDD International Conference on Knowledge Discovery and Data Mining. San Francisco, California USA: ACM, pp. 1135-44. https://doi.org/10.1145/2939672.2939778.

Robbins, H./Stone, T./Bolte, J./van den Hoven, J. (2021): "Legibility as a Design Principle: Surfacing Values in Sensing Technologies". Science, Technology, & Human Values, 46 (5), pp. 1104–35. https://doi.org/10.1177/0162243920975488.

Rosamond, E. (2016): "'All Data Is Credit Data'. Reputation, Regulation, and Character in the Entrepreneurial Imaginary". Paragrana, 25 (2), pp. 112–24. https://doi.org/10.1515/para-2016-0032.

Rouvroy, A./Berns, T./Libbrecht, L.C. (2013): "Algorithmic Governmentality and Prospects of Emancipation". Reseaux, 177 (1), pp. 163–96.

Seyfert, R. (2022): "Algorithms as Regulatory Objects". Information, Communication & Society, 25 (11), pp. 1542–58. https://doi.org/10.1080/1369118X.2021.1874035.

Spradley, J.P. (1980): Participant Observation. New York: Holt, Rinehart and Winston.

Stanica, M. (2016): "Portraits of Delegation". The Eighteenth Century, 57 (2), pp. 235–49.

TransUnion. (2023): "Get Your Free Score and More". Intuit Credit Karma. https://www.creditkarma.com/tools/credit-score-simulator.

Tsing, A.L. (2005): Friction: An Ethnography of Global Connection. Princeton, N.J: Princeton University Press.

Verbeek, P-P. (2006): "Materializing Morality: Design Ethics and Technological Mediation". Science, Technology, & Human Values, 31 (3), pp. 361–80. https://doi.org/10.1177/0162243905285847.

Waibel, D./Peetz, T./Meier, F. (2021): "Valuation Constellations". Valuation Studies, 8 (1), pp. 33–66. https://doi.org/10.3384/VS.2001-5992.2021.8.1.33-66.

Wark, M. (2019): Capital Is Dead. London, New York: Verso.

Wulff, K/Finnestrand, H. (2023): "Creating Meaningful Work in the Age of AI: Explainable AI, Explainability, and Why It Matters to Organizational Designers". AI & SOCIETY, January. https://doi.org/10.1007/s00146-023-01633-0.

Ziewitz, M. (2013): "What Does Transparency Conceal?" Working paper, Privacy Research Group, New York University. https://zwtz.org/files/Notes-on-transparency.pdf

Zuboff, S. (2020): The Age of Surveillance Capitalism: The Fight for a Human Future at the New Frontier of Power. First Trade Paperback Edition. New York: PublicAffairs.

Conflicting Values in Epidemiological Modelling, Simulation, and Dashboard-Design

A Contribution to the Analysis of the Epistemisation of Pandemic Politics

Jens Hälterlein

Abstract

Mathematical models and computer simulations played a crucial role in dealing with the COVID-19 pandemic. Political decision-makers regularly justified their actions by referring to a knowledge derived from modelling and simulations of infection dynamics. However, as pandemic politics were contested and have become the focal point of societal value conflicts, modelling expertise was contested as well. The paper aims to contribute to the understanding of the anticipatory practices of epidemiological modelling and simulation and their entanglement with digital practices of evaluation, conflicting societal values and the epistemisation of politics. First, I will stress that models and simulations enable the prospective evaluation of political options. I will then show how different modelling approaches relate to different concepts of society and how they may or may not depict the diversity of people's lives in and individual reactions to the pandemic situation. Thereby, central value conflicts and the unequal distribution of risks that come to light in a social crisis situation are either considered or concealed. Their consideration in modelling can be understood as a starting point for a reflexive politicisation of epistemology that openly addresses conflict, controversy and friction as part of the political—especially in times of crisis. Next, a critical examination of an interface design of a simulation software will illustrate how the plurality of dimensions of a pandemic can be considered and how, at the same time, the digital evaluation of both the present situation and possible measures can follow a scientistic ideal and thus play into the hands of an epistemisation of politics. Finally, I will discuss problematic effects deriving from this scientistic ideal and briefly refer to the few existing proposed solutions.

Keywords

Modelling, Simulation, Dashboard-Design, Prospective Evaluation, Epistemisation

DOI 10.14361/dcs-2023-0209

Pandemic Modelling and the Epistemisation of Politics

The COVID-19 pandemic was the first pandemic in history that has come to be known in mathematical models and simulations. This is not so much an effect of new forms of science communication (rapid publication and release of modelling studies) but of media stories and social media attention (Rhodes/Lancaster 2020: 180). On 14 March 2020, the Washington Post published the online story *Why outbreaks like coronavirus spread exponentially and how to "flatten the curve"* (Stevens 2020). It featured several live simulations of the spread of a fake disease called "simulitis" in a town of 200 people, represented by 200 bouncing blue balls inside a square. When an infected individual, a red ball, hits a blue ball, the latter would be infected and turn red as well. The story is based on four scenarios. In scenario one, no measures to "flatten the curve" are in place and "simulitis" is able to spread quickly across the entire population. In scenario two, a forced quarantine is imposed but proves largely ineffective because, as it is assumed, not all social contacts can be prohibited. In scenario three, three-quarters of the population practice social distancing which flattens the curve significantly compared to the first two scenarios. In scenario four, seven of every eight people practice social distancing and the curve remains even flatter than in scenario 3. Even though the exact results of the simulations are random and will change with every restart or revisit of the page, the overall results remain the same, sending a clear message: social distancing is the best way to flatten the curve. And just as "simulitis" spread through the networks of bouncing balls, the story spread through networks of communication. It was tweeted by Barack Obama to his 114 million followers and generated 122 million retweets. Venezuelan President Nicolas Maduro even presented the simulations on state television.

However, simulations did not only play a central role in media communication during the COVID-19 pandemic. Political decision-makers regularly justified their actions by referring to knowledge derived from mathematical modelling and computer simulations of infection dynamics. For example, a model that simulated the spread of SARS-CoV-2 in the British population in different scenarios had a decisive influence on the actions of the British government. At the beginning of the pandemic, the government initially relied on the strategy of "herd immunity". However, given a simulated scenario in which the UK public health system would quickly be overburdened by SARS-CoV-2 infections and up to 500,000 deaths could occur, the British government decided to take measures. For the U.S., a scenario of up to 2.2 million deaths was simulated based on the same model. Confronted with these figures, the White House decided to take immediate action and issued, among other things, rules for social distancing (Adam 2020). The influence of modelling on political decision-making processes can also be observed in Germany. In a statement of the German Society for Epidemiology from 18 March 2020 (Deutsche Gesellschaft für Epidemiologie 2020), recommendations for action were made to decision-makers at the federal and state levels based on the results of a computer simulation. The recommendation stated that although results were "associated with numerous uncertainties" due to limited knowledge, the simulations could nevertheless provide a "representation of a broad spectrum of possible developments as well as the effect of infection control measures" based on which "recommendations for infection control" could be derived. Given the estimated capacity limits of the German healthcare system, it was strongly recommended that existing measures (bans on large events and school shutdowns) be supplemented by further restrictions on social contacts. A few days later, concerning these recommendations, the German Federal Government and the German States decided on a comprehensive package of measures including general contact restrictions. Accordingly, former German Science Minister Anja Karliczek (2020), referring to the approach of the German Federal Government to manage the crisis, stated that: "Scientific findings guide politics and guide us as rarely before."

This entanglement of epidemiological expertise based on modelling and simulation and pandemic politics can be seen as a manifestation of general development in recent decades, in the course of which scientific knowledge has gained enormously in societal importance and also represents a central resource for political decision-making. However, this development has taken on new characteristics. Alexander Bogner has coined the term "epistemisation of politics" (2021) to describe the current trend towards the reframing of political controversies that are inherently value conflicts into conflicts of scientific knowledge. Societal controversies and normative problems are gradually replaced by epistemic disputes that appear to be solvable by better knowledge and better science communication. In view of the COVID-19 pandemic, Bogner states thats: "Even though many experts repeatedly stressed that they had no political mandate whatsoever, the idea became widely established in the Coronavirus crisis that whoever listens to science, whoever follows the majority of experts, will make the right policy." (2022: 127) What is easily overlooked in this submission to the truth claims of (certain forms of) science is that "issues as diverse as availability of intensive-care hospital beds, employment and civil liberties are simultaneously at play, even if they cannot be simply quantified and then plugged into the models." (Saltelli et al. 2020: 484)

This epistemisation of politics, however, harbours considerable potential for the polarisation of political controversies—and equally has consequences for scientific expertise. As pandemic politics became contested in public, epidemiological models, simulations and entangled expertise became contested as well. In media stories, we are warned of "self-appointed data analysts" and "armchair epidemiologists" (Rhodes/Lancaster 2020: 185). On 4 December 2021, the German daily newspaper BILD referred to Dirk Brockmann, Viola Priesemann and Michael Mayer-Hermann, three experts for modelling who were consulted by the German Government for some time during the Covid-19 crisis, as "The Lockdown-Makers" ("Die Lockdown-Macher"), declaring them responsible for the "hard-hitting measures" that the Government had announced the previous day (BILD 2021).

Contrary to what is implied by BILD, the results of epidemiological modelling and simulations have of course not determined the political decisions taken by governments. However, it is indisputable that the knowledge generated by these techniques has played a crucial role in political decision-making. As Andrejevic and O'Neill stress, "pandemic response was a thoroughly mediated phenomenon" (2024: 1165). But how exactly are the anticipatory practices of epidemiological modelling and simulation to be understood, and what is their entanglement with digital practices of evaluation, conflicting societal values and the epistemisation of politics?

In the following section, I first want to stress that epidemiological models and simulations enable the prospective evaluation of political options. My thesis here is that we should regard the application of epidemiological computer simulations in crisis management as a process of algorithmic decision-making. I will then show how different modelling approaches relate to different concepts of society and may or may not depict the diversity of people's lives *in* and individual reactions *to* the pandemic situation. Thereby, central value conflicts and the unequal distribution of risks that come to light in a social crisis situation and create societal frictions are either considered or concealed. Their implicit consideration in modelling can be understood as a starting point for a reflexive politicisation of epistemology that openly addresses conflict, controversy and friction as part of the political—especially in times of crisis. Next, a critical examination of the interface design of a simulation software will illustrate how the plurality of dimensions of a pandemic and the values associated with them can be considered (plurality-by-design) and how, at the same time, the digital evaluation of both the present situation and possible measures can follow a scientistic ideal and thus play into the hands of an epistemisation of politics. Finally, I will discuss problematic effects deriving from this scientistic ideal and briefly refer to the few existing proposed solutions.

While the first two sections are conceptual in nature and serve to elaborate the political dimension of models and simulations as well as to illustrate a fundamental difference within these politics of knowledge production, the third section is based on a qualitative study of a government-funded research and development project on modelling and simulation of infection dynamics in the context of pandemic management. As part of the study, I conducted six semi-structured interviews with the actors involved in the project between October 2021 and January 2022, analysed publications resulting from the project and observed the public presentation of the project results. The material was analysed using qualitative methods, drawing heavily on strategies developed in grounded theory (Strauss/Corbin, 1998). The analytical process started with a close line-by-line reading of the material, during which codes were developed that describe every syntactic unit. The text was then broken down by developing empirically grounded concepts. While the codes at first were closely attached to the manifest meaning of a syntactic unit, they quickly became increasingly abstract. Codes that seemed to belong to a higher-level code (category) were grouped, which made it possible to capture higher-level relationships and argumentative structures. New codes were assigned to already established categories, if possible.

Epidemiological Models and Simulations as Algorithmic Decision Support Systems

How exactly are the anticipatory practices of epidemiological modelling and simulation to be understood? In order to answer this question, it is instructive to delineate them from other technologies used in the context of pandemic control and infectious disease management in the first place. Epidemiological models and simulations do not aim to reconstruct past infection events (as in the case of tracing apps), to monitor the current development of an infectious disease (as in the case of surveillance systems such as the *Global Outbreak Alert and Response Network*), nor to predict outbreaks (as in the case of early warning systems[1]). Instead, they enable the creation of different scenarios of possible future states of a complex social system. While tracing apps, surveillance systems and early warning systems are intended to provide insights into a specific section of reality (chains of infection and identification of infected individuals / identify an emerging epidemic / predicting an outbreak), an epidemiological simulation creates a duplication (Esposito 2007) or multiplication of reality that is not a reflection or mirror of an independent reality. Rather, simulations create technologically mediated versions of realities, whose relationship to an empirical reality must, however, by no means be arbitrary. Computer simulations have to be "realistic" because only then it is possible to translate insights from simulated realities into knowledge about an empirical reality. The specific realism of computer simulations corresponds to the principle of mathematical modelling: mathematical models are formalised descriptions of a section of reality, which they do not aim to reproduce 1:1. It is about a reduction in complexity that makes it possible to carry out certain operations or experiments in and with a model. The same applies to epidemiological models and computer simulations which can thus be understood

---

1   Such early warning systems should either automatically detect conspicuous events in the data of surveillance systems or analyse search engine queries and posts in social media for relevant words and statements (Ginsberg 2009). However, the performance of these technologies has so far fallen short of expectations (Lazer et al. 2014). In addition, the use of machine learning in the detection of pathogens should enable pre-emptive action by predicting the emergence of new infectious diseases through transmission from animals to humans (Morse et al. 2012; Salama et al. 2016).

as virtual laboratories in which scientists produce knowledge about the possible futures of a pandemic. They are transforming "time-depended system states into easily accessible formats of pictures, diagrams and numbers." (Kaminski et al. 2023: 14) These "easily accessible formats" are of course of interest to policymakers.

Although many empirically unsubstantiated assumptions as well as mere estimates of numerical values (reproduction number, incubation time, duration of infection, mortality rate, etc.) are included in an epidemiological model, its simulation allows for contingency management in dealing with uncertainty. "By producing information about what has not yet happened", models and simulations "reduce social complexity and constitute problems for acting in the present" (Aykut et al. 2019: 2). A central motivation for investigating the unknown through modelling and simulating is, hence, to tame the uncertainties of the present (Hacking 1990). Evidence-based politics become possible even when empirical evidence is at best uncertain. Through models and simulations, "we move from limited actuals—based on emergent case reports and empirical observations in particular sites—to detached abstractions—based on a mix of biosocial plausibility and mathematical probability—to materialised practices—wherein projections are actualised and particularised in social practices of the everyday." (Rhodes/Lancaster 2020: 178–179) As materialised practices, these anticipatory actions "close down unknowns into a governable present" and are therefore "lived as anticipated potentials, affecting actions, publics and policies in-the-now." (Rhodes et al. 2020: 253) Epidemiological models and simulations can hence be understood as "technologies of preparedness" (Adey/Anderson: 2012), analogous to, for instance, disaster exercises (Barrett et al. 2005).

Furthermore, epidemiological models enable the testing and prospective evaluation of pharmaceutical and non-pharmaceutical measures regarding their (potential) effectiveness in managing a pandemic situation. Epidemiological computer simulations can thus support political decision-making processes by making it possible to anticipate and assess the consequences of possible decisions. This algorithmically enabled prospective evaluation of options for action can reduce a second type of uncertainty that is connected to but not identical to the uncertainty regarding the future unfolding of a pandemic: the uncertainty that accompanies the unpredictability of the effects of action in political practice (Opitz 2017). Models and simulations "help to simplify decision making in exigent and complex conditions, substituting in effect the 'speculative forecast' for the messy sciences of the actual." (Anderson 2021: 177) They support decision-making processes in a crisis in which previous experience can only be drawn on to a limited extent and in which non-deciding is not an option. „Decisions about prognostic futures have to be made despite all the complexity of the sociotechnical system, possible path dependencies and uncertainties as well as non-knowledge about (un-)intended economic, ecological and societal consequences of these decisions." (Kaminski et al. 2023: 14) When a global health crisis turns into a crisis of decision-making, technological promises meet political desires. The entanglement of practices of modelling and simulating with pandemic politics is hence "an act of mutual adaptation, of promotion or inhibition, as well as it is a demand for understanding and a threat of misunderstanding" (ibid: 12)

For this reason, I proposed to regard the application of epidemiological computer simulations in crisis management as a process of algorithmic decision-making (Hälterlein2023). The degree of automation varies within ADM. In the case of epidemiological computer simulations, these are Algorithmic Decision Support (ADS) Systems that are not intended to make decisions themselves, but merely to support them. Just as any other ADS system, ADS systems designed for pandemic management are embedded in wider socio-technical practices and work in contextual and contingent ways. The use of these systems is regularly embedded in processes of human-centred formation of judgement and sensemaking that may follow their own logics. This starts with the collection and preparation of data and ends with the interpretation of visualisations of the output of these systems. Thus,—pandemic management understood as a complex sociotechnical practice—amalgamates different forms of knowledge production, different rationalities and different valuations. Keeping in mind this "messy" reality, an essential part of the critical endeavour to engage with the entanglement of algorithmically mediated evaluation practices and pandemic politics is to take a closer look at the different approaches to modelling and simulation.

From Equation-based to Agent-based Modelling

To simulate infection dynamics in scenarios, so-called equation-based models that identify variables of a system and evaluate or integrate sets of equations relating to these variables usually take the form of the SIR compartmental model (or a variation of it). This model divides a population into different compartments: the susceptible, the symptomatically infectious, and the recovered. Possible infection dynamics can then be modelled in terms of transitions between these variables. In an SEIR model, the model underlying the aforementioned statement of the German Society for Epidemiology, the compartment of infected but not yet infectious persons (exposed) is included as well. One of the main advantages of equation-based models is that they are relatively simple to construct and implement (Hunter et al. 2017). However, in recent years more and more doubts have been expressed whether the methods and tools currently used to test and evaluate epidemiological policies do actually work (Bruch/Atwell 2015). This failure has been attributed, among other factors, to the fact that individuals adapt their behaviour to the epidemic (Epstein et al. 2008). For instance, they would avoid mass events or would take hygiene measures even in situations when they are not legally required. These adaptations, in turn, affect infection dynamics. Hence, model-based predictions that do not consider individual behaviour are doomed to fail (ibid.). One of the reasons for this abstraction from individual behaviour is that equation-based models simply assume a homogeneous population consisting of identical members without any traits except their health status (S/E/I/R). The reason for this methodological reductionism is that a more differentiated representation of multiple populations would have to be reflected in much more complex mathematical equations, making these models difficult to construct and implement (Frias-Martinez et al. 2011). In addition, equation-based SIR models only need a small amount of current population data (primarily the number of new infections). Hence, with the availability of such data for an entire population, these models can be used for overall statements about countries.

However, so-called agent-based models and simulations (ABMS) are now increasingly seen as a promising alternative to these macro-models, as they would allow the modelling of individual behaviour and therefore enable a much more sophisticated and, to that extent, more realistic simulation of scenarios (Lorig et al. 2021). In ABMS, compartments and the transitions between them are still considered, but the inhabitants of an entire city can now be modelled as individual actors (=agents) who (inter-)act in a modelled environment according to the logics of action assigned to them. This modelled environment can be, for example, a digital twin of a city. In most cases, the agents' logics of action are modelled according to the daily routines of individual subpopulations that are considered typical. For this purpose, the model population is divided into age cohorts, households, or occupational groups, each of which is assigned a specific mobility and social behaviour. These behaviours result in risk encounters that can lead to infections. The behaviour of individual agents is modelled either in the form of "random walks", i.e. randomised movement in virtual space (as in the simulation of "simulitis") or according to the methods of distributed artificial intelligence (Epstein 2009). In the latter case, agents are programmed as rational actors, i.e. they follow certain predefined strategies and react to changing environmental conditions with, again, predefined, modified behaviours, e.g. they would avoid certain places if the risk of infection would be too high. It is also possible to program agents that evaluate and weigh up different options according to their benefits, just as the actors of rational choice theory. Accordingly, Flache and Macy (2011: 248) suggest thinking of agent-based simulation as a method in which "a single unified model of the population" is replaced with "a population of models each of which is an autonomous decision-maker."

In this "artificial world", the outbreak of an infectious disease is simulated to observe how the virus spreads geographically and demographically as a result of the mobility and interactions of the individual agents. As agents interact with each other and with their environment, their behaviour influences the behaviour of other agents—either directly or mediated by changes in environmental conditions, while it is still possible to observe how the distribution of the population in compartments is changing in a simulated scenario. Equation-based models, on the contrary, are unable to account for interactions and their effects. And because the mutual adaptation of behaviour can lead to system states that cannot be predicted in advance due to nonlinear processes and emergent effects (Weyer/ Roos 2017), equation-based models are prone to unrealistic assumptions and tend to create incorrect predictions of future developments. This is all the more problematic as the promise of prediction strongly shapes expectations of modelling and computer simulations in both the public and policy arenas (Ioannidis et al. 2022). However, this does not necessarily mean that ABMS produces correct predictions of future developments. Since ABMS are statistical models in which the relationships between variables are stochastic, multiple runs of a simulation may produce different results. Such variance can be conceptualised as a range of outcomes within a possibility range. Thus, while the output of ABMS can be understood as a more realistic representation of complex social systems, the outcome of a simulation is not necessarily identical to the outcome of social interactions in the "real world". The simulated futures are not necessarily identical with the futures as they unfold. Thus, ABMS can generate an awareness of contingency vis-à-vis the evaluations of political measures which might also go hand in hand with a more modest understanding of the role of scientific expertise in political decision-making.

Another difference that is central to the topic of this paper is that the two different approaches to epidemiological modelling relate to two different concepts of society (homogenous vs. heterogenous). While equation-based models differentiate individuals only in terms of their health status (S/E/I/R) and hence methodically exclude the social, ABMS has the potential to consider differential risks within a population associated with different realities of everyday life (home-schooling, home office, commuting, etc.) and different individual reactions to the pandemic (risk avoiding or risk-taking, depending on a given situation). Thus, ABMS can account for central value conflicts (security vs. freedom, that is: either putting public health over individual rights such as freedom of movement and freedom of assembly or putting these individual rights over public health-related concerns) and the unequal distribution of risks (e.g., based on occupation or family status), that usually become more apparent in a social crisis situation. During the COVID-19 pandemic, these factors have contributed to the creation or reinforcement of societal frictions (Nijhuis & van der Maesen 2021).

Potentials and Pitfalls of Dashboard Design

But what role does this acknowledgement of value conflicts and differential risks in modelling as well as the non-predictive character of simulations play in the development of Algorithmic Decision Support Systems for pandemic management? As an answer to this question, I will now turn to the demonstrator of the dashboard that was developed in the researched project. While the following analysis exclusively refers to just one dashboard developed in a specific Research & Development project, it can nonetheless be seen as a paradigmatic example of how design choices can either conceal or consider value conflicts and epistemic uncertainty. In the project, ABMS was used to produce knowledge about local infection dynamics. This knowledge was then translated into the information presented on a dashboard. The project aimed to support municipalities in managing crisis situations by creating a situational picture based on the analysis of smart city data (provided by a city involved in the project as a cooperating partner) and simulating as well as visualising possible effects of local, non-pharmaceutical measures. It is important to emphasise at this point, however, that although this is clearly application-oriented research, no operational technology was developed and no real political decision-making took place as part of the project. This would not be possible let alone for reasons of funding policy, which cannot be discussed here.

In the project, a specific type of ABMS called *cognitive social simulation* was used. Here, human beings are seen as active elements that create a mental representation of a situation, act according to individual motivation, experiences and aims and interact with other members of the social system based on these cognitive factors. Therefore, the availability of information, the assessment of the situation within the population and the mutual influence of groups of people in their behaviour are included in the modelling and simulation of a situation. The behaviour of the agents is therefore more differentiated and less stochastic. In the project, even deviant behaviour (refusal to wear a mask when it is mandatory, joining illegal gatherings, etc.) and voluntary self-quarantine in the event of perceived symptoms were programmed as options for action at the level of individual agents. In one of the project's publications, this is expressed as follows: "We do not assume automatic conformity, but model conflicting interests of actors that must be resolved in the decision-making situations." However, the no longer purely stochastic character of agent modelling does not change the fact that the simulated system processes are non-linear and emergent and thus, albeit generating a "more realistic" picture of reality, can never be used to predict future system states. In one of the interviews, this is interpreted as a break with the promise of prediction:

Because we have a range, I don't like to talk about forecasting there because essentially, yes, we can't actually predict the future. Ultimately, we can only give an order of magnitude or open up the range between 'this is the worst case that we've observed' and 'this is the best case that we've observed.' And then, with some plausibility, the reality is probably somewhere in between.[2]

However, the statement "with some plausibility" already points out that under conditions of emergence and nonlinearity, this range represents only a part of the possible realities, i.e., system states. The interviewee illustrates this epistemic -

---

2   The interviews were conducted in German. Quotes have been translated by the author.

and thus also political - risk by using the example of "throwing a dice", which is paradigmatic for stochastic procedures:

We threw a dice a hundred times, we observed outcomes between 1 and 6, but when we throw the dice the hundred and first time, and we throw the dice in reality, so to speak, we don't know which of those outcomes will come. And it may well be that it was a ten-sided dice and yet we only observed 6 of the possible outcomes and then the real outcome in the end is even outside of that.

But how are these societal and epistemological reflections translated into the information presented on the dashboard? The dashboard developed in the project basically functions as a human-machine interface through which users can interact with the simulation software. *Figure 1* shows the dashboard. One of the interviewees describes it as analogous to an aeroplane cockpit:

Ultimately, the idea is that [...] if you imagine an aeroplane cockpit, for example, several people work together in a team with distributed roles to bring the plane to its destination. And then there are different possibilities or different instruments that these people can use, namely display instruments to assess the situation and also control instruments to be able to influence the situation. And in our case, the display instruments are something like the compilation of information about the actual state [of the pandemic, J.H.]. And the control instruments are the possibility to select [...] what possible measures we could decide to introduce, and also which measures we would like to take back, so to speak, when the situation eases; and then just to gain an impression via the simulations, how the whole thing would play out.

Due to its acclaimed capability of presenting epidemiological findings and providing opportunities for experimental testing and prospective evaluation of possible measures, the dashboard reflects both the actual state and hypothetical what-if states. Both types of states of the simulated situation are summarised in a so-called pandemic pressure score (PPS). The PPS is generated considering numerous values and weightings for the following four dimensions:

- General Health (of the Population)
- Healthcare system
- Industry and Economy
- Critical infrastructures

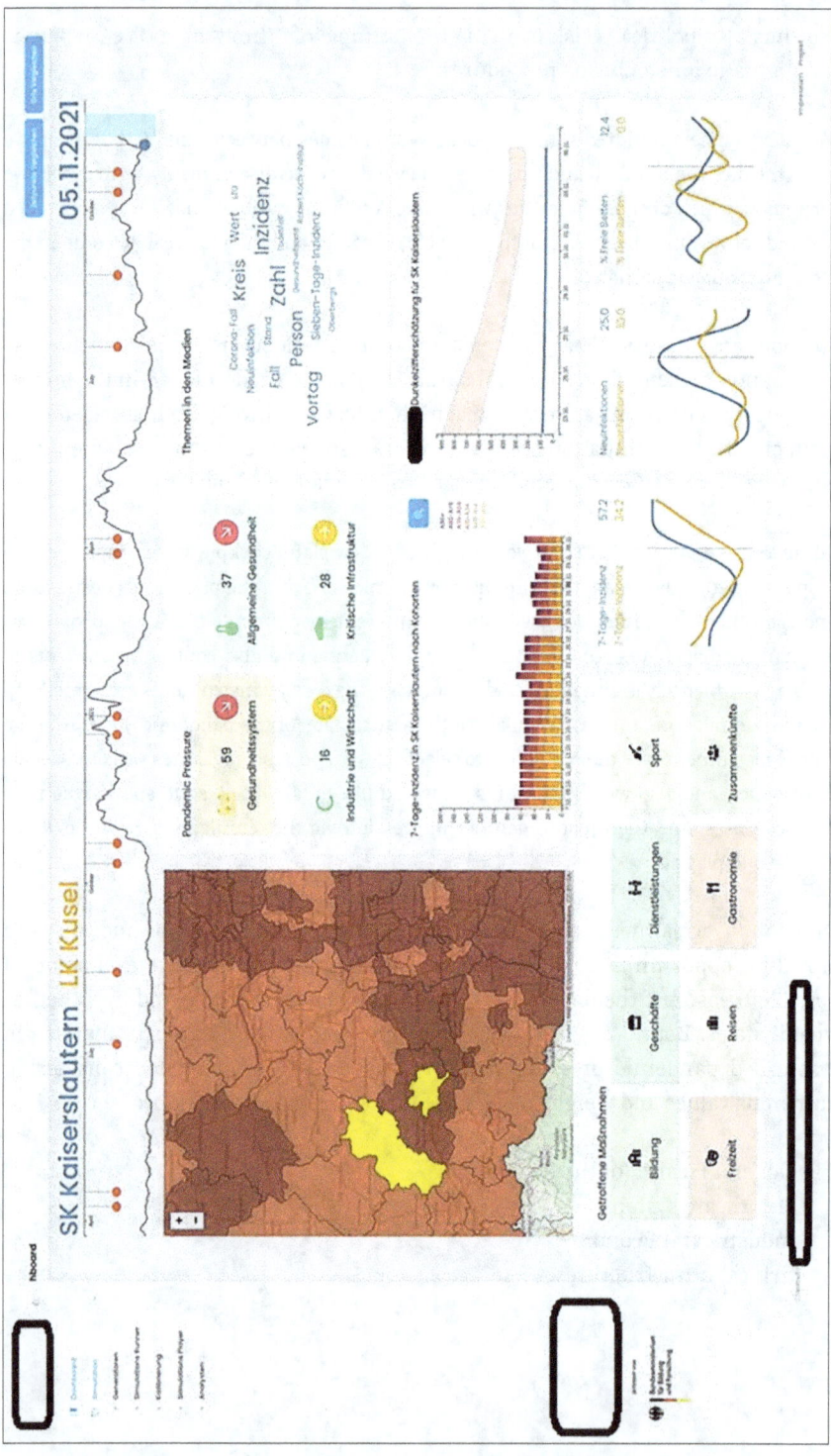

Figure 1: Dashboard (Source: publication of the project under study)

In the publications of the project and the interviews I conducted, it was always emphasised that the PPS captures non-medical factors of a pandemic in addition to incidence and hospitalisation rates, and thus stands out from comparable services and tools in its degree of differentiation. Following on from concepts of *privacy-by-design* and *ethics-by-design*, I therefore propose to refer to the design concept of the dashboard as *plurality-by-design*. Plurality-by-design should be seen as a new type of value-sensitive design (Friedman et al 2008) or value-based engineering (Spiekermann 2023) respecting human values and societal consequences of algorithmic systems as these are planned and in early development stages. Applied to the dashboard, plurality by design means that the plurality of effects of the pandemic as well as the plurality of effects of pandemic politics is reflected already during the design of the system. With regard to the use of the system for Algorithmic decision-making, this design might, at least in principle, counteract an epistemisation of politics and foster a reflexive politicisation of epistemology. Decision-makers would be confronted with the different value dimensions of their potential decisions. Instead of entrusting themselves to supposedly objective scientific expertise, they would need to acknowledge the conflictual nature of societal values and the irreducible political dimension of their decisions.

While this fact, at least to some extent, is brought to light by the design of the dashboard, other things are concealed though. Firstly, the four dimensions hardly reflect the diversity of values and realities of everyday life integrated into the model. The choice of the four dimensions displays a systemic bias, a strong focus on certain functional systems of society that are considered systemically relevant while ignoring those aspects of individual and collective experience of the pandemic that cannot be reduced to its life-threatening and purely economic consequences. Secondly, instead of openly communicating the non-predictive nature and limitations of the simulation results that are displayed, its design fosters the belief in the objectivity of predictive knowledge about the future. This is because the PPS of what-if scenarios does not convey the range of possible future system states, but its metric scaling (the PPS can take a value between 1 and 100) suggests that it is a definite and exact result in each case, which ultimately has a prognostic character. Building on a deeply rooted 'trust in numbers' (Porter 1995), quantified results of computation like the PPS tend to "obscure underlying uncertainties and suggest a level of accuracy which is often not adequate to reality." (Kaminski et al. 2023: 15)

Besides the PPS, there is a second element of the dashboard that suggests an objectivity that simply does not exist. A traffic light system is meant to evaluate both the present pandemic situation and the what-if scenarios. The traffic light colours serve as a background for the PPS and display the criticality of the actual state or the anticipated state of the four dimensions General Health, Healthcare System, Critical Infrastructure, and Industry and Economy. Criticality either refers to the incidence in a population or the burden on the respective functional system of society. A green light indicates a low, a yellow light a moderate, and a red light has a high criticality. As it was explained to me, this approach was chosen with the needs of policymakers in crisis situations in mind. One of the interviewees points out that the project was asked to develop such a traffic light system as a basis for decision-making by one of the project's partner cities. On the one hand, this desire is quite understandable because, given the abundance of potentially relevant information, a decision can only be made, especially under time pressure, if it does not have to reflect all the information. To prevent an "information overflow", a traffic light system can therefore be quite useful. On the other hand, this reduction of complexity leads to an evaluation (red/yellow/green light), which cannot be derived from the PPS itself, but always remains a question of the values underlying an evaluation. In the form of a traffic light, however, these evaluations are equipped with the authority of scientific objectivity. The question of when a situation or state can be considered critical and by what standard such criticality should be measured is suspended and dissolved in the unquestionable authority of a traffic light colour that forms a unit with the metric objectivity of the PPS. In view of this rather naïve scientism, the impression prevails that the design of the dashboard would play far more into the hands of an epistemisation of politics if used in real-life political decision-making. Existing approaches to value-based engineering, which could promote a reflexive politicisation of epistemology, would ultimately fade into the background.

Problematic Effects and Possible Solutions

While there are many good reasons to criticise the epistemisation of politics from a democratic theory or social theory perspective, it could be argued from a scientistic perspective that politics based on scientific knowledge instead of values is still the best option we have under conditions of uncertainty. However, scholarship on the impacts of the use of (algorithmic) decision support systems (Skitka et al. 1999) can help us to identify several problematic effects that such a wrongly ascribed objectivity might have. One of the key findings of this research is that users hardly question the output of the systems critically and even tend to regard it as infallible, the so-called automation bias. This bias often leads to two types of errors: In a commission error, users follow an erroneous recommendation of an assistance system, while in an omission error, on the other hand, users overlook critical system states if these are not identified by the system. When the knowledge produced by modelling and simulation is used in an Algorithmic Decision Support System for pandemic management, erroneous recommendations could arise because the data is faulty or empirical values have been incorrectly estimated. In addition, in the case of ABMS, incorrect assumptions about agent behaviour and inaccurate representation of population structure and environmental conditions for agent behaviour can become a source of erroneous evaluations. This source of error becomes even more likely when models are imported from other scientific disciplines or application contexts, thereby ignoring that assumptions which are adequate in one place can become misleading in another (Saltelli et al. 2020: 483). Finally, a city, a county, or even an entire society cannot be mapped in all its empirical details. Therefore, relevant aspects must always be distinguished from irrelevant ones. This, however, contributes to the error-proneness nature of ABMS since the omission of even minor components in a simulated environment can lead to significant biases in the results of the simulations. Thus, the great advantage of ABMS over equation-based models in being able to better represent the diversity of social reality also gives rise to one crucial disadvantage of ABMS (Andrae/Pobuda 2021: 13–14). Although the risk for omission errors is reduced by the multidimensionality of the PPS, critical system states that are not captured in one of the four dimensions remain invisible to the users. Moreover, the dashboard only captures (and consequently makes available for evaluation) those measures that have already played a role in the context of infectious disease control. Thus, the scope of the dashboard is limited to the scope of state-of-the-art crisis management. Alternative approaches to pandemic management are made invisible by design (Littoz-Monnet 2020). This, however, is hardly surprising as any dashboard or—more general—any graphical user interface renders its underlying database and software protocols invisible while at the same time rendering visible only particular representations of that data (Jarke/Macgilchrist 2021). The understanding of the interface as an enabling media structure has long been replaced by an understanding according to which interfaces visibly or invisibly set limits for their users pre-structuring human-machine interactions in many ways. Consequently, media studies have pleaded for a critical perspective on interfaces (Andersen/Pold, 2011; Hadler/Haupt, 2016).

Saltelli and colleagues have elaborated on how such a critical perspective could be cultivated within epidemiological modelling and simulations. In their manifesto *Five ways to ensure that models serve society* (2020) they demand a shared commitment to be transparent about the values that guide the construction of models. No matter what exact shape claims for precision and objectivity take, "all presuppose a set of values about what matters — sustainability for some, productivity or profitability for others. Modelers should not hide the normative values of their choices." (ibid.: 483) Getting to the heart of their concerns, the authors state that "[m]odels' assumptions and limitations must be appraised openly and honestly. Process and ethics matter as much as intellectual prowess." (ibid.) The best way to reveal the values and assumptions that guide modelling, simulation and design of dashboards alike would be a set of social norms that cover "how to produce a model, assess its uncertainty and communicate the results. International guidelines for this have been drawn up for several disciplines. They demand that processes involve stakeholders, accommodate multiple views and promote transparency, replication and analysis of sensitivity and uncertainty. Whenever a model is used for a new application with fresh stakeholders, it must be validated and verified anew." (ibid.: 484) However, a literature review by Heath et al. (2009) showed that 65 percent of the investigated articles presenting agent-based models lacked such a thorough validation.[3] In the meantime, there is a guideline for describing agent-based and other simulation models—the Overview, Design concepts and Details (ODD) protocol (Grimm et al. 2020). It however remains an open question whether voluntary guidelines will be enough to pave the way towards a politicisation of epistemology and, thus, provide new modes of addressing value conflicts within—and arising from—pandemic politics.

List of References

Adam, D. (2020): "Special report: The simulations driving the world's response to COVID-19." Nature 580(7803), pp. 316–318.

Adey, P./Anderson, B. (2012): "Anticipating emergencies: Technologies of preparedness and the matter of security." Security Dialogue 43(2), pp. 99–117.

Andersen, C.U./Pold, S.B. (2011): Interface Criticism: Aesthetics Beyond the Buttons. Aarhus: Aarhus University Press.

Anderson, W. (2021): "The model crisis, or how to have critical promiscuity in the time of Covid-19." Social Studies of Science 51(2), pp. 167–188.

Andrae, S./Pobuda, P. (2021): Agentenbasierte Modellierung: Eine interdisziplinäre Einführung. Wiesbaden, Heidelberg: Springer Gabler.

Andrejevic, M./O'Neill, C. (2024): "Automated responses to the coronavirus disease-19 pandemic: An overview." New Media & Society 26(3), pp. 1165–1182.

Aykut, S./Demortain, D./Benboudiz, B. (2019): "The Politics of Anticipatory Expertise: Plurality and Contestation of Futures Knowledge in Governance — Introduction to the Special Issue." Science & Technology Studies 32(4), pp. 2–12.

Barrett, C.L.B./Eubank, S.G./Smith, J.P. (2005): "If Smallpox Strikes Portland …" Scientific American 292(3), pp. 54–61.

BILD (2021): "Experten-Trio für harte Maßnahmen: Die Lockdown-Macher." BILD, 4 December, available at: https://www.bild.de/politik/inland/politik-inland/experten-trio-die-lockdown-macher-78437086.bild.html (accessed 2 November 2023).

Bogner, A. (2021): Die Epistemisierung des Politischen. Wie die Macht des Wissens die Demokratie gefährdet. Ditzingen: Reclam Verlag.

Bogner, A. (2022): "What can science do in the face of pandemics?" Culture, Practice & Europeanization 7(1), pp. 122–135.

Bruch, E./Atwell, J. (2015): "Agent-based models in empirical social research." Sociological Methods & Research 44(2), pp. 186–221.

---

3   The author has no information on whether this situation has changed since then.

Deutsche Gesellschaft für Epidemiologie (2020): Aktualisierte Stellungnahme der Deutschen Gesellschaft für Epidemiologie (DGEpi) zur Verbreitung des neuen Coronavirus (SARS-CoV-2), available at: https://www.dgepi.de/de/berichte-und-publikationen/stellungnahmen-offene-briefe-etc/ (accessed 31 May 2024).

Epstein, J.M. (2009): "Modelling to contain pandemics." Nature 460(7256), p. 687.

Epstein, J.M./Parker, J./Cummings, D./Hammond, R.A. (2008): "Coupled contagion dynamics of fear and disease: mathematical and computational explorations." PloS one 3(12), p. 3955.

Esposito, E. (2007): Die Fiktion der wahrscheinlichen Realität. Frankfurt am Main: Suhrkamp.

Flache, A./Macy, M. (2011): "Social Dynamics from the Bottom Up." In: P. Bearman/P. Hedström/A. Flache/M. Macy (eds.), The Oxford Handbook of Analytical Sociology. Oxford: Oxford University Press, pp. 245–268.

Frias-Martinez, E./Williamson, G./Frias-Martinez, V. (2011): "An Agent-Based Model of Epidemic Spread Using Human Mobility and Social Network Information." 2011 IEEE Third International Conference on Privacy, Security, Risk and Trust and 2011 IEEE Third International Conference on Social Computing, Boston, MA, 09.10.2011 - 11.10.2011, IEEE, pp. 57–64.

Friedman, B./Kahn, P. H./Borning, A. (2008): "Value Sensitive Design and Information Systems." In: K. E. Himma (ed.), The handbook of information and computer ethics. Hoboken, New Jersey.: Wiley, pp. 69–101.

Ginsberg, J./Mohebbi, M. H./Patel, R. S./Brammer, L./Smolinski, M. S./Brilliant, L. (2009): "Detecting Influenza Epidemics Using Search Engine Query Data." Nature 457(7232), pp. 1012–1014.

Grimm, V./Railsback, S.F./Vincenot, C.E./Berger, U./Gallagher, C./DeAngelis, D.L./Edmonds, B./Ge, J./Giske, J./Groeneveld, J./Johnston, A.S./Milles, A./Nabe-Nielsen, J./Polhill, J.G./Radchuk, V./Rohwäder/M.-S./Stillman, R.A./Thiele, J.C./Ayllón, D. (2020): "The ODD Protocol for Describing Agent-Based and Other Simulation Models: A Second Update to Improve Clarity, Replication, and Structural Realism." Journal of Artificial Societies and Social Simulation 23(2), 7.

Hacking, I. (1990): The Taming of Chance. Cambridge: Cambridge University Press.

Hadler, F./Haupt, J. (eds.) (2016): Interface Critique. Berlin: Kulturverlag Kadmos.

Hälterlein, J. (2023): "Agentenbasierte Modellierung und Simulation im Pandemiemanagement." TATuP 32(1), pp. 30–35.

Heath, B., Hill, R./Ciarallo, F. (2009): "A Survey of Agent-Based Modeling Practices (January 1998 to July 2008)." Journal of Artificial Societies and Social Simulation 12(4), 9.

Hunter, E., Mac Namee, B./Kelleher, J.D. (2017), "A Taxonomy for Agent-Based Models in Human Infectious Disease Epidemiology." Journal of Artificial Societies and Social Simulation 20(3), 2.

Ioannidis, J.P.A./Cripps, S./Tanner, M.A. (2022): "Forecasting for COVID-19 has failed." International journal of Forecasting 38(2), pp. 423–438.

Jarke, J./Macgilchrist, F. (2021): "Dashboard stories: How narratives told by predictive analytics reconfigure roles, risk and sociality in education." Big Data & Society 8(1), https://doi.org/10.1177/20539517211025561.

Kaminski, A./Gramelsberger, G./Scheer, D. (2023): "Modeling for policy and technology assessment: Challenges from computerbased simulations and artificial intelligence." TATuP—Zeitschrift für Technikfolgenabschätzung in Theorie und Praxis 32(1), pp. 11–17.

Karliczek, A. (2020): "Jetzt schlägt die Stunde der Erklärer." Frankfurter Allgemeine Zeitung, 2 April, available at: https://www.faz.net/aktuell/wissen/forschung-politik/corona-krise-schafft-zugaenge-fuer-politische-entscheidungen-16704373.html (accessed 31 May 2024).

Lazer, D./Kennedy, R./King, G./Vespignani A. (2014): "Big Data. The Parable of Google Flu. Traps in Big Data Analysis." Science 343(6176), pp. 1203–1205.

Littoz-Monnet, A. (2020): "Depoliticising through Expertise. The Politics of Modelling in the Governance of Covid-19", available at: https://globalchallenges.ch/issue/special_1/depoliticising-through-expertise-the-politics-of-modelling-in-the-governance-of-covid-19/ (accessed 8 April 2022).

Lorig, F., Johansson, E./Davidsson, P. (2021): "Agent-Based Social Simulation of the Covid-19 Pandemic: A Systematic Review." Journal of Artificial Societies and Social Simulation 24(3), 5.

Morse, S. S./Mazet, J. A. K./Woolhouse, M./Parrish, C. R./Carroll, D./Karesh, W. B./Zambrana-Torrelio, C./Lipkin, W. I./Daszak, P. (2012): "Prediction and Prevention of the Next Pandemic Zoonosis." The Lancet 380(9857), pp. 1956–1965.

Nijhuis, H. G. J./van der Maesen, L. J. G. (2021): "Editorial. The Societal Impact of the COVID-19 Pandemic Explained via Three Frameworks." The International Journal of Social Quality 11(1-2), pp. v–xx.

Opitz, S. (2017): "Simulating the world." European Journal of Social Theory 20(3), pp. 392–416.

Porter, T.M. (1995): Trust in Numbers: The Pursuit of Objectivity in Science and Public Life, Princeton: Princeton University Press.

Rhodes, T./Lancaster, K. (2020): "Mathematical models as public troubles in COVID-19 infection control: following the numbers." Health Sociology Review: The journal of the Health Section of the Australian Sociological Association 29(2), pp. 177–194.

Rhodes, T./Lancaster, K./Rosengarten, M. (2020): "A model society: maths, models and expertise in viral outbreaks." Critical Public Health 30(3), pp. 253–256.

Salama, M. A./Hassanien, A. E./Mostafa, A. (2016): "The Prediction of Virus Mutation Using Neural Networks and Rough Set Techniques." EURASIP. Journal on Bioinformatics & Systems Biology, 10.

Saltelli, A./Bammer, G./Bruno, I./Charters, E./Di Fiore, M./Didier, E./Nelson Espeland, W./Kay, J./Lo Piano, S./Mayo, D./Pielke, R./Portaluri, T./Porter, T.M./Puy, A./Rafols, I./Ravetz, J.R./Reinert, E./Sarewitz, D./Stark, P.B./Stirling, A./van der Sluijs, J./Vineis, P. (2020): "Five ways to ensure that models serve society: a manifesto." Nature 582(7813), pp. 482–484.

Skitka, L.J./Mosier, K.L./Burdick, M. (1999): "Does automation bias decision-making?" International Journal of Human-Computer Studies 51(5), pp. 991–1006.

Spiekermann, S. (2023): Value-based engineering. A guide to building ethical technology for humanity. Berlin, Boston: De Gruyter.

Stevens, H. (2020): "Why outbreaks like coronavirus spread exponentially, and how to 'flatten the curve'." The Washington Post, 14 March, available at: https://www.washingtonpost.com/graphics/2020/world/corona-simulator/ (accessed 2 November 2023).

Strauss, A. L.,/Corbin, J. M. (1998): Basics of Qualitative Research: Techniques and Procedures for Developing Grounded Theory. 2nd ed. Thousand Oaks, CA: Sage.

Weyer, J./Roos, M. (2017): "Agentenbasierte Modellierung und Simulation." TATuP - Zeitschrift für Technikfolgenabschätzung in Theorie und Praxis 26(3), pp. 11–16.

Why is it so Complicated?

Cooperation, Conflicts, and Frictions in the Digitalisation of Healthcare

Karolin Kappler, Florian Neft and Katharina Ebner

Abstract

In the context of an increasingly digitised society, theoretical approaches have emerged to address the frictions created by digital technologies in a data-centric culture. Those theoretical approaches focus on aspects like order, subject understanding and socio-cultural changes. Other approaches examine the power asymmetries and polarisations inherent in digital cultures under labels, such as surveillance capitalism, digital disenfranchisement and exploitation 4.0. Contributing to this theoretical view, the current article presents the Economics/Sociology of Conventions (E/SC) as a prism to study these above-mentioned situations, focusing in particular on the emergence and stabilisation of cooperation, frictions and conflicts in the context of decision-making in collaborative situations with health analytics. The digitalisation of healthcare, especially the introduction of AI-based health analytics, presents a notable case study, with technologies like AI (artificial intelligence) and big data aiming to optimise healthcare delivery. This article utilises the E/SC framework to dissect frictions encountered during the adoption of health analytics, and is based on 45 expert interviews. The findings illuminate how health analytics disrupt existing conventions, leading to novel frictions and contributing to the broader dialogue on healthcare's digital future.

Keywords

Health Analytics, Digitalisation of Healthcare, Economics/Sociology of Conventions, Conflict, Friction

1. Introduction

The ongoing digital transformation is reshaping nearly every facet of our society, ushering in a new era often referred to as the "Data Society" (Houben/Prietl 2018; translation by author), algorithmic cultures (Seyfert/Roberge 2016) or the platform society (van Dijck et al. 2018), and challenging sociological theoretical thinking (Block/Pohle 2023). Most of the theoretical approaches to digitalisation deal with the degree of frictions created by the introduction of digital technolo-

DOI 10.14361/dcs-2023-0210

DCS | Digital Culture and Society | Vol. 9, Issue 2 | © transcript 2025

gies, be it Nassehi's (2024) paradigm of frictionless differentiation theory, which understands digitalisation as a problem of order, or Reckwitz's (2020) singularisation theory, which is based on practice theory and addresses the frictions on questions of subject understanding and socio-cultural change. Other authors, in turn, focus on specific frictions that become a central momentum in digitality, among others: surveillance capitalism (Zuboff 2019), digital disenfranchisement (Mühlhoff 2018), cybernetic proletarianisation (Schaupp 2021), the Lumpenscoretariat (Fourcade 2022) and exploitation 4.0 (Greffrath 2021). With this focus on frictions and underlying contradictions, power asymmetries and polarisations penetrating digital cultures, both sociology and science and technology studies of digital transformation stand out when it comes to the promise of a frictionless technology. This article aims to supplement this state of research by adopting the theoretical standpoint of the Economics/Sociology of Conventions (E/SC). As a pragmatic research programme, the E/SC has proven itself as a theoretical approach to illuminate digitalisation processes (Cappel/Kappler 2022; Diaz-Bone 2015). It focuses on critiques and justifications that occur regularly through minor disagreements, debates or the resolution of inconsistencies, conflicts, contradictions, irritations and annoyances. In situations where routines are disrupted, i.e. by digital technologies, and coordination breaks down, there is necessity to fundamentally address how something can and ought to be executed in an appropriate way (Diaz-Bone 2018). Hence, the E/SC considers sociotechnical entanglements as (sometimes cooperative, sometimes conflictual) negotiation processes over value and quality, emphasising how actors collaborate in situations where their objective is to attain a common good, share a common goal and clarify uncertainties regarding qualities and meanings involved.

Up till now, there is no common or standardised wording that describes the above-mentioned conflicts and irritations from an E/SC-perspective. By adding the term *frictions*, the current article focuses on the proximity generated in the negotiation processes between different understandings of quality and justifications in relation to common goods.

Such frictions and the associated negotiation processes are particularly prevalent in the course of digital transformation processes, especially in the area of the digitalisation in healthcare (Haring 2019; Cappel/Kappler 2022). New technologies are poised to revolutionise the way healthcare is organised and conceived. Concepts, such as telemedicine, eHealth, digital health, smart health, big data and robotics have become integral to discussions surrounding this transformative shift, being often framed within the context of economic considerations, with a primary focus on the frictions between providing high-quality healthcare for individuals and making it financially sustainable (Lux 2017; Lux/Breil 2017). In response to this dilemma, the digitalisation of healthcare is frequently suggested as a solution strategy. Information and communication technologies are expected to enhance the quality of healthcare while simultaneously reducing costs (Kankanhalli et al. 2016). Artificial intelligence (AI) and big data are lauded as pivotal technologies of the future, with the potential to enable early disease detection, improved risk assessment and optimisation of diagnosis and treatment processes. In addition, health analytics, defined as a data-driven approach to generate automated, algorithm-based analyses providing valuable decision-making support (Berente et al. 2021; Bygstad et al. 2020; Kankanhalli et al. 2016), is envisioned as a means to address the shortage of healthcare professionals by lightening the workload of physicians through assistance systems (Oesterreich et al. 2020; Cohen et al. 2014; Berente et al. 2021).

However, the introduction of health analytics is not without challenges and resistances. In digitised healthcare, coordination is centred on the essence of providing "good" treatment for the patients. Actors must reach consensus on the standards and norms which dictate this assessment and the attributes that define the results of their collaboration. This practically justifies the implementation, use and rejection of health analytics by referencing supra-individual categories and evaluation schemes, anchoring them through the utilisation of artefacts and subjecting them to quality tests (Diaz-Bone 2015). Hence, this article delves into the intricate valuation arguments and justifications that are used to weigh, legitimise, and critique the advantages and disadvantages associated with the digitalisation of healthcare, specifically the implementation and use of health analytics. Examining the frictions arising during the implementation of health analytics from a pragmatic standpoint within the E/SC framework, we ask which frictions around justifications for "good" treatment involving health analytics appear in an ever more digital medical culture. It explores the dynamics of quality tests, their legitimacy and criticisms while also considering whether the digitalisation of healthcare might shift or solidify certain orders of worth. Conducting a case study on the provision of health analytics and the frictions encountered during its introduction as a socio-material practice of decision-making, we consider both the legal and managerial contexts, as well as the daily challenges faced by physicians in their everyday practices. Utilizing an extensive review of the literature and a deductive analysis of 45 expert interviews, this article provides a unique perspective on how health analytics affect existing justifications, serving mainly as an amplifier of already existing frictions in digital medical culture. However, health analytics do not only accentuate the "industrialization of healthcare" (Da Silva 2020), but also contributes to emergent frictions arising around the role of physicians, their competences and learning processes. This article expands the boundaries of E/SC studies, shedding light on various forms of valuation and quality tests, and also on the related frictions between orders of worth, ultimately influencing the adoption or rejection of health analytics. In doing so, this paper refines the ongoing pragmatic research on current developments in healthcare and broadens the discussion on the future of the medical profession. The article offers valuable insights into how health analytics are situationally legitimised and criticised, thereby providing a comprehensive exploration of current developments and frictions within the realm of digital health.

2. Pragmatic View on the Digitalisation of Healthcare

2.1 Frictions in Medical Practice through Health Analytics

The integration of health analytics into the field of medicine has marked a significant shift in the way healthcare organisations operate and how medical professionals make decisions. Health analytics use a data-driven approach that processes large amounts of health data to create automated analyses that provide valuable support for decision-making (Berente et al. 2021; Bygstad et al. 2020; Kankanhalli et al. 2016). They include applications such as systems for automatic sepsis detection or image recognition methods in radiology. The application of health analytics are associated with the potential to transform the healthcare landscape by enhancing efficiency, improving patient care and optimising resource allocation.

The promises of health analytics—as described in the literature—are extensive. They are said to accelerate medical treatment processes and enhance the diagnoses and treatment quality (Kankanhalli et al. 2016). By processing and interpreting patient data swiftly, health analytics can provide summaries, visualisations, predictions and recommendations based on historical patient data and, therewith, assist physicians in making accurate diagnoses and treatment plans more rapidly than traditional methods (Oesterreich et al. 2020). These tools facilitate the identification of disease patterns, early disease detection and the customisation of treatment approaches (Wang et al. 2018). They contribute to precise medical decision-making and, as a result, reduce hospitalisation durations and associated costs (Baird/Angst/Oborn 2018; Boytcheva et al. 2015; Cohen et al. 2014). This acceleration in decision-making is particularly crucial in healthcare where time is often of the essence and swift interventions can be life-saving. A further promise refers to the enhancement of organisational transparency and profitability. It provides healthcare administrators with valuable insights into the operational efficiency of their facilities and the allocation of resources (Shaban-Nejad et al. 2021). This newfound transparency can lead to improved resource allocation, ultimately optimising cost-effectiveness. However, the introduction of health analytics adds a layer of complexity to clinical decision-making, challenging physicians' traditional ethos, the Hippocratic Oath (Meskó/Spiegel 2022). Physicians are confronted with the need to balance their clinical judgement and experience with the data-driven insights provided through health analytics.

Health analytics may introduce a set of new frictions into the healthcare domain or they may make existing frictions more salient. The frictions usually pertain to the roles and perceptions of medical professionals. Physicians, who have traditionally held positions of authority and expertise in the realm of healthcare, now find themselves confronted with the growing influence of health analytics challenging their credibility and hierarchy (Shaban-Nejad et al. 2021). While these systems aim to augment medical decision-making, physicians perceive them as a potential threat to their credibility and hierarchical position. Physicians operate in an environment characterised by inherent time pressures and uncertainty, which are natural aspects of their profession (Fang et al. 2013; Trimble/Hamilton 2016). The complexities of individual patient cases and the limited availability of comprehensive health data further compound this uncertainty. In such a context, health analytics may be viewed with scepticism, as they introduce an additional layer of complexity and data-driven decision-making (Shahbaz et al. 2019; Trimble/Hamilton 2016). Moreover, physicians may worry about their decisions being subjected to scrutiny, potentially leading to personal liability in cases of malpractice (Shahbaz et al. 2019). The integration of health analytics into their practice may reinforce these existing frictions surrounding physicians' professional responsibilities.

In conclusion, while health analytics promise to revolutionise healthcare by enhancing efficiency, improving patient care and optimising resource allocation, they also introduce frictions into the medical field. These frictions revolve around the perceived threat to physicians' credibility, the challenge to traditional hierarchical structures and the transformation of clinical decision-making and professional ethos. To shed light on these frictions, the article focuses on justifications, conventions, quality tests and orders of worth raised by actors in healthcare.

2.2 Conventions and Health

The research approach of the E/SC represents a notable departure from Bourdieu's structuralist research paradigm (Boltanski/Thévenot 2006). Over the course of almost four decades, the E/SC has evolved into a transdisciplinary academic movement marked by diverse theoretical concepts, all grounded in a shared pragmatic foundational theory (Diaz-Bone 2015). The E/SC has proven particularly adept at critiquing neoclassical economics (Eymard-Duvernay/Thévenot 1983; Eymard-Duvernay et al. 2011; Eymard-Duvernay 2012; Thévenot 1984); however, its applicability extends to various domains, including healthcare. In healthcare, the focus has increasingly shifted towards welfare considerations, alongside economic concerns (Da Silva 2018; Batifoulier et al. 2018). Within the EC framework, conventions are conceptualised as situational and pragmatic coordination logics embedded in the practices of competent actors. The E/SC shifts this actor-centric approach and incorporates a new perspective focusing on the situation enriched with various conventional sediments. This shift, focusing less on actors and more on the situation, is precisely what this article aims to achieve.

Coordination in healthcare, much like in other domains, often involves the mobilisation of arguments by actors to defend their viewpoints. Boltanski and Thévenot (2006) outline two critical conditions for mapping justifications and criticisms: the presence of a divergence and a willingness to seek a peaceful response to criticism. Through the organisation of these arguments, actors construct orders of worth or conventions, which are registers of justification aligned with higher common principles. These conventions are pluralistic but limited in number, as they must possess a sufficient level of generality to be accepted. These higher common principles serve as models of evaluation or judgement, enabling the assignment of value—often termed greatness or grandeur—to people and things (Batifoulier et al. 2016; Diaz-Bone 2015).

Boltanski and Thévenot (2006) identify six such principles or orders of worth: the market, civic, industrial, domestic, opinion and inspired conventions. Later, they were complemented by two further principles: the network convention (Boltanski/Chiapello 2013) and the green convention (Lafaye/Thévenot 1993). These frameworks can be applied in the healthcare sector to qualify individuals or institutions. Batifoulier's example (2020) is a theoretical elaboration of an analysis of the coordination between a doctor and a patient and exemplifies six conventions, each with a corresponding higher common principle, quality criteria and equivalent quality tests.

Order of worth/ Convention	High common principle	Political philosophy	Qualified good doctor (justification)	Disqualified doctor (critique)
Market	Competition, self interest	Smith	Market competitiveness, good price, value for money	Business, profit
Civic	General will, collective action	Rousseau	Welfare policy, solidarity	Irresponsibility, wasting resources
Industrial	Efficiency performance	Saint Simon	Expert, scientist, technical efficiency	Protocolisation, standardisation
Domestic	Proximity, neighbourhood, tradition	Bossuet	Family doctor, regular physician	Personal dependencies, routinisation
Opinion	Popularity, audience, public recognition	Hobbes	Notoriety, celebrity (charismatic)	Expensive, not available
Inspired	Imagination, inspiration	Saint Augustin	Researcher, innovation, creativity	Publish or perish, cutting off from reality

Table 1: Healthcare E/SC adapted from Batifoulier (2022: 10)

Building on these conventions, Sharon (2016; 2018; 2021) explored the Googlisation of health (research), identifying another emergent order of justification—the convention of vitality around the value of health (Sharon 2016). Furthermore, she addresses the E/SC's normative deficit and purely descriptive "multiple-sphere ontology" (Sharon 2021: 315) by developing a "normative pragmatics of justice" (Sharon 2021: 315) based on the dynamic interaction of conventions and spheres focusing on sphere transgressions, contradictions and instrumentalisations.

In Cappel and Kappler (2022), the mobilisation of health as a category is brought into focus by showing situationally how forms, conventions and objects change in the context of digital transformations. By focusing on the negotiation process in coordination situations, the E/SC can thus counteract a truncated and one-dimensional perspective on health by taking a plurality of moral interests as a basis. In this sense, Lenz (2021), in her interview study with developers of digital health technologies, showed possible solutions for the tensions (and frictions) between the growing commercialisation of the healthcare system and ethical-professional expectations. Nonetheless, she also revealed that digital technologies might compromise physicians' pursuit of medical autonomy, a fundamental aspect of their medical ethos. Grön (2021: 1) sheds light on the "ambiguity and plurality" of common goods in data-intensive healthcare, outlining possible frictions between the upcoming purposes and goals.

Furthermore, Da Silva and Rauly (Da Silva/Rauly 2016; Da Silva 2020) depict how healthcare is changing from a domestic convention and logic of inspiration to an industrial market convention due to datafication processes, the advance of evidence-based medicine, the ever-increasing implementation of digital technologies and new digital practices. This conflict in healthcare influences, among other things, the use of these newly introduced digital technologies.

Applying the E/SC to healthcare offers a relevant conceptual framework not only for understanding, on a global level, the main conceptions of health in global politics (Hanrieder 2016), but also for understanding, on a local level, the criteria defining a setting in healthcare for doctors, hospitals, medical techniques, networks of care, health funding systems, solidarity and priorities (Da Silva/Rauly 2016; Da Silva 2020; Batifoulier et al. 2018). In essence, the E/SC framework delves into the fundamental question of what defines quality in healthcare, shedding light on the plural and diverse nature of conventions that underpin different notions of value and quality. Moreover, from an E/SC perspective, it is imperative to recognise the inherent diversity of coordination logics in the context of digitalisation in healthcare. If actors cannot converge on a shared understanding of a common good and its quality, frictions will inevitably arise. This implies that for effective coordination to take place, actors must arrive at a mutual consensus regarding a common good and the quality standards aligned with it, which equally has implications for the conventions healthcare organisations are in.

3. Methodological Approach

Investigating complex phenomena such as frictions from an E/SC perspective requires a comprehensive and nuanced dataset. To accomplish this, we adopted a qualitative deductive interview framework, following the methodology advocated by Patton (2015). This methodological approach is particularly suited for illuminating previously unexplored facets of the subject matter, allowing for the discovery of "contradictory observations to change what we know" as suggested by Gilgun (2001: 3).

Our research involved two iterative rounds of data collection, each with its specific focus and objectives. These rounds of data gathering allowed us to systematically uncover areas of discord and incongruities, shedding light on the justifications behind the nuanced perceptions of medical practices involving health analytics. In the initial interview cycle, which centred on telemedical consultations during the COVID-19 pandemic, we aimed to elucidate the initial frictions and quality tests related to trustworthiness, innovations and competence. To delve more comprehensively into these contradictions, the second interview cycle focused on justifications, critique and frictions in ongoing processes of change affecting medical practices and socio-digital situations. This iterative approach allowed us to corroborate established knowledge concerning the utilisation of and resistance to health analytics while simultaneously revealing new insights originating from latent frictions. We ensured a diverse dataset by employing a theoretical sampling strategy, including a wide variety of interviewees ranging from recent medical graduates to medical directors, affiliated and multi-hospital physicians, as well as national and international medical consultants. This includes different medical specialities, such as radiology, intensive care and surgery. In total, we conducted 45 interviews, with 22 in the first round and 23 in the second. The saturation point in the second round was reached when interviews with the 22nd and 23rd participants yielded no new insights, indicating that we had explored the subject matter comprehensively (Rowlands/Waddell/McKenna 2016).

We conducted all interviews virtually via video meetings, allowing us to analyse both verbal and non-verbal cues. This approach facilitated a rich understanding of participants' perspectives. To mitigate potential social desirability bias, we utilised the proxy subject technique, asking respondents about hypothetical situations and issues they have observed with colleagues. Owing to the diverse sample, we asked about health analytics in general, as applications can differ in the respective specialisations. Furthermore, all interviews were recorded, transcribed and independently coded by two authors. Our case analysis adhered meticulously to established qualitative data analysis directives for deductive inquiries, as promulgated by Miles et al. (2020) and Patton (2015). This rigorous analytical process ensured that our findings were grounded in sound methodological principles. To ensure the validity and reliability of our findings, we followed well-established qualitative research guidelines articulated by Dubé and Paré (2003),

Roulston (2018) and Schultze and Avital (2011). These guidelines provided a robust framework for our research design and data analysis.

Data collection	Round 1	Round 2
Context	22 physicians	23 physicians
Position	1 medical director, 2 heads of department, 7 attending physicians, 11 chief residents, 1 pharmacist	2 medical directors, 1 head of department, 6 attending physicians, 4 chief residents, 5 fellows, 2 interns, 1 pharmacist, 1 IT expert, 1 project manager
Duration	August 2021–February 2022	May 2023–September 2023
Average age	43.5 years	43.0 years
Average experience	17.6 years	14.2 years
Gender	10 males, 12 females	16 males, 7 females

Table 2: Data Summary Chart

In conclusion, our methodology, involving two iterative rounds of data collection, adherence to qualitative data analysis directives and validation through established qualitative research guidelines (Miles/Huberman/Saldaña 2020) ensured the robustness of our study. The dataset's depth and diversity of participants, combined with a meticulous analytical process, allowed us to explore the complex landscape of health analytics and the frictions they introduce within the healthcare domain.

4. Intra- and Inter-conventional Frictions: To Function or Not to Function and What For

The interview analysis revealed frictions both within and particularly between conventions. The results follow these identified frictions.

4.1 Failing the Market and Industry Quality Test: It Must Not Cost Anything

In the realm of the market convention, the predominant focus revolves around assessing competitiveness, with the primary criterion being price. While the existing literature often portrays health analytics as a means to achieve cost savings

(Baird et al. 2018; Boytcheva et al. 2015; Cohen et al. 2014), it is worth noting that numerous interviewees have expressed concerns regarding health analytics' lack of adaptation and optimisation when it comes to the hospitals' specific requirements. The quality test of the market convention—defined as competitiveness (Diaz-Bone 2015: 162)—does not seem to apply here, as the so-called healthcare market does not fully guarantee the demand for customised products through exchange. An interviewee (I26) notes, for example, that hospitals, as relatively small customers, often lack the flexibility to configure or influence system adjustments. In this context, I26 criticises the alphabetical listing of medications and recounts an unsuccessful request for a more user-friendly grouping. Without these adjustments, the promised cost savings cannot be achieved, as they do not make work any easier. This is even an impediment to using the new system. Prior to this, physicians listed medications topic-wise, which allows them to better replicate a patient's disease and condition.

Another issue raised pertains to the absence of crucial add-ons, such as an automated medication entry or transfer capabilities, also due to associated costs in development and customisation (I28). Consequently, the manual input of each individual medication into the system becomes a labour-intensive necessity, as "every single medicine has to be entered manually into a programme" (I28). Both examples outline how digital technologies bring about increasing efforts for physicians, affecting the market convention.

However, the interviewees refer not only to frictions within the market convention, but also to frictions regarding the alignment with the industrial convention whose quality test refers to stability and competence with regard to a higher functionality (Diaz-Bone 2015: 62).

"Hard to say. Efficiency, hm. The thing is, that is also a technical matter. As far as IT is concerned, the hospitals are an absolute disaster. For example, we have two image viewing programmes, of which one is outdated and a backup, and the other one is a new one. I haven't had access to our new image viewing programme since February. And IT doesn't care. They can't figure out why. So now I'm working with the old one. [...] But someone has to pay for the maintenance" (I28).

As reported by I28, the information systems are sometimes outdated, do not work and are not maintained properly. It seems that the necessary price incentives or investments are lacking to meet the quality standards set by the industrial convention, particularly in terms of efficient performance, functionality, effectiveness and stability. This partially contradicts the findings of Da Silva (2020), who has mapped out the interdependence of the market and the industrial convention in what he calls the "industrialization of healthcare" (Da Silva 2020). Our interview data reveal frictions in this often expected harmonious alignment between the market and the industrial convention (Da Silva 2020), as—from an E/SC-perspective—health analytics often fail to fulfil the promised quality tests of the market and industrial convention: cost saving, stability and competence. In general, health analytics seem to function according to the market and industrial convention and their criteria of product quality and time savings, described as an inexpensive and efficiently produced product whose quality consists in the adequacy of technical standards for mass consumption (Diaz-Bone 2015: 162). Our interviewees are not satisfied with these quality tests, which raises frictions in terms of time and quality management.

4.2 Challenging the Industrial Quality Test: The Persistence of Manual Labour

Although the literature refers to an acceleration of processes and more accurate diagnoses through health analytics as seen in Chapter 2, the interviews show a more nuanced picture. This is because health analytics might fulfil the quality test criteria of the industrial convention, promising efficiency and productivity in relation to scientific data and statistics (Diaz-Bone 2018, 62) according to technical standards for mass consumption. In contrast, the interviewees challenge this quality test. For example, interviewee I36 refers to the manual input of medication schedules during the patient transfer to other intensive care units. In addition to the laborious manual data entry, interviewees also raise concerns about the issue of over-alerting (mentioned by I36, I35, I26). This phenomenon is described as "inflationary" (I26) and may lead to situations where important alerts, such as indications of drug interactions, are no longer given the attention it deserves, especially in high-pressure environments like emergency departments:

"So, there was support coming from the system that you didn't perceive as support; you perceived it as a time eater and clicked it away" (I26).

The precise configuration of warning and prognosis systems plays a pivotal role for our interviewees. However, when it comes to health analytics like sepsis early warning systems (I36) or scoring systems in the emergency department (such as the Manchester Triage System) (I43), concerns have been raised about their reliability and dependability, pointing out that these systems do not fulfil the quality test of the industrial convention. As one of the interviewees (I36) articulates, there is a desire for these systems to provide early alerts, possibly even before human perception. Yet, the current reality falls short of being reliably supportive:

"We would certainly like these systems to alert us relatively early, perhaps even before we perceive the medical alert ourselves. But as I said, although that is theoretically conceivable, those systems are currently not quite so reliable to the extent that we can really say: 'Yes, that system really supports us now'" (I36).

In terms of reporting, health analytics appear to lack the precision needed to meet the quality standards of systematic reporting (I38). An interviewee states:

"Well, my expectations, if I were to actually automate it and no longer check it, would be for the reporting to be in the form that I use in everyday life, so that it would be complete and accurate and so that nothing would be overlooked. But in reality, that is not the case. So there are a few things that the device recognises, but that is not a systematic diagnosis" (I38).

The excessive need for manual adjustments and physician oversight negates the promised simplification of work by these systems (i.e. Liang/Xue 2021). As one of the interviewees points out:

"And if you have to control the system too much manually as a human being, then it doesn't help you anymore. So, somehow it has to make work easier without a lot of control. Exactly. I think that's a bit of a problem" (I42).

Despite these critical voices, health analytics appear to garner a level of acceptance and hold promise for the future in some medical domains and related fields characterised by high standardisation (such as medication interactions and radiology), where time for contemplation may be limited (I44), or where there is a rapid and industrial-like volume of findings (as seen in radiology (I33)). For instance, health analytics integrated into defibrillators can provide guidance not only to laypersons, but also to medical professionals during resuscitation efforts, ensuring safety in stressful and often chaotic situations (I31). This provides a more nuanced picture of "the industrialization of healthcare" (Da Silva 2020), as medical specialities should be differentiated on the basis of the standardisation capability of their activity profiles and their corresponding proneness to health analytics.

Radiology stands out as a field that is particularly poised to benefit from health analytics. As I37 suggests, computerised systems can be highly beneficial in radiology, especially when interpreting multiple findings, particularly during night shifts when fatigue is a factor. In clinical settings where active involvement and hands-on work are required, these systems may be less useful (I24). However, for tasks like analysing data, reviewing laboratory values and interpreting findings, these systems are seen as valuable tools that can assist in explanations and decision-making. However, as elucidated by I29, the current potential of health analytics seems to be predominantly in supporting standardised reporting.

"In essence, there are three stages or steps [...]. Firstly, detecting that there is a finding. Secondly, formulating possible diagnoses and, thirdly, making recommendations. In the best-case scenario, we are still primarily at stage one in our clinical everyday practice. The issue is that this type of finding detection primarily works for standardised findings and those with minimal external contextual factors. The second aspect is the formulation of diagnoses. Ideally, it could yield a list of potential diagnoses. However, the challenge lies in the fact that the same finding can be interpreted quite differently based on the available clinical data. For the development of differential diagnoses, we are still at least several years away from achieving that, but it is undoubtedly a prospect for the future"(I29).

As articulated by I29, the challenge arises when further contextual information becomes relevant, such as previous medical history or additional illnesses. In such cases, health analytics struggle to interface effectively with and integrate all pertinent data, weigh the factors and provide comprehensive interpretation—and this leads us to the third friction.

4.3 Industrial versus Inspired and Domestic Convention: When Complexity Becomes Too Big

Despite the increasing implementation of medical guidelines and standards in recent decades (I2)—what Da Silva (2020) calls "the industrialization of health-care"—it seems that only a few domains can truly be standardised in line with the industrial convention; instead, many domains are still marked by a high degree of individual case complexity, aligning more with the domestic convention where manual intervention and individual case reasoning are pivotal. This describes the friction between the still ongoing "industrialization of healthcare" (Da Silva 2020), with the upcoming industrial convention, and the inspired and domestic convention of healthcare quality, which link the medical activity to creativity, innovation and deliberation in line with the inspired convention and trust, tradition and individual case analysis in correspondence with the domestic convention.

Several interviewees, including I25, I36, I44 and I41, emphasise the intricacy of decision-making, wherein factors beyond clinical parameters, such as medical history, individual circumstances and patient preferences, must all be considered. One of the interviewees expressed it as follows:

"Yes, I haven't found them very beneficial so far. They are very limited. They can't make such complex decisions yet. And when we really have questions, they are usually relatively complex problems. The simple things can be quite helpful for a beginner, I think. But when you've been doing it for a while, those are not the things where that's helpful. They really have to be things where more complex contexts can be taken into account. We will probably get there at some point. But so far we are not there yet. In this respect, these systems are decision support tools because they can help contextualise data to some extent. However, in practical application, it's not yet satisfactory enough to rely on it completely. There's still plenty of room for improvement" (I36).

I34 also holds the view that health analytics might be helpful in scoring and providing alerts, but when it comes to actionable insights, human expertise surpasses the system's capabilities. I41 goes even further, stating, "if the algorithm can't do something, it's the clinical judgement of an experienced doctor that will do something" (I41). Here, the conflict between domestic and industrial convention leads to doubts and less trust in the socio-digital system.

The interviewees thus describe the friction that can be seen in the literature as an almost classic conflict in relation to the reforms of the healthcare system (Liang/Xue 2021). However, the study shows how these influence the everyday working life of doctors in hospitals and which hierarchy and role discussions and possible shifts can be associated with this.

4.4 The Domestic and Industrial Convention: Shifting Roles of Health Analytics from Secretary to Decider

Linked to these reflections on standardisation and complexity, interviewees have varied perspectives on health analytics functioning as an expert system. Some, with reference to the industrial convention and its valuation criteria of efficiency and productivity, view health analytics as an assistant or secretary offering valuable support aimed at saving time, particularly in administrative and logistical tasks (I34, I35). This assistance would enable physicians to refocus on their core medical duties, ultimately alleviating their overall workload. While health analytics could assume the routine and standardisable tasks (in an industrial understanding), the physicians ponder their way back to professional values of deliberations oriented towards the complexity of the individual case, as supported by the inspired and domestic convention (Da Silva 2020). As an interviewee aptly put it,

"Then I wouldn't come home so exhausted because, at the end of the day, I would have someone beside me, like a ward secretary, who supports me. And that's why I would welcome that" (I37).

These supportive activities could encompass a range of tasks as outlined in the interviews, including scanning medication slips (I43), streamlining the processing of notes and case documentation (I39) and the (semi-)automated generation of physicians' reports (I40). An interviewee outlines the need for an application that can summarise relevant information:

"There must be an application that condenses this for me, that recognises the case and says, 'for this clinical picture, there are ten pieces of information that were important to Ms. [I34] in the last six months.' I present them to her now, also with some form of progression and assessment" (I34).

Conversely, some interviewees envision an alternative future scenario in which physicians assume the role of administrators tasked with implementing the diagnoses and decisions generated by health analytics. I44 claims that health analytics imply a reduced need for personal diagnosis and assessment, potentially transforming physicians into administrators—or industrial (health assembly line) workers—who primarily manage the information provided to them.

"[W]e are a conservative subject. We don't operate. And if we were to be relieved of the diagnostics by health analytics, well, then we would still have a therapy decision. But that's another thing. If that were to be taken away from us, then we would somehow almost only be administrators. Then this medical competence, as each physician experiences it now on a personal level, would be lost" (I44).

Within this industrial logic associated with competence, being either associated with scientifically trained physicians or, in the second case, with data-driven health analytics, the role of physicians could also develop into a supervisory role. On the one hand, recommendations originating from health analytics can assist physicians in doublechecking their opinion and treatment proposal. Physicians can use their and other cases to learn how to diagnose or make adequate treatment proposals. On the other hand, health analytics can take a more important role, should physicians rely more strongly on the results of health analytics. This is partially even necessary as I29 describes for the case of radiology where factors such as forensic interests result in a surplus of work and an increasing amount of imaging, which can no longer be managed by humans alone. In these assigned roles, there exists an ongoing negotiation when it comes to decision-making hierarchies and the allocation of decision-making authorities (I29). This negotiation extends to determining the ultimate responsibility for decisions, particularly in relation to potential legal ramifications and disputes arising from these decisions (I28; I33). Furthermore, these discussions also revolve around matters of control (I26) and transparency (I23; I24).

Hierarchy as well as authority are central valuation criteria of the domestic convention, characterised by a clear hierarchy akin to that of a master and apprentice in the spirit of the craft. Furthermore, significant emphasis is placed on control and trust as central dimensions within the domestic convention (I26; I41). This dynamic is exemplified in the following quotation, which pertains to an electrocardiogram (ECG) app:

"At the end of the day, I still do not fully trust this type of technology because it is not really widely available yet. So, as a cardiologist I will still be able to keep an overview to some extent when I have an app like this, and I will be able to see that it is a super support for me because it takes care of some aspects more quickly, for example, measuring things in the ECG, that can be done faster automatically. But in the end, I can still check the app with my expertise in the last instance, whereas if I were to imagine that a colleague [...] [...] who doesn't have a lot of experience with ECGs and lacks the routine and gets and uses this app, then he would perhaps more easily overlook aspects that the app has perhaps not assigned correctly. So, I think you still have to control that" (I41).

The hierarchical arrangement of the two expert systems, namely physicians and health analytics, leaves space for what I27 describes as a "fundamental apprehension of other expert systems" (I27) among physicians. This apprehension can be viewed as a challenge to the "professional ethos" (I23) held dear by physicians. However, delegating tasks and forwarding responsibility and tasks to an opaque system contradict this professional ethos. This friction and the collaboration between these two entities, i.e., physicians and systems, are only feasible when there is a foundation of mutual transparency, information exchange, the intelligibility of proposals and recommendations and the sharing of outcomes. This cooperative endeavour also entails a process of mutual learning (I27; I34) and the friction that "a software is supposed to tell me that it knows better than I do" (I25) despite the physician having studied for a long time. In part, this discussion about competence, expertise and the ultimate decision-making power of expert systems—physician or health analytics—also reflects the conflict between evidence-based and hierarchy-guided medicine (I40).

"We have certain medical procedures that are, sort of, clearly guideline-backed. Yes, and if a score now brings you these procedures, these guidelines, it is a game changer, so to speak. It's just like a cardiology guideline that says: you have a legal burden, you have to do this and that, then that's what I'll do. Yes, or I change to the area of eminence-based medicine and say: I don't care, I'm the boss here and I've always done it this way and then we'll continue to do it this way. And that's how a score would be. A score is like a red flag" (I40).

Even if, as described by I40 when discussing the negotiation of decision-making authority between a score and the physician, it is concluded that neither the fundamental structure nor the organisational processes within a hospital would undergo significant change, several questions emerge. These questions revolve around the prioritisation of decision-making criteria—either following an industrial/market or an inspired/domestic logic, encompassing aspects like the quality of treatment and resource allocation (I39), legal considerations (I28) and the allocation of responsibilities (I23).

Above all, the question of trust—which is a central aspect of the relationship not only between physicians and patients (I23), but also between medical colleagues, and which is a central dimension in the domestic convention—is affected by this, since trust, at least thus far, is based on personal contact and positive experiences (I24). "The only thing that works (...) is when you know each other personally" (I28).

Trust is of great importance for the use of health analytics, as I35 suggests that the acceptance of clinical decision support systems (CDSSs) in healthcare is significantly lower when there is no accompanying explanation or guidance. When the CDSS suggests actions like "reduce dose", the implementation rate is low when there is no one to explain its purpose. However, when a pharmacist provides input, clarifies system functions and emphasises their importance, the outcomes are more positive. I35 highlights the inefficiency of simply installing such systems and conducting one-time training sessions regarding the usage of the systems and their impact on decision-making.

Hence, settings that promote the embedding of health analytics in (lifelong) learning—which is an important building block in medicine (I45)—is crucial. In this context, health analytics are also evaluated against this question, because, as already briefly mentioned above, health analytics are classified as helpful above all for inexperienced residents (I38), since the support provided by the systems decreases for more experienced physicians (I36; I38). I33 poses the question of how learning and experience acquisition processes will be shaped for physicians who work with health analytics from the beginning. Hence, and in addition to the hierarchy and role friction already discussed above, many new questions of joint learning, as well as the exchange between physicians and health analytics, need to be clarified.

5. Discussion of Friction Lines: Saving Time, Data Quality, Trust and Status Shift

As described in Chapter 4, intraconventional frictions appear mainly when the corresponding quality tests are not met, as seen with the market and industrial convention. Medical specialties show differentiations. In some disciplines, such as radiology, it is easier to standardise tasks. Here, health analytics, analysing the mass of images, appear to be easier to introduce with fewer frictions than in the field of intensive care where many different parameters have to be included in the decision-making process. The interviewed physicians found some health analytics, for example, the sepsis early warning system, to be rather disruptive due to insufficient fit and reliability creating the problem of over-altering. This, in turn, leads us to inter-conventional frictions. In Chapter 4.1, the interviewees note that the quality test of the industrial convention—stability and competence in functioning processes—is not fulfilled, as the product quality corresponds to that of industrial mass consumption, whereas they themselves make a (case-by-case) assessment. Here, trust and trustworthiness are at the centre of the quality test, in line with the domestic convention.

Trust as the relational logic of the domestic convention is one central friction line along which the interconventional friction between the industrial and the domestic convention is manifested. Physicians actively build trust and discern which tasks can be delegated to health analytics and what should remain within their purview (I23; I24; I34; I36). This trust-building process extends to consulting expert colleagues whose judgment they trust, emphasising the importance of human collaboration in healthcare decision-making (I24; I34; I36; I40). While health analytics may assist with certain tasks, the final decision-making authority primarily rests with human actors and major decisions are typically made collaboratively within medical teams (I26; I33). Physicians maintain a reliance on personal experience, trust in experienced colleagues within their networks and a degree of scepticism towards patient data received from other physicians (I7; I16; I26; I28; I43). These examples show the crucial role of trust as the building block of physicians' practices. In this complex trust-concentrated culture with a long history in the domestic convention (Da Silva 2020), health analytics instead of sole decision-makers seem to serve as quality checks, with physicians continuing to exercise control and oversight (I26; I36; I37; I41). In this friction between the domestic and industrial convention, the relationship logics of domestic trust and of industrial functionality thus confront each other. Functioning often is not enough, as mistrust in automatically generated diagnoses and prognoses by health analytics stems from their perceived black box nature, making it challenging for physicians to fully rely on these systems (I23; I29; I33). In this context, Al-Amoudi and Latsis (2019) also referred to the obfuscation of normative choices by (AI-based) health analytics.

"While AIs as we currently know them are not capable of participating in normative discussions as discussants, we can expect their outputs to increasingly be the object of normative discussions between humans" (Al-Amoudi/Latsis 2019: 119).

This nuanced approach reflects the acknowledgement that health analytics can complement medical practice but not replace the crucial role of human expertise (I31; I40). Looking at trust, not from a psychological perspective but as a relational concept linked to the domestic convention, sheds new light on historically grown hierarchies, dynamics and logics. Hence, health analytics in less industrialised medical specialities must meet other quality tests than health analytics in more industrialised medical specialities.

     Data quality, which is closely linked to trust, is another friction line within the evolving landscape of healthcare, shaping physicians' perceptions and practices in the context of health analytics integration. On the one hand, data quality—following the industrial convention—does not always pass the corresponding quality test, while, on the other hand, questions surrounding responsibility and accountability arise (Liang/Xue 2021), which are aligned with the domestic convention. Physicians retain ultimate responsibility for medical decisions, but the delegation of tasks to health analytics introduces intricate (quality) challenges (I26). This delegation raises the question of how physicians define their field of expertise and navigate the incorporation of external expertise into their decision-making process (I34). There is a spectrum of physician attitudes towards the use of health analytics, ranging from those who solely rely on their own judgment to those who embrace health analytics as a complementary tool (I40). The question that arises from this friction line is a (re)definition of quality. With the introduction of health analytics, physicians are increasingly uncertain about which quality tests they should rely on and, furthermore, about how to deal with normative choice (Al-Amoudi and Latsis 2019).

This leads to physicians' fear of a status shift and the loss of professional competence within the evolving landscape of healthcare, linked to health analytics inhibiting "the practical wisdom of medical practitioners, patients, and policy-makers" (Al-Amoudi/Latsis 2019: 136). Within this friction line, physicians grapple with the shifting dynamics of their roles, transitioning from traditional roles as caretakers—following the domestic logic of recognition, reputation and authority (Diaz-Bone 2015: 162-163)—to potentially becoming managers or case managers within healthcare teams (I26). This idea follows the industrial logic of professional scientific competence. It implies a shift in competences, which necessitates a re-evaluation of physicians' professional identities and status within the healthcare hierarchy. The acceptance of these changes is multidimensional, shaped by complex interplays of professional roles and the evolving landscape of healthcare (I26). These dimensions highlight the ongoing negotiation of roles and competences, reflecting the challenges and opportunities posed by the integration of health analytics into medical practice, along inter-conventional frictions.

In the realm of medical industrialised (Da Silva 2020) practice, the pursuit of time efficiency remains a paramount concern, with health analytics emerging as a double-edged sword. On the one hand, there is an enduring hope that health analytics can alleviate the burden of documentation efforts, prompting physicians to seek innovative workarounds (I34; I41), following an industrial logic. This aspiration is fuelled by a desire to refocus on what most of our interviewees regard as the core tenets of the medical profession—the physician-patient relationship (I23) with its foundation in the domestic and inspired convention (Da Silva 2020). One of the physicians poignantly captures the time imbalance, lamenting and highlighting the urgency for a rebalancing act within the medical field, with its basis in the interconventional friction, which is shown at the friction line concerning time:

"How much time do we spend on the patient? That's minutes a day. How much time do we spend on the computer? That's hours" (I36).

Paradoxically, the introduction of health analytics has, in certain aspects, amplified the struggle against time as already outlined in, for example, Lyle (2021). Physicians perceive health analytics as introducing time pressures stemming from the need for meticulous double-checking (I38; I43), the constant barrage of alerts (I30), the requisite investment in learning the system (I34), interoperability challenges (I26; I36) and limited perceived added value (I26). Curiously, the reduced dependence on external networks, often considered a potential source of relief, is viewed with apprehension bordering on a sense of threat (I40; I41). A physician poignantly reflects:

"(i)f the system says, 'Take a look at this', then you're practically forced to do so because if you don't (...), you get three prompts after ten hours and 27 prompts after two days" (I30).

Furthermore, inefficiencies in data transfer processes, such as the manual input of patient medication into intensive care programs, are deemed superfluous and frustrating (I36). While some simple tasks have been expedited (I24; I29), the broader impact of health analytics seems to reinforce the notion that physicians are increasingly expecting to maximise their time economically, placing a heightened emphasis on economic considerations and subsequently contributing to resistance (I40; I41). These frictions between the market and industrial convention versus the domestic convention are also shown by Da Silva (2020) and Batifoulier (2020) in their seminal work on the industrialisation of healthcare. This might also be a practical example of what Zuboff's "Be the Friction" (2019) aims to convey. This is because, in the pursuit of time efficiency, the introduction of health analytics has unveiled a complex interplay between aspirations for streamlined medical practice and the time pressures that come hand in hand with this transformative technology.

6. Conclusion

In conclusion, our study sheds light on the complex dynamics surrounding the implementation and use of health analytics in the medical field. We have observed that while many physicians appreciate the potential benefits of health analytics, there is also hesitation and resistance. In line with Sharon (2021), the findings show that the market convention in healthcare faces multiple frictions and includes other logics, partly in contrast to Da Silva (2020), Da Silva and Rauly (2016) and Batifoulier, Da Silva and Domin (2018) who claim an ongoing industrialisation of healthcare closely linked to the industrial and market conventions.

Nevertheless, the pressure on resources—both human and monetary—is mentioned several times in the interviews, with the promise that health analytics might ease some of physicians' (time) pressure. However, the interviewees have challenged this market-driven paradigm in the interviews, as there have been painful realisations, most notably the understanding that health analytics, despite its promises, do not always deliver the desired output. This shortcoming underscores a friction between the market and the industrial convention, as the development, training and adaptation of the health analytic systems are not enough to guarantee a satisfactory functioning. Furthermore, in addition to some standardised and routine tasks, medicine is primarily determined by case-by-case analyses and decisions as well as the inclusion and weighting of many different aspects in keeping with the domestic convention. Thus, the traditional role of a physician is characterised by the deliberative consideration of the individual case, in a combination of the domestic and deliberative (inspirational) conventions (Da

Silva 2020). Despite a general trend in medicine towards guideline conformity, evidence-baseness and standardisation—in the sense of the industrial convention (Da Silva 2020)—the interviewees still insist on the relevance of the domestic convention, also with regard to the distribution of roles between health analytics and physicians. As outlined by some interviewees, health analytics are ideally positioned as efficient assistants that handle routine tasks and data analysis, thereby enabling physicians to focus on core medical aspects, particularly caring and communicating more with their patients. In this sense, the interviewees hope that health analytics perform standardised as well as industrialised tasks, while they may (re)turn to being a helpful assistant system in the future.

In contrast to Siffels, Sharon and Hoffman's paper on "the rise of the civic" (2021), the civic convention was not mentioned in our interviews. This may come as an surprise at first, but it could be due to us not focusing on "data-intensive medical research" (Siffels et al. 2021) or patients in our interview guideline. Our emphasis was on physicians' daily working routines. The interviewees within this study only marginally address overarching patterns of justification, referring to health policy issues or individual motivational patterns and attitudes regarding professional ethos.

To be able to assess these results correctly, it is important to acknowledge that our research has certain limitations. However, these constraints pave the way for further investigative opportunities. Our data collection was majorly limited to Germany, but to mitigate potential biases we incorporated insights from physicians with experience in multiple countries including the USA, Denmark and Switzerland. These findings may therefore serve as a foundation to explore similar dynamics within other healthcare systems. Regarding our data collection methodology, the initial interviews were concentrated on telemedical consultations and were concise due to the time constraints physicians faced during the COVID-19 pandemic. In contrast, our subsequent interviews were more extensive and broader in scope. Although we achieved a comprehensive understanding from our interviews, the primary clinical areas represented were radiology, cardiology and intensive care, leaving other domains unexplored. While we have highlighted certain frictions, future studies should delve into other possible frictions and their evolutions, potentially including perspectives from various medical professionals. To further substantiate our observations on friction development, a longitudinal study would be instrumental in deepening our grasp of the existing contradictions, shedding light on evolving patterns. The role of health analytics as investment in forms (Thévenot 2016, 1984) could be the starting point for further research. In this study, we concentrate our analysis on conventions only. It might be helpful to expand and refocus the findings based on Sharon's ideas on spheres (Sharon 2021), adding a normative layer on frictions and conflicts between spheres.

In closing, our research has demonstrated the significance of latent frictions in understanding the evolving healthcare landscape, examining the orders of justifications and conventions, cited by physicians with regard to their experiences with health analytics. The E/SC does not yet have an elaborated terminology to address such forms of cooperation and conflict within and between conventions. Therefore, the current study proposes the term *frictions* to describe the ongoing negotiation between the plural order of justifications. Friction arises at close range, in direct encounters, as this is where conflicts crystallise. These frictions manifest in negotiations and justifications within and between conventions, particularly with regard to competence shifts and trust dynamics. In addition, considerations about legal accountability and responsibility in medical decisions are intrinsic to the domestic convention. Questions about who holds the ultimate responsibility, who can be considered the expert and whether physicians' risk of becoming mere administrators are central to these discussions, pertain to the core characteristics of the medical profession and touch on fundamental questions of professional ethics. In this sense, the question that arises is *who or what is the friction*, to paraphrase Zuboff's (2019) claim. To be more precise, it seems that it is not humans who bring friction into the digitalisation process, but the technology itself— here, health analytics—that brings about friction. In this sense, the healthcare sector presents a unique and normative cultural landscape where contradictions, ambivalences and value clashes are prevalent. These conflicts and controversies in relation to hierarchical changes and learning processes offer opportunities to envision alternative designs for an adjusted digital medical culture, respecting and embedded in the moral tissues of healthcare. The integration and implementation of health analytics serve as a supreme example to show the essential role of justifications and negotiations in the digitalisation process and the contribution that the E/SC can make in gaining insights into digital culture.

List of References

Al-Amoudi, I./Latsis, J. (2019): "Anormative Black Boxes: Artificial Intelligence and Health Policy." In: I. Al-Amoudi/E. Lazega (eds.), Post-Human Institutions and Organizations: Confronting the Matrix, London: Routledge, pp. 119–142.

Baird, A./Angst, C./Oborn, E. (2018): "Health Information Technology." In: MIS Quarterly Research Curations.

Batifoulier, P. (2022): "Health, Conventions, and Society.". In: R. Diaz-Bone/G. de Larquier (eds.), Handbook of Economics and Sociology of Conventions, pp. 1–23.

Batifoulier, P./Bessis, F./Ghirardello, A./Larquier, G. de/Remillon, D. (eds.) (2016): Dictionnaire des conventions, Villeneuve d'Ascq: Presses Universitaires du Septentrion.

Batifoulier, P./Da Silva, N./Domin, J.-P. (2018): Économie de la Santé, Paris: Armand Colin.

Berente, N./Gu, B./Recker, J. et al. (2021): "Special Issue Editor's Comments: Managing Artificial Intelligence." MIS Quarterly, 45, pp. 1433–1450.

Block, K./Pohle, J. (2023): "Digitalisierung als Herausforderung für die soziologische Theorie." Berliner Journal für Soziologie, 33, pp. 189–195.

Boltanski, L./Chiapello, È. (2013 [1999]): Der neue Geist des Kapitalismus. Konstanz: UVK.

Boltanski, L./Thévenot, L. (2006): On Justification: Economies of Worth. Princeton, Oxford: Princeton University Press.

Boytcheva, S./Angelova, G./Angelov, Z./Tcharaktchiev, D. (2015): "Text Mining and Big Data Analytics for Retrospective Analysis of Clinical Texts from Outpatient Care." Cybernetics and Information Technologies, 15, pp. 58–77.

Bygstad, B./Øvrelid, E./Lie, T./Bergquist, M. (2020): "Developing and Organizing an Analytics Capability for Patient Flow in a General Hospital." Information Systems Frontiers, 22, pp. 353–364.

Cappel, V./Kappler, K. (eds.) (2022): Gesundheit - Konventionen - Digitalisierung. Eine politische Ökonomie der (digitalen) Transformationsprozesse von und um Gesundheit. Wiesbaden: Springer VS.

Cohen, I. G./Amarasingham, R./Shah, A./Xie, B./Lo, B. (2014): "The Legal and Ethical Concerns that Arise from Using Complex Predictive Analytics in Health Care." Health affairs (Project Hope), 33, pp. 1139–1147.

Da Silva, N. (2020): "The Industrialization of Healthcare and Its Critiques." In: R. Diaz-Bone/G. de Larquier (eds.), Handbook of Economics and Sociology of Conventions, pp. 1–25.

Da Silva, N./Rauly, A. (2016): "La télémédecine, un instrument de renouvellement de l'action publique ? Une lecture par l'économie des conventions." Economie & Institutions.

Diaz-Bone, R. (2015): Die "Economie des Conventions". Grundlagen und Entwicklungen der neuen französischen Wirtschaftssoziologie. Wiesbaden: Springer VS.

Diaz-Bone, R. (2018): "Valuation an den Grenzen von Datenwelten. Konventionentheoretische Perspektiven auf Quantifizierung und Big Data." In: J. Kropf/S. Laser (eds.), Digitale Bewertungspraktiken: Labore der Grenzziehung in vernetzten Welten. Wiesbaden: Springer VS, pp. 69–94.

Diaz-Bone, R/de Larquier, G. (eds.) (2020): Handbook of Economics and Sociology of Conventions. Cham: Springer International Publishing.

Dubé, L./Paré, G. (2003): "Rigor in Information Systems Positivist Case Research: Current Practices, Trends, and Recommendations." MIS Quarterly, 27, pp. 597–635.

Eymard-Duvernay, F. (ed.) (2012): Epreuves d'évaluation et chômage. Toulouse: Octarès Editions.

Eymard-Duvernay, F./Favereau, O./Orléan, A./Salais, R./Thévenot, L. (2011): "Werte, Koordination und Rationalität: Die Verbindung dreier Themen durch die 'Économie des conventions'." In: R. Diaz-Bone (ed.), Soziologie der Konventionen. Grundlagen einer pragmatischen Anthropologie. Frankfurt am Main/New York: Campus, pp. 203–230.

Eymard-Duvernay, F./Thévenot, L. (1983): Les investissements de forme. Leur usage pour la main d'oeuvre. Working Paper, Paris.

Fang, X./Gao, Y./Jen-Hwa Hu, P. (2013): "A Prescriptive Analytics Method for Cost Reduction in Clinical Decision Making." MIS Quarterly, 45, pp. 83–116.

Fourcade, M. (2022): Zählen, benennen, ordnen: Eine Soziologie des Unterscheidens. Hamburg: Hamburger Edition.

Gilgun, J. (2001): "Case-Based Research, Analytic Induction, and Theory Development: The Future and the Past." 31st Annual Theory Construction & Research Methodology Workshop: Proceedings.

Greffrath, M. (2021): "Ausbeutung 4.0—Die Digitalisierung des Menschen." Blätter für deutsche und internationale Politik, 66, pp. 105–113.

Grön, K (2021): "Common good in the era of data-intensive healthcare." Humanities & Social Sciences Communications, 8(230), pp. 1–10.

Hanrieder, T. (2016): "Orders of Worth and the Moral Conceptions of Health in Global Politics." International Theory, 8(3), pp. 390–421.

Haring, R. (ed.) (2019): Gesundheitswissenschaften. Berlin, Heidelberg: Springer Nature.

Houben, D./Prietl, B. (eds.) (2018): Datengesellschaft. Einsichten in die Datafizierung des Sozialen. Bielefeld: transcript.

Kankanhalli, A./Hahn, J./Tan, S./Gao, G. (2016): "Big Data and Analytics in Healthcare: Introduction to the Special Section." Information Systems Frontiers, 18, pp. 233–235.

Liang, H./Xue, Y. (2021): "Save Face or Save Life: Physicians' Dilemma in Using Clinical Decision Support Systems." Information Systems Research, 33(2), pp. 737–758.

Lafaye, C./Thévenot, L. (1993): "Une Justification Écologique? Conflits dans l'aménagement de la nature." Revue française de sociologie, 34, pp. 495–524.

Lenz, S. (2021): ""More like a Support Tool": Ambivalences around digital health from medical developers' perspective." Big Data & Society, 8(1), pp. 1–13.

Lux, T. (2017): "E-Health-Begriff und Abgrenzung." In: S. Müller-Mielitz/T. Lux (eds.), E-Health-Ökonomie, Berlin, Heidelberg: Springer Gabler, pp. 3–23.

Lux, T./Breil, B. (2017): "Digitalisierung im Gesundheitswesen - zwischen Datenschutz und moderner Medizinversorgung." Wirtschaftsdienst, 97, pp. 687–692.

Lyle, K. (2021): "Interventional STS: A Framework for Developing Workable Technologies." Sociological Research Online, 26(2), pp. 410–426.

Meskó, B./Spiegel, B. (2022): "A Revised Hippocratic Oath for the Era of Digital Health." Journal of Medical Internet Research, 24, e39177.

Miles, M. B./Huberman, A. M./Saldaña, J. (2020): Qualitative Data Analysis: A Methods Sourcebook. Los Angeles: Sage.

Mühlhoff, R. (2018): "Digitale Entmündigung und User Experience Design: Wie digitale Geräte uns nudgen, tracken und zur Unwissenheit erziehen." Leviathan, 46, pp. 551–574.

Nassehi, A. (2024): Patterns: Theory of the Digital Society. Paris, London: Polity Press.

Oesterreich, T. D./Fitte, C./Behne, A./Teuteberg, F. (2020): "Understanding the Role of Predictive and Prescriptive Analytics in Healthcare: A Multi-Stakeholder Approach." Proceedings of the 28th European Conference on Information Systems (ECIS), An Online AIS Conference, June 15–17.

Patton, M. Q. (2015): Qualitative Research and Evaluation Methods: Integrating Theory and Practice. Los Angeles: Sage.

Reckwitz, A. (2020): The Society of Singularities. Cambridge, Medford: Polity Press.

Roulston, K. (2018): "Qualitative Interviewing and Epistemics." Qualitative Research, 18, pp. 322–341.

Rowlands, T./Waddell, N./McKenna, B. (2016): "Are We There Yet? A Technique to Determine Theoretical Saturation." Journal of Computer Information Systems, 56, pp. 40–47.

Schaupp, S. (2021): Technopolitik von Unten. Algorithmische Arbeitssteuerung und Kybernetische Proletarisierung. Berlin: Matthes & Seitz.

Schultze, U./Avital, M. (2011): "Designing Interviews to Generate Rich Data for Information Systems Research." Information and Organization, 21, pp. 1–16.

Seyfert, R./Roberge, J. (eds.) (2016): Algorithmic Cultures: Essays on Meaning, Performance and New Technologies. London, New York: Routledge.

Shaban-Nejad, A./Michalowski, M./Brownstein, J./Buckeridge, D. (2021): "Guest Editorial Explainable AI: Towards Fairness, Accountability, Transparency and Trust in Healthcare." IEEE Journal of Biomedical and Health Informatics, 25, pp. 2374–2375.

Shahbaz, M./Gao, C./Zhai, L./Shahzad, F./Hu, Y. (2019): "Investigating the Adoption of Big Data Analytics in Healthcare: The Moderating Role of Resistance to Change." Journal of Big Data 6.

Sharon, T. (2016): "The Googlization of Health Research: From Disruptive Innovation to Disruptive Ethics." Personalized Medicine, 13, pp. 563–574.

Sharon, T. (2018): "When Digital Health Meets Digital Capitalism, How Many Common Goods Are at Stake?." Big Data & Society, 5(2), pp. 1–12.

Sharon, T. (2021): "From Hostile Worlds to Multiple Spheres: Towards a Normative Pragmatics of Justice for the Googlization of Health." Medicine, Health Care and Philosophy, 24, pp. 315–327.

Siffels, L.E./Sharon, T./Hoffman, A.S. (2021): "The Participatory Turn in Health and Medicine: The Rise of the Civic and the Need to 'Give Back' in Data-Intensive Medical Research." Humanities and Social Sciences Communications, 8, p. 306.

Thévenot, L. (1984): "Rules and Implements: Investment in Forms." Social Science Information, 23, pp. 1–45.

Thévenot, L. (2016): "From Social Coding to Economics of Convention: A thirty-year Perspective on the Analysis of Qualification and Quantification Investments." Historical Social Research, 41, pp. 96–117.

Trimble, M./Hamilton, P. (2016): "The Thinking Doctor: Clinical Decision Making in Contemporary Medicine." Clinical Medicine (London, England), 16, pp. 343–346.

van Dijck, J./Poell, T./Waal, M. d. (2018): The Platform Society: Public Values in a Connective World. New York: Oxford University Press.

Wang, J./Cao, B./Yu, P. S./Sun, L./Bao, W./Zhu, X. (2018): Deep Learning Towards Mobile Applications, https://arxiv.org/pdf/1809.03559.pdf.

Zuboff, S. (2019): The Age of Surveillance Capitalism: The Fight for a Human Future at the New Frontier of Power, London: Profile Books.

Domestic Discords

Frictions in Smart Speaker Valuation

Lukas Schmitz

Abstract

In the contemporary landscape of interconnected technologies, the smart home emerges as a symbol of progress, revolutionising domestic life by seamlessly integrating and optimising tasks for modern dwellers. Smart speakers, while epitomising this transformation, serve as conduits for managing various connected devices. However, the process of integrating smart speakers is not frictionless; as a new type of technology, smart speakers are, above all, to be implemented into everyday life. It is only during this adaptation process, in which individuals incorporate these smart technologies into their daily routine, that the actual value of the smart home becomes apparent. This paper, therefore, addresses the appropriation processes of smart speakers through a qualitative study, exploring frictions in the valuation of smart speakers within households. Drawing on a micro-sociological perspective and a pragmatist valuation framework, the paper examines the valuations guiding persons in using, avoiding, or rejecting smart speakers in everyday domestic life. By analysing data from ten households, the paper reveals how valuations of smart speakers express specific attachments and are legitimised through different regimes of justification. The unfolding of this valuation process creates friction as smart speakers challenge existing attachments, and it is carried out through various justifications that are often in tension with each other. Establishing this dual perspective on friction, the study sheds light on how people navigate the integration of new technology in their domestic environment and realise the promise of the smart home individually.[1]

Keywords

Smart Speaker, Smart Home, Sociology of Valuation, Attachments, Justifications

---

1 I thank Susann Wagenknecht (TU Dresden) for the motivating and inspiring conversations, many helpful hints and extensive support in writing this essay.

1. Introduction

In the era of interconnected technologies, the smart home concept has emerged as a beacon of convenience, efficiency, and connectivity. From controlling household appliances to managing security systems, the smart home has changed how people interact with their living spaces, making tasks easier, more efficient, and increasingly personalised. It embodies a vision of interconnectedness, where every aspect of domestic life is seamlessly integrated and optimised for the modern dweller's convenience. The smart home holds the promise that integrating smart technology into the domestic environment will create a success story from which everyone can benefit in their everyday lives. As the vision of increased productivity and efficiency, the smart home is constructed in opposition to a supposed "dumb home" of inefficiency (Dahlgren et al.: 2021, p.1160). It conveys the vision of an optimised future where the domestic space is characterised by an aesthetic experience that is fun and stylish, customised, controllable, convenient, and energy-efficient (Strengers et al. 2020).

Smart Speakers like Amazon Echo or Apple Home Pod act as conductors of the smart home, offering users intuitive access to a plethora of services and functionalities through voice commands. They serve as the central hub through which users interact with and orchestrate various connected devices, ushering in an era of unprecedented convenience and efficiency in smart home management. Smart speakers, therefore, play a vital role in the current transformation of the domestic and have become the epitome of the smart home.

The promise of the smart home as an industrial vision has already been critically scrutinised. Yolande Strengers et al. (2020) show, for example, that smart control for energy efficiency can have the opposite effect: the appliances themselves increase energy output in terms of consumption. At the same time, the smart home itself requires work in the sense of *digital housekeeping* (Strengers et al. 2019).

This raises the question of what value the smart home actually has. Where could an answer be found if not where the smart technology is used? It is the domestic sphere, where people integrate the technology and customise it for their individual use. But how does smart technology's appropriation process occur in everyday life? How do people negotiate their relationship with smart technology? How does the promise of the smart home materialise in the domestic?

Based on a qualitative study, drawing on ethnographic observations and interview data in ten households, this paper deals with the friction in the appropriation process of smart speakers in the domestic. From a micro-sociological perspective using a pragmatistic valuation framework, I ask which valuations guide people in using—also avoiding, eschewing, or ignoring—smart speakers in everyday domestic life. With the help of Antoine Hennion and Laurent Thévenot, I show how valuations of smart speakers are to be understood as expressions of specific attachments (Gomart/Hennion 1999; Hennion 2011/2013/2017) and how these valuations are legitimised by recourse to different justifications (Boltanski/ Thévenot 2006). This valuation process is structured frictionally: as a new technology, the smart speaker challenges the person and collides with attachments; this leads to an individual valuation. To legitimise their valuation of the smart speaker, people refer to various justifications that are also in tension with each other. This dual perspective on frictions in the appropriation process helps to understand more precisely how people integrate new technology in their domestic environment and realise the promise of the smart home in the domestic.

To this end, after briefly summarising existing research on smart speakers (2), I will present the theoretical framework based on valuation studies (3) and then describe my methodological approach (4). Subsequently, I will closely analyse the different frictions that arise in Smart Speaker appropriation (5). The analytical focus will be on the friction between attachment and the smart speaker (5.1) and justifications used for legitimisation (5.2). After discussing the results (6), this paper ends with a short conclusion (7).

2. Why People Use Smart Speakers: Research Insights

This section first provides an overview of the research literature that aims to understand what drives people to appropriate smart speakers in the home. After more than a decade, a field of research has developed that deals with smart speakers from various perspectives, including discussions of privacy issues (Lau/Zimmermann/ Schaub 2018; Pridmore/Mols 2020; Modaresnezhad/Nemati 2020; Maccario/ Naldi 2023), the interactions between people and smart speakers (Humphry/ Chesher 2020; Kudina 2021), usage studies (Kiseleva et al. 2016; Rzepka 2019) and questions about the consequences of smart speaker use (Hernandez-Ortega/ Ferreira 2020; Atkinson/Barker 2021).

Thus, there is some research on what motivates people to use smart speakers in the domestic sphere. Graeme McLean and Kofi Osei-Frimpong (2019) show that the use of smart speakers is motivated by utilitarian, symbolic, hedonic, and social benefits, and "users turn to voice-controlled technology due to their usefulness and convenience to aid them in the completion of tasks" (19). Emily Buteau and Joonghwa Lee (2021) show that efficient support in the organisation of work is a driving motive for using smart speakers. At the same time, several publications emphasise that the perception of smart speakers is negotiated via privacy concerns (McLean/Frimpong 2019; Buteau/Lee 2021; Pospisil et al. 2022).

In their qualitative study on motives for using smart speakers, Josephine Lau, Benjamin Zimmermann, and Florian Schaub (2018) also show that privacy issues play a role in rejecting smart speaker use, primarily for non-users. Conversely, convenience is a driving motive for users, while non-users would not see this benefit. Saba Brause and Grant Blank (2020) identified usage genres "that go beyond 'convenience' and 'entertainment'", namely "companionship, self-control, and productivity, health care support, better sleep, peace of mind and improved accessibility" (757). Christine Rzepka (2019) comes to a similar conclusion, differentiating usage motives into "efficiency, convenience, ease of use, minimal cognitive effort, and enjoyment" (5).

However, little research exists about the complex background against which people negotiate their relationship with smart speakers. The focus of this paper lies in how these valuations are made—the aim is to show that the appropriation process needs to be understood as a complex negotiation worth taking a closer look at. This makes a broad theoretical approach necessary to contextualise how people deal with smart speakers. To this end, I put this into perspective as a valuation procedure. Therefore, in the next section, I develop a theoretical concept that describes valuation as driven by specific attachments and carried out by referring to justifications.

3. A Pragmatist Program of Valuation

This section will present my theoretical approach, establishing a nuanced perspective on valuations. I am grounded in the program of valuation studies and focus on the theoretical approaches of Antoine Hennion, Laurent Thévenot, and Luc Boltanski. First, I outline the basic features of a sociology of valuation. I then sketch Antoine Hennion's concept of *attachment*, which illustrates the many ties that make up and constitute a person. Finally, to differentiate these attachments, I draw on Laurent Thévenot's *regimes of engagement*. The regimes describe different ways of meaningfully locating one's actions concerning a specific value. As a result of the theoretical discussion, I argue that friction is a term that, on the one hand, is suitable for conceptualising the confrontation between the smart speaker and the attachment and, on the other hand, helps to illuminate the tensions between the justifications used for the valuation.

To analyse the valuation of smart speakers, I draw on conceptual resources developed in Valuation Studies, an interdisciplinary field with an affinity to Science and Technology Studies (Antal/Hutter/Stark 2015; Lee/Helgesson 2019). The starting point of this perspective is to describe "valuation as a social practice" (Helgesson/Muniesa 2013: 4). What is valued is not inherent to the objects or a pure result of social construction. Instead, this valuation can "be seen as the outcome of a process of social work and the result of a wide range of activities" (ibid: 6). Valuations are always inherent in projections; Dewey (1939) speaks of an "intellectual factor" that identifies a deficiency and values objects and actions for their suitability to resolve the conflict by projecting them into the future (34).

Valuation takes place only when there is something the matter; when there is some trouble to be done away with, some need, lack, or privation to be made good, some conflict of tendencies to be resolved by means of changing existing conditions (ibid).

This perspective illuminates the empirical observation that valuations of smart speakers are something different for each person; it emphasises that valuation is not just about getting to know the "true" value of things but happens when something is at stake, when it is necessary to project a value onto something that has not previously sought valuation.

To illustrate the breadth of references people draw on when valuing smart speakers, I work with Antoine Hennion's concept of attachment. Building on his studies of taste, which he describes as a form of valuation (Hennion 2017a), he develops a theory of attachment that illustrates how people, in a processual engagement with the world, draw on a structure that reflects their respective position in this world. For Hennion, a pragmatic theory is not a classical theory of practice but refers, in particular, to an inclusion of things (Hennion: 2013: 23). Hennion describes social reality as "bodies and things in a web of attachment, affection and connectedness" and thus refers to the close connection between actors and their environment (Hennion 2011:93*).[2] He points out that in this sense, one cannot assume an intentional agent who consciously carries out actions, but that in their relationship to the world, humans oscillate between active—as a conscious mode of execution—and passive—in the sense of being exposed to the effects of the things that constitute the environment (Hennion/ Gomart 1999: 243). For Hennion, persons continuously engage with their environment against the background of the attachment, thereby constantly producing and conceptualising themselves as coherent beings on the foundation of their past (Hennion 2007: 102). Accordingly, he understands attachment as "what we hold to and what holds us [...] and [...] a way of keeping unseparated our objects of attachment and our ways of keeping us attached to them" (Hennion 2017a: 71). For him, the attachment reflects the individual development of the person, "it is what links us, constrains us, holds us, and what we love, what binds us, that of which we are a part" (Hennion 2007: 109), and is thus to be understood as the "account that the past presents to the present" (Hennion 2011: 94*).

Attachment thus forms the background against which a person acts; the action is at the same time also a result of the attachment itself:

"To hold to something is a relationship which is fundamentally reciprocal—it is not that easy to say who holds what or what holds whom, what is determining and what is determined. Attachment is neither a cause nor an effect; it is rather an action and its results, seized together, a performance." (Hennion 2017a: 74)

---

2   Citations marked with * have been translated from German into English by the author.

Attachment, therefore, refers to an individual bond to materialities, personal relationships, ideas, and discourses that are performatively actualised; in this way, persons model and reflect themselves in a way that is their own.

Attachment is a performative category for discussing what a smart speaker can be for a person, as the object takes shape in the relationship that persons maintain with it (Hennion 2013: 22). This relationship is always based on a valuation: "Things only exist to the extent that they are worth something, to the extent that they are 'for' something" (Hennion 2017a: 72). This performative attribution of value takes place in the confrontation with the object; Hennion argues here for a perspective on subject-object relationships that understands them "as beings in formation, open, resistant, making each other in a reciprocal fashion, acting reflexively on those who cause them to come into being" (ibid: 74). Valuing is "a way of sustaining their openness and not of domesticating their plurality" (ibid: 72).

Having presented the concept of attachment, I next follow Laurent Thévenot for more conceptual nuance. Equally rooted in the pragmatic tradition, his *regimes of engagement* outline different modes of how people relate to their environment. In the following, the main features of the theory are outlined before the individual regimes are discussed.

Thévenot uses the concept of regimes of engagement to develop a heuristic that captures the different ways people's actions are linked to meaning through valuations. He argues that not every engagement—a way of relating to the environment—is grounded in valuations of the same quality and scope. Some engagements are merely expressions of certain habits, where the inherent valuation does not claim overarching validity but reflects a highly individual attribution of value. In contrast, other actions are more closely linked to references that can claim supra-individual validity. Thévenot describes these ways of linking actions with valuations of different scopes through the regimes of engagement. For him, "each regime of engagement is characterised not only by the modality of a realistic adaptation to the world but also by the nature of the goods of different importance that allow this adaptation to be valued" (Thévenot 2019b: 85*). He emphasises "the person's dependence on the environment she relies on while grasping it by means of a certain cognitive format" (Thévenot 2007: 415). This heuristic thus focuses less on the human actor and more on the dynamics of the relationship between the actor and his environment (Thévenot 2010: 3), aiming to overcome "two-term oppositions" such as "individual vs. collective" or "lifeworld vs. social norms" (Thévenot 2007: 416).

Thévenot now claims to depict this "dynamic confrontation with the world" (Thévenot 2001a: 56) through different regimes of engagement. For him, social practices are not regular and stable but are to be understood as "realistic adjustment to a resistant, changing and transformed world" (Thévenot 2001a: 58). He observes that people must constantly "change the scope of their engagement, shifting along a scale between greater or lesser generality" (Thévenot 2001a:

57). Persons are accordingly composed of a plurality of engagements (Thévenot 2010). To do justice to this dynamic, Thévenot distinguishes three regimes, each of which places different references centrally: (1) *the regime of personal familiarity*, (2) *the regime of an individual plan*, and (3) *the regime of public justification*, which are presented below. These regimes describe different modes of meaningfully relating to the world, as they contain different "notion[s] of the good" (Thévenot 2001a: 59): (1) comfort in the personal sphere, (2) the realisation of a plan or (3) public recognition (for a concise overview, see Thévenot 2019a: 8).

The *regime of personal familiarity* describes engagements in the personal sphere of proximity, where people constantly engage with their surroundings; in this highly individual relationship to the world, persons value and organise their surroundings according to comfort criteria. The result is an environment that is a specific expression of the person, appropriated through a mode of "familiarising oneself in a milieu shaped by use (Thévenot 2010: 6). In particular, the relationship between "bodily gestures" and the material environment plays a role in this regime (Thévenot 2001a: 62). In their immediate surroundings, people are "guided by a wide range of sensorial data, including not only visual but also tactile, auditory, and olfactory clues, as well as indications from spatial positioning" (ibid). For Thévenot, the shape of the personal sphere is an exclusive expression of the person and not the result of collectively shared convictions (Thévenot: 2007: 416).

On the other hand, the *regime of an individual plan* aims to understand the intentionality with which people perform actions as an interpretative attitude aimed at realising goals through planning (Thévenot 2001a: 62; Thévenot 2007: 417). In contrast to the first regime, personal comfort is not the good that is valued here. Instead, this regime formulates a greater claim to plausibility; an action is valued according to whether it serves a certain purpose, i.e. whether it is good *for* something. This engagement is thereby linked to the ability to project oneself into the future through a plan (Thévenot 2007: 417). However, the purpose to which the action is directed is not up for discussion in the regime of an individual plan, as it is negotiated in the third regime.

In the *regime of public justification*, valuations are based on orders oriented towards the common good. In their joint book *On Justification*, Laurent Thévenot and Luc Boltanski identify six different overarching modes of justification that can be referred to in public discourse, such as, e.g., the industrial regime, which describes efficiency as a value, or the civil regime, where something is valued according to how it satisfies civic demands (Boltanski/Thévenot 2006: 159ff.). These modes of justification—so-called *orders of worth*—describe various historically evolved frames of reference or a "grammar of common good" (Thévenot 2001a: 70), which can claim a high degree of legitimacy. This regime is oriented towards the interests of the public order and must, therefore, serve its interests (Thévenot 2007: 417).

I argue that using the concepts of attachment and regimes of engagement provides some insight into the valuation process and criteria of smart speakers.

Although Thévenot also mentions the concept of attachment, he does not elaborate on it but simply describes it as the relationship between person and environment in the first regime (Thévenot 2007: 416). For me, however, the concept of attachment is also suitable for putting valuations in the other regimes into perspective because the reference to specific justifications and the alignment of actions with these can also be read as an expression of an attachment. With the orders of justification, Boltanski and Thévenot claim to create an overarching grammar of worth that serves as a frame of reference, understandable and usable by all. However, empirical evidence shows that the reference to justifications has a highly individual character and refers, for example, to a localisation in certain discourses.[3] The declination of this justification in the sense of a transfer into plannable action also always has an individual character. Attachment, as I understand it, encompasses the regimes of engagement, as it is suitable for conceptualising this individuality. The regimes, in turn, emphasise that this interplay consists of various forms of rational reference—un-reflected (in the sense that the regime of the familiar does not require being justified), plan-related, and oriented towards socially shared justifications. Both heuristics are suitable for treating the complexity and inconsistency of social action differently.

This is where friction comes into play: valuations are "sites and moments of dispute and contention" (Hutter/Stark 2015: 4). Something is challenged—in this paper, the smart speaker confronts attachments, which initially leads to friction and, thus, to valuation. The resulting valuations are legitimised through justifications, which in turn stand in a frictional relationship to one another because the invoked "orders of worth" form frames of reference that are incompatible or even incommensurable (Boltanski/Thévenot 2006: 216). Now, people are fundamentally integrated into different social contexts in which justifications have different validity; they must, therefore, be able to recognise which justification is appropriate in each situation (ibid.). As will be shown later in the analysis, this leads to different justifications that are in tension.

4. Method

To reveal the valuations of smart speakers in the domestic sphere, I rely on an interpretative analysis of my qualitative data according to Grounded Theory (Corbin/Strauss 2008; Charmaz 2014).

For the data collection, an ethnographic approach was combined with an interview study to broaden the contextualisation of smart speaker appropriation.

---

3   Criticising Boltanski/Thévenot, Axel Honneth has already pointed out that different social contexts may require different references to normative principles (Honneth 2010: 380).

On the one hand, the domestic environment, particularly the smart home infra-structure, was ethnographically logged. On the other hand, a reflexive perspec-tive on the smart home was recorded through ethnographic in-depth interviews. This combination of the ethnography of technical arrangements and the reflexive discussion in the interviews follows Hine's recommendations for ethnographic research into the smart home (Hine 2019).

The ethnographic focus on the arrangements smart speakers are integrated into aimed "to bring into the public space the elements constituting the (often hidden) pragmatic condition of individuals" (Baszanger/Dodier 2004: 25). Such an approach is essential to understand how valuations are made: Greeson (2020) has shown that valuations are always "part of an ecology of interconnected spaces and material flows [...] [and] cannot be fully understood if not considered alongside the conditions in which the goods being valued are produced" (168). Therefore, a 'technology tour' was conducted at the beginning of the home visits, where the study participants showed which technological devices are present in the household, where they are located, how they are connected, and for what purpose.[4] Of interest were also the reasons that the interviewees gave for their arrange-ments, to understand "the intimacy of technology, the relationships and feelings it is bound up in, and the understanding that technology contributes dynami-cally and dramatically to the performance of everyday life" (Kein 2008: 1103). The "technology tour" was recorded with a tape recorder. Field notes and photographic material were collected simultaneously to be able to reconstruct the domestic arrangement as accurately as possible.

Subsequently, in-depth, open-ended interviews were conducted, which were recorded and ethnographically logged simultaneously (Spradley 1979). The inter-views aimed to be as open as possible about the interviewees' relationship with smart speakers and technology in general. Additional field protocols were created after the home visits to record central observations.

The data collection took place between December 2021 and November 2022 and contains material from home visits to ten households.[5] The sample includes users between the ages of 25 and 75, in a balanced gender ratio, living in urban

---

4   The guidelines for the 'technology tour' were developed by an interdisciplin-ary research team from the research project "Disruptions of Networked Privacy (DIPCY)". The project (duration 10/21-8/25) is based at the TU Dresden and deals with privacy-related issues in smart speaker use from a sociological, media sci-ence and computer science perspective. Project website: https://tu-dresden.de/gsw/forschung/exzellenzmassnahmen/tudisc/projekte/dipcy.

5   Due to the COVID-19 pandemic, the first four interviews were conducted via Video Call. The author of this article was not part of the research team then. After joining in March 2022, he used this interview material as a starting point and continued to collect data, conducting home visits according to the research program outlined above.

and rural areas. This resulted in a diverse corpus of data, consisting of transcripts of around twenty hours of audio, field notes, and protocols.

For the analysis, I proceeded according to Grounded Theory, i.e., while the material was coded openly, I continuously documented insights and results in memos (Corbin/Strauss 2008; Charmaz 2014). Building on the analytical observation that different uses of Smart Speakers can be distinguished sociologically in terms of valuation, I used this as a "sensitising concept" to get "a general sense of reference and guidance in approaching empirical instances" (Blumer 1954: 7). The sociology of valuation therefore formed a "framework for [...] developing a deep understanding of social phenomena" (Bowen 2006: 20). The perspective on frictions allowed taking a nuanced approach to these valuation processes as complex negotiations. The following section refers to empirical examples to show which frictions arise in the valuation of smart speakers.

5. Analysis: On Attachments and Justifications

The analysis section demonstrates how people value smart speakers against the background of their attachments and make them plausible by referring to various justifications. It becomes clear that frictions occur in the structuring of smart speaker valuation. Frictions in valuation arise:

(a) Between the attachment and the smart speaker: People value smart speakers against the background of their attachment; the attachment is a condensate of a person's experience and thus features an individual pattern to be aligned with the smart speaker's agency. The attachment includes habits and routines that manifest in a particular relationship to the (material) environment. This adaptation is structured in a frictional manner. The smart speaker confronts the attachment—it is at the fault lines of the frictions where the valuation of the smart speaker is negotiated. These frictions, as irritations of habit and routines, lead to an individual selection of the features of a smart speaker that are used. Thus, using smart speakers takes shape in processing the frictions that arise during the appropriation process.

(b) Between the justifications used to legitimise a perspective on smart speakers: People refer to various justifications to render plausible their perspective on smart speakers. These include, in particular, motives of sustainability, efficiency, and social inclusion. These reflect the individual projection of the situation in which the justification is made. The justifications have different scopes and are in tension with each other. The empirical material shows the flexibility of people's referring to various and even incommensurable orders to justify their smart speaker use. The regimes of engagement form the hinge upon which a given justification is offered—from the overarching motive of justification to a purpose-oriented implementation. Central to this is the motive of competence through which justifications are made plannable.

5.1 Non-Fits: Frictions in Smart Speaker Appropriation

The first ethnographic vignette demonstrates how the features provided by the smart speaker can create friction with a person's attachment, leading to a valuation that results in the non-use of these features. During a home visit, I sit on the couch with my interview partner, a male in his mid-40s who works in an electronics store. He enthusiastically explains the advantages of smart speakers, emphasising their ability to connect media devices and provide entertainment efficiently. For him, checking the weather or news via voice commands is convenient. However, when I ask whether he also uses voice commands to send text messages via the smart speaker, he categorically denies it. "I'm a typer", he says, explaining that he grew up "with an old Nokia" and can send messages in his trouser pocket without even looking at the device. This physical practice of typing has become a deeply ingrained habit that he is unwilling to give up. The option to send messages via voice command holds no value for him as it conflicts with his long-established communication practice.

In the second ethnographic vignette, it becomes apparent that the smart speaker's general mode of operation—controlled by voice and requiring an active user—leads to friction with the person's attachment, encompassing a haptic relation to media objects and a passive role in media use. Here, the friction causes not only the non-use of specific features but also a rejection of the smart speaker.

I visited a young family that had equipped their kitchen, living room, and office with smart speakers. I speak to both parents—while the father of the family is the driving force behind the purchase of the smart speakers, the mother remains sceptical. In the conversation, my interviewees tell me that they originally also had a smart speaker in the bathroom, which, however, was now replaced by an older radio device. This is how the mother explains their decision:

"[...] So this very old-fashioned, push the button and turn on the radio was somehow cool to have. Something haptic and not...we have already been very technically equipped, so again, this...I felt the need to press a button to turn the radio on, in an old-school fashion. Not to always have to say what you want, what you want to watch [or] to listen to. To hear what is on the program and not what you have chosen, so...that was the background.[6]"
(transcript home visit 7)

Here friction also occurs due to the confrontation between attachment and the smart speaker. Firstly, the attachment once again comes into sight as a specific

---

6   The excerpts from the transcripts are translated from German to English by the author.

practice of media use, which here, however, articulates itself in different dimensions: on the one hand, as a haptic reference ("press on a button"); on the other hand, in taking a passive role in media consumption. The transition to a technology that does not require a haptic reference while forcing the person into an active position leads to friction with the interviewee's attachment. Adjusting to modify and evolve the attachment requires work the person does not want to do. This is not justified by a general attitude of refusal but rather by the abundance of technical equipment—in the case of the bathroom radio, there is simply a desire to remain in the habit and not have to frequently adapt to the requirements of technological innovation.

The third ethnographic vignette also illustrates that people's valuations are grounded in their attachment. The smart speaker's facilitating potential is in friction with established practices—in this case, plant-caring, which doesn't tolerate facilitation via technical support. Again, this leads to non-use, particularly concerning aspects of everyday practice as layers of the person's attachment.

My interviewee is in her early 20s, works in academia, and lives in an extensively "smart" household. Hence, there are smart speakers in almost every room. She uses them for tasks like listening to the news and making shopping lists. Noticing her many plants in the apartment, I ask if she uses an app linked to the smart speaker to manage their care—I had learned about this possibility during another house visit. She responds:

"I see [smart speakers] as a technology that should support me in my life, but plants... in the end, Alexa should help me facilitate my daily tasks and structure them. But I don't want to have my hobby structured; I want to live it out... I don't need anyone to help me structure it. I think for people who have plants in their home, just because they think it's beautiful, that reminder might be helpful—if they don't have a green thumb —but I mean, I have a laundry basket full of seedlings [...] I do it for the joy of it. When I have time, I repot a plant and don't want Alexa to tell me to repot it." (transcript home visit 8)

Two motives stand in contrast here: on the one hand, the smart speaker as a technical artefact to which the function of support and optimisation is attributed. On the other hand, plant care, which requires a particular form of care that cannot be technically optimised—attachment is expressed here in a unique way; its implementation is not organised according to efficiency criteria (Hennion 2011: 94). The practice of plant care as described has a value for the person which she sees threatened when using the smart speaker. Part of my interviewee's everyday life is to walk attentively through her home and engage with the plants. By observing and touching them, she recognises their needs and, therefore, she knows when to water or repot them. The relationship to plants as an expression of a particular sensual attachment is ascribed to a value lost when it is mechanised. To put it with Thévenot:

"The good of the nearest is both important for preserving the person based on relationships with the environment and central to a loving appreciation that pays no less attention to their particularities than to what influences their particularities. The commitment clarifies that any threat to the environment and the most important bonds concerning used objects or living areas also violate the person's intimacy." (Thévenot 2010: 7*)

The interviewee's handling of the plants in her flat is therefore not only aimed at keeping these plants alive but should be understood as an engagement with the environment that is familiar to my interlocutor as a practice that provides her with stability and, in this way, constitutes her as a person. Integrating the smart speaker, therefore, causes friction: the smart speaker collides with the attachment, which is expressed here as a sensual relation to the domestic environment.

Valuations of smart speakers can accordingly be understood as "reflexive work performed on one's own attachments" (Hennion 2007: 98), which is in tension with a potentially more efficient organisation that, however, has no value in itself. In this way, individual processes of smart speaker appropriation emerge, shaped by the frictions between personal attachment and the smart speaker as an object, functional device, and projection surface.

5.2 Navigating Justifications

While frictions between attachment and smart speakers were identified in the previous section, the following section focuses on the justifications used to value smart speakers. These justifications reflect a variety of references, including motives of sustainability, efficiency, and social inclusion, each rooted in distinct orders of worth (Boltanski/Thévenot 2006). Notably, these references do not always form coherent arguments; instead, especially in interview situations, persons often feel pressured to legitimise their choices using various justifications (Hennion 2011: 94). This often results in a combination of justifications that are in tension with each other, realised in different ways within the *regime of an individual plan*. Focusing on the frictions between justifications reveals that people appropriate justifications to perform valuations and apply them situationally to legitimise their perspectives on smart speakers.

In the following excerpt, I talk to the person already introduced in the previous vignette about the advantages of smart control in general, and smart speakers in particular:

"[T]hat's why I find these things quite practical because I also know that I don't have the awareness for it, and right now, with the Ukraine crisis and with the energy thing, I'm already curious if there is a benefit at all, so we bought them last year. Unfortunately, we don't have our energy audit from last year yet, so I don't know if there is a benefit but... it's just such a relief; it's the same as with Alexa's shopping lists or something, that you don't have to write down anything, you save paper (laughs), and then you don't have to think about it anymore. And that would also, I think, be quite pleasant with a robot vacuum cleaner because you can just...you can go to work, you set it up, and it does it. And you don't have to return to the apartment and vacuum [...]" (Excerpt from transcript of home visit 8).

Here, the interviewee references multiple justifications, each claiming its own validity. Firstly, sustainability and energy-saving are highlighted as justifications for smart control, particularly relevant in light of current political events. Thévenot has already shown that justification via a green order of worth is now well established (Thévenot 2019b: 89). However, the interviewee quickly de-emphasises this, questioning its validity. She then introduces another justification: efficient planning in everyday life, which is comprehensible in an entirely different way. These two justifications—sustainability and efficiency—are not linked; they are in tension. The listener decides which justification to accept as plausible for valuing smart speakers.

The motives are combined to achieve the highest possible legitimisation, demonstrating the interviewee's ability to adapt justifications to the situation (Boltanski/Thévenot 2006: 216; Thévenot 2019b: 100). These justifications are then translated into the *regime of an individual plan* differently: energy consumption becomes plannable for sustainability, while household activities are automated for efficiency. Remarkably, competence plays a central role in valuing smart speakers, as dealing with them makes the person competent in facing challenges.

In the following empirical vignette, different justifications come into play and are carried out via the motive of competence, too. In a video conference with a woman of around 70, who is retired and single, she reports on a remarkable practice involving technical devices. When asked what role technology plays in her life, she replies:

"Actually, the biggest. The biggest role—what I do, which might not be right, is this: when something new is on the market, it doesn't matter whether it's a video camera or not, I order it from Amazon, it has to be new, I must not be familiar with it yet. I try it out, then I know how it works and I send it back, I don't want to keep it, I just want to get to know the technology. And [...] not that the dear men think that women are all stupid when it's about technology. (laughs) They think I'm a bit crazy because, let's say, I'm actually out of the age, but...it has nothing to do with age!" (transcript remote house visit 4)

The interviewee is not primarily a user but only test-drives the devices: she orders them, tests them and then sends them back because she cannot afford them. This is justified with a motive of technical competence, which is then combined with two justifications. Firstly, technical competence is described as an emancipatory project, so my interviewee, in this way, becomes an emancipated subject. Secondly, a justification motive of social inclusion is introduced: my interviewee continuously proves her ability to participate in social events despite her advanced age through her adept use of technology. Here, too, technology forms the vehicle for gaining competence about the justifications mentioned—albeit with entirely different justifications than in the previous example.

The friction between the stated justifications is not just that they are incommensurable or incompatible. Instead, justifications can also be connected, as in the case where an efficient household organisation is combined with reference to the Ukraine crisis and a new urgency for sustainability awareness. Not only are the different justifications crucial, but also the creative and flexible ways they are used. The mode of rational appropriation becomes visible in this switching between different modes of justification, which cover very different scopes. Thus, rationality does not refer to some consistent argumentation but rather to the diversity of references to various justifications suitable for valuing smart speakers differently.

6. Discussion: A Friction-Guided Perspective on Valuing Smart Speakers

The analysis so far identified various frictions, on the one hand, as a non-fit between a person's attachment to a particular form of smart speaker use and, on the other hand, in the interrelationships among the justifications as legitimisations of valuations. I will now summarise and discuss the insights.

It was first shown that valuations of smart speakers must be understood as "reflexive work performed on one's attachments" (Hennion 2007: 98). The attachment represents a unique profile: it reflects the routinised form of engaging with the environment, its connection with objects, and its reference to ideas, interpretations and discourses a person has appropriated through experience. At the same time, these experiences create a restriction in that new things are not simply adopted but must be harmonised with what already exists as an attachment. In this respect, people are exposed to their attachment to a certain extent (Hennion/Gomart 1999: 243). The smart speaker does not fit in seamlessly but creates friction by interposing itself between a person and her environment, thus interrupting familiar structures of engagement; this leads to a valuation of the smart speaker in an individual and experience-led negotiation, which is often in tension with the motive of efficient organisation. This applies, e.g., to the case of the fully-equipped salesperson who prefers to type in his messages rather than dictate them verbally to the smart speaker; and to the young mother who feels the need to press a button in old-school fashion. What Hennion has elaborated on in the context of taste also applies to valuation: it "implies an engagement by the body" (Hennion 2005: 6), suggesting that people relate to their environment through material practices. This sensory connection to the environment, understood as part of an attachment, leads to specific valuations of objects and practices within that environment—such as the smart speaker in my study. As a result, efficient organisation is not considered an intrinsic value but must be harmonised with these existing attachments. Therefore, the specific organisation of the domestic environment should be seen as a sanctuary that plays a central role in the constitution of the person. The frictions that arise in the smart speaker adaptation within the domestic sphere can accordingly be understood as tensions with the person themselves (Thevenot 2010: 7). Attachment as "what links us, constrains us, holds us, and what we love, what binds us, that of which we are a part" (Hennion 2007: 109) forms the background of valuations and shapes them. This performative, frictional negotiation either adapts or rejects the smart speaker. Therefore, valuations are not merely reflexive attributions by rational actors but situated performances that express specific attachments.

While the concept of attachment was suitable for analysing the valuation background against which people encounter smart speakers, the cognitive processing mode of the valuations was analysed via the concept of justifications. It became clear that people tend to combine different justifications to legitimise their relationships with smart speakers. This was due to a person's ability to recognise the situational validity of some justification in a differentiated society, and to adapt accordingly (Boltanski/Thévenot 2006: 216; Thévenot 2019b: 100). The smart speaker, as an object of projection, relates to various orders of worth, which, depending on the attachment, have different values for the person on the one hand, and are suitable for public legitimisation in different ways on the other. The interview situation, in particular, may trigger references to specific justifications because one "only gives reasons for a bond or attachment if one is explicitly asked to defend [...] a behaviour" (Hennion: 2011: 94*). This is the ex-post rationalisation that Thévenot describes as "opposition between the truth of the course of action and the subsequent interpretation, which produces a behaviour determined by the subject" (Thévenot 2019b: 90*).

As a new technical artefact, the smart speaker prompts people to engage with it and may, therefore, be valued according to different modes of justification—be it motives of efficiency or social connection. The justifications reflect a person's attachment and ability to relate to various orders of worth. Justifications may be smoothly combined, or they may, quite in contrast, occur in an incommensurable way—for example, when scepticism about technology collides with the convenience of an efficient organisation. They can even appear to be structured as an inherent paradox, such as when the reasoning suggests that efficient control of smart apps leads to lower energy consumption—despite the fact that the overall energy output may still increase due to the increased use of the technology itself.

Furthermore, justifications are variably drawn upon via the motive of competence in the various regimes of engagement. The modes of justification do not form distant points of reference but rather convey a claim for a person to competently face challenges of the present. They are realised in the regime of an individual plan by translating the justification motives into concrete action: Saving energy through automation or social inclusion through technical skills. Competence, therefore, functions as a track to bring together attachments and justifications by translating the overriding motive into practice.

Valuations, thus, take place against the background of the attachment, are orientated towards justifications, and are transferred into plannable action via the motive of competence. This leads to an individual valuation process that produces diverse results. Justifications do not necessarily form the starting point for action but are available to a person and used to create situational personal consistency (Thevenot 2019b: 100). While the smart speaker challenges the person on several levels, people negotiate their relationships to it in the appropriation process through individual valuations. The complex process of coming to terms with the smart speaker thus becomes evident in the frictions of adaptation—frictions with people's attachment, as well as frictions among the various modes of justification drawn upon in the process.

7. Conclusion

In this article, I used the case of smart speakers to show how people value the promise of the smart home in the domestic sphere. It became clear that the appropriation of smart speakers is frictionally structured. On the one hand, the smart speaker collides with existing attachments and thus leads to friction. The attachment comprises individual experience, which condensed in a unique way of relating to the environment. As a new type of technology, the smart speaker offers usage options that collide with these habits and require individual adaptation. On the other hand, it was shown that the various justifications that are used to legitimise perspectives on smart speakers are in tension with each other—different justifications, as reflexive ex-post rationalisations, have different validity and they are used in a flexible and interrelated way to create plausible legitimisations of the smart speaker use. The justifications are then translated into an individual plan via the motive of competence: people use smart speakers to react competently to challenges they consider relevant due to their social situatedness. The double perspective of friction offers a differentiated perspective on the complex valuation processes of smart speakers, and thus helps to understand how the promise of the smart home is negotiated in the domestic sphere.

List of References

Antal, A./Hutter, M./Stark, D. (2015): Moments of Valuation: Exploring Sites of Dissonance. Oxford: Oxford University Press.

Atkinson, P./Barker, R. (2021): "'Hey Alexa, What Did I Forget?': Networked Devices, Internet Search and the Delegation of Human Memory." Convergence: The International Journal of Research into New Media Technologies, 27 (1), pp. 52–65.

Baszanger, I./Dodier, N. (2004): Ethnography: Relating the Part to the whole. In: D. Silverman (ed.), Qualitative Research: Theory, Method, and Practice. London: SAGE, pp 9-34.

Blumer, H. (1954): "What Is Wrong with Social Theory?" American Sociological Review, 19(1), pp. 3–10.

Boltanski, L./Thévenot, L. (2006): On Justification: Economies of Worth. Princeton: Princeton University Press.

Bowen, G. (2006): "Grounded Theory and Sensitizing Concepts". International Journal of Qualitative Methods 5 (3), pp.12–23.

Brause, S./Blank, G. (2020): "Externalized Domestication: Smart Speaker Assistants, Networks and Domestication Theory." Information, Communication & Society 23 (5), pp. 751–763.

Buteau, E./Lee, J. (2021): "Hey Alexa, Why Do We Use Voice Assistants? The Driving Factors of Voice Assistant Technology Use." Communication Research Reports 38 (5), pp. 336–345.

Charmaz, K. (2014): Constructing Grounded Theory. Introducing Qualitative Methods. Los Angeles: Sage.

Corbin, J./Strauss, A. (2008): Basics of Qualitative Research: Techniques and Procedures for Developing Grounded Theory. Los Angeles: Sage.

Dahlgren, K./Pink, S./Strengers, Y./Nicholls, L./Sadowski, J. (2021): "Personalization and the Smart Home: Questioning Techno-Hedonist Imaginaries." Convergence: The International Journal of Research into New Media Technologies 27 (5), pp. 1155–1169.

Gomart, E./Hennion, A. (1999): "A Sociology of Attachment: Music Amateurs, Drug Users". The Sociological Review 47 (1pl): 220–247.

Greeson, E. (2020): "Ecologies of Valuation." Valuation Studies 7 (2), pp. 167–196.

Helgesson, C./Muniesa, F. (2013): "For What It's Worth: An Introduction to Valuation Studies." Valuation Studies 1 (1), pp. 1–10.

Hennion, A. (2005): "Pragmatics of Taste." In: M. Jacobs/N. Weiss Hanrahan (eds.), The Blackwell Companion to the Sociology of Culture. Oxford: Blackwell, pp. 131–144.

Hennion, A (2007): "Those Things That Hold Us Together: Taste and Sociology." Cultural Sociology 1 (1), pp. 97–114.

Hennion, A (2011): "Offene Objekte, Offene Subjekte?: Körper und Dinge im Geflecht von Anhänglichkeit, Zuneigung und Verbundenheit.". Zeitschrift für Medien- und Kulturforschung 2 (1), pp. 93–110.

Hennion, A (2013): "Von einer Soziologie der Mediation zu einer Pragmatik der Attachements: Rückblick auf einen soziologischen Parcours innerhalb des CSI. " Zeitschrift für Medien- und Kulturforschung 4 (2), pp.11–35.

Hennion, A (2017a): "From Valuation to Instauration: On the Double Pluralism of Values." Valuation Studies 5 (1), pp. 69–81.

Hennion, A (2017b): "Attachments, You Say? ... How a Concept Collectively Emerges in One Research Group". Journal of Cultural Economy 10 (1): pp. 112–121.

Hernandez-Ortega, B./Ferreira, I. (2021): "How Smart Experiences Build Service Loyalty: The Importance of Consumer Love for Smart Voice Assistants." Psychology & Marketing 38 (7), pp. 1122–1139.

Humphry, J./Chesher, C. (2021): "Preparing for Smart Voice Assistants: Cultural Histories and Media Innovations." New Media & Society 23 (7), pp. 1971–1988.

Kien, G. (2008): "Technography = Technology + Ethnography: An Introduction." Qualitative Inquiry 14 (7), pp. 1101–1109.

Kudina, O. (2021): "Alexa, Who Am I?: Voice Assistants and Hermeneutic Lemniscate as the Technologically Mediated Sense-Making." Human Studies 44 (2), pp. 233–253.

Lau, J./Zimmerman, B./Schaub, F. (2018): "Alexa, Are You Listening?: Privacy Perceptions, Concerns and Privacy-Seeking Behaviors with Smart Speakers." Proceedings of the ACM on Human-Computer Interaction 2 (CSCW), pp. 1–31.

Lee, F./Helgesson, C.F. (2020): "Styles of Valuation: Algorithms and Agency in High-Throughput Bioscience." Science, Technology, & Human Values, 45 (4), pp. 659–685.

Maccario, G./Naldi, M. (2023): "Alexa, Is My Data Safe? The (Ir)Relevance of Privacy in Smart Speakers Reviews." International Journal of Human-Computer Interaction, 39 (6), pp. 1244–1256.

Malodia, S./Islam, N./Kaur, P./Dhir, A. (2022): "Why Do People Use Artificial Intelligence (AI)-Enabled Voice Assistants?" IEEE Transactions on Engineering Management, pp. 1–15.

McLean, G./Osei-Frimpong, K. (2019): "Hey Alexa ... Examine the Variables Influencing the Use of Artificial Intelligent In-Home Voice Assistants." Computers in Human Behavior, 99, pp. 28–37.

Modaresnezhad, M./Nemati, H. (2020): "Participatory Sensing or Sensing of Participation: Awareness and Privacy Concerns with Smart Device Applications." International Journal of Technology and Human Interaction, 16 (3), pp. 124–143.

Pospisil, B./Sauter, T./Treytl, A./Huber, E./Sebock, W. (2022): "'Totally Unnecessary' or 'Simply Convenient'—About Users and Non-Users of Voice Assistants". 15th International Conference on Human System Interaction (2022), p. 1–7.

Pridmore, J./Mols, A. (2020): "Personal Choices and Situated Data: Privacy Negotiations and the Acceptance of Household Intelligent Personal Assistants." Big Data & Society, 7 (1).

Rzepka, C. (2019): "Examining the Use of Voice Assistants: A Value-Focused Thinking Approach." Twenty-fifth Americas Conference on Information Systems, Cancun.

Spradley, J. P. (2016): The Ethnographic Interview. Long Grove: Waveland.

Strengers, Y./Hazas, M./Nicholls, L./Kjeldskov, J./Skov, M. (2020): "Pursuing Pleasance: Interrogating Energy-Intensive Visions for the Smart Home." International Journal of Human-Computer Studies 136.

Strengers, Y./Kennedy, J./Arcari, P./Nicholls, L./Gregg, M. (2019): "Protection, Productivity and Pleasure in the Smart Home: Emerging Expectations and Gendered Insights from Australian Early Adopters.". Proceedings of the 2019 CHI Conference on Human Factors in Computing Systems, pp. 1–13.

Thévenot, L. (2001a): "Pragmatic Regimes Governing the Engagement with the World.". T. Schatzki/K. Knorr-Cetina/E. v. Savigny (eds.), The Practice Turn in Contemporary Theory. London/New York: Routledge, pp. 56-73.

Thévenot, L (2001b): "Organized Complexity: Conventions of Coordination and the Composition of Economic Arrangements.". European Journal of Social Theory, 4 (4), pp. 405–425.

Thévenot, L (2007): "The Plurality of Cognitive Formats and Engagements: Moving between the Familiar and the Public.". European Journal of Social Theory, 10 (3), pp. 409–423.

Thévenot, L (2010): "Die Person in ihrem vielfachen Engagiertsein.". Trivium, Nr. 5.

Thévenot, L (2019a): "What Engages? The Sociology of Justifications, Conventions, and Engagements, Meeting Norms". La Revue des droits de l'homme 16.

Thévenot, L (2019b): "Vielfältige Formen des Engagiertseins als Grundlage von Gemeinschaft und Persönlichkeit: Erweiterung einer pragmatisch-kritischen Soziologie im Anschluss an 'De la justification'". In: S. Nicolae/M. Endreß/O. Berli/D. Bischur (eds.), (Be)Werten. Beiträge zur sozialen Konstruktion von Wertigkeit. Wiesbaden: Springer, pp. 81–112.

Biographical Notes

Marcus Burkhardt is professor of Media, Algorithms and Society at Paderborn University. He is also PI at the DFG Collaborative Research Center "Media of Cooperation". His research interests include the history and theory of digital media, especially the logi(sti)cs of database technologies, big data and algorithmic media as well as digital methods.

Katharina Ebner is researcher and postdoc at the Chair of Business Information Systems at University of Hagen. Before that she did her Ph.D. at EBS Business School in Oestrich-Winkel and holds a diploma in Computer Science from University of Jena. Her research and teaching interests centre around digital transformation with intelligent systems, and information technology adoption and adaptation, for which she has been awarded with multiple research and teaching awards. She is a member of the editorial board of Electronic Markets and serves regularly as associate editor and reviewer for the most renowned IS conferences and journals. Her research has been published, among others, at ICIS, ECIS, HICSS, and in renowned journals such as IEEE Transactions on Engineering or Information & Management.

Miriam Fahimi is currently a visiting fellow at Cornell University's Digital Due Process Clinic within the Department of Science and Technology. Previously, she was a fellow at the Center for Advanced Internet Studies (CAIS) in Bochum and a Marie Skłodowska-Curie Fellow in the "NoBIAS – Artificial Intelligence without Bias" project. Miriam is pursuing her PhD in STS at the University of Klagenfurt. Her research focuses on the intersections of AI, discrimination, and social justice.

Sascha Friesike is co-director of the Weizenbaum Institut Berlin and principal investigator of the research group "Reorganization of Knowledge Practices".

Carolin Gerlitz is professor of Digital Media and Methods at the University of Siegen. She is also a member of the Digital Methods Initiative Amsterdam, the Public Data Lab and the App Studies Initiative. Her research concerns data intensive media, platforms, valuation, social media, data critique, quantification, sensory media, inventive methods and controversy/issue analysis. She got her PhD from Goldsmiths, University of London. Currently she is spokesperson of the DFG Collaborative Research Center "Media of Cooperation" and PI at the DFG Collaborative Research Center "Transformations of the Popular".

DOI 10.14361/dcs-2023-0212

DCS | Digital Culture and Society | Vol. 9, Issue 2 | © transcript 2025

Jens Hälterlein is a research associate at the Department of Media Studies at Paderborn University. He is coordinating the project "Meaningful Human Control. Autonomous Weapon Systems between Regulation and Reflection". He was PI of the project "AI and Civil Security – A study on the effects of the future vision 'Artificial Intelligence made in Germany' on applied security research". His research focuses on security, war, resilience, surveillance technologies, artificial intelligence and technopolitics.

Karolin Kappler is professor of Digitality at the Catholic University of Applied Sciences North Rhine-Westphalia. Previously, she researched and taught as a postdoc at the Chair of Business Information Systems, as well as at the Department of Sociological Contemporary Diagnoses at the University of Hagen and at the Technological Research Center in Catalonia (EURECAT). Her research interests include digital transformation and digitality in social and health care and the sociology of valuation with a focus on the Economics / Sociology of Conventions. She has authored numerous papers in the fields of sociology, information systems, informatics, and philosophy.

Katharina Kinder-Kurlanda is professor of Digital Culture at the Digital Age Research Center (D!ARC) at the University of Klagenfurt in Austria. She studied cultural anthropology, computer science and history in Tübingen and Frankfurt in Germany and received her PhD from Lancaster University in the UK in 2009. Her research interests are in digital humanities, STS, internet studies, and web science and topics include AI & knowledge, datafication, interdisciplinarity, and play & culture.

Sebastian Koth is PhD student at the Weizenbaum Institut Berlin in the research group "Reorganization of Knowledge Practices".

Jonathan Kropf is postdoctoral researcher and head of the research project "Music Analytics: Data Valuation in the Music Industry" (funded by Fritz Thyssen Stiftung) in the Department of Sociology at University of Kassel.

Anne K. Krüger is head of the research group "Reorganization of Knowledge Practices" at the Weizenbaum Institut Berlin.

Carsten Ochs (PD Dr.) is postdoctoral researcher and coordinator of the research project "User Advice: Boosting Informational Self-Determination Through Work Alliances in Digital Consumer-Protection", Department of Sociology/ University of Kassel.

Lukas Schmitz studied Governance and Public Policy and Sociology at the Universities Passau and Dresden. He currently is a doctoral student and Research Associate at TU Dresden.

Tatjana Seitz is a PhD researcher in the DFG Collaborative Research Center "Media of Cooperation" at the University of Siegen. She holds an M.A. in Digital Media and Culture from the Centre for Interdisciplinary Methodologies at the University of Warwick, UK. Her dissertation on the politics and power of APIs (Application Programming Interfaces) is situated at the intersection of critical economic, aesthetic, and data driven concepts within the context of corporate social interfaces.

Florian Neft is a PhD student and research assistant at the Chair of Business Information Systems at the University of Hagen. His research interests are focused on knowledge management in health information systems and their acceptance, with emphasis on personal and cultural factors influencing the use of telemedicine. He has authored papers in information systems related conference proceedings, such as the Hawaii International Conference on Systems Sciences, and practice journals such as HMD. Besides his academic pursuits, Florian Neft has been holding various positions in the healthcare industry at Siemens Healthineers since 2013, including his current role in project management.

Felix Raczkowski is a post-doc researcher/assistant professor with the department for media studies at University of Bayreuth. He is currently writing a book on fakes and faking in digital cultures and co-editing a handbook on the methods of digital media research. His research interests cover the history and theory of digital media with a special emphasis on social media as well as game studies, the theory of play and educational and office media.

Oliver Ruf is research professor for Media Aesthetics, Principal Investigator and Co-Speaker of the Rhine Ruhr Center for Science Communication Research of the Institute for Advanced Study in the Humanities Essen, the TU Dortmund, the University of Bonn and the Bonn-Rhine-Sieg University of Applied Sciences in cooperation with the Science Media Center Germany and the German Science Press Conference, funded by the Volkswagen Foundation. Main focus: Theories of contemporary media, media aesthetics of digitality, intermediality, transdisciplinary aesthetic practice. He is also co-director of the Institute for Media Research and Development, scientific director of the Media Aesthetics Laboratory, academic coordinator of the International Media Studies programme in cooperation with Deutsche Welle and the Department of Media Studies at the University of Bonn, and dean of studies of the Digital Communication and Media Innovation Master of Arts program.

Christian Schulz is a research associate at the DFG Collaborative Research Center TRR 318 "Constructing Explainability" and a member of the Digital Cultures team at the Department of Media Studies at Paderborn University. His research interests are social media and its media theories, algorithms and data practices, theories of the subject, and digital photography. He recently published his dissertation, in which he takes the introduction of the like button as a point of departure for developing a general theory of social media platforms from a media historical perspective.

Lena Teigeler is a research associate in the DFG Collaborative Research Center "Transformations of the Popular" at the University of Siegen. Her dissertation focuses on Twitter's regulation of automation since 2006. She is interested in digital methods, quantification and platform governance.

Aleksandra Vujadinovic is a research assistant in Media Cultural Studies at the Bonn-Rhine-Sieg University of Applied Sciences and a PhD student at the Rhine Ruhr Center for Science Communication Research. Her research focuses on media aesthetics and media culture, format theory, memes in science communication, forms and formats of science communication for the humanities and social sciences.

GPSR Authorized Representative: Easy Access System Europe, Mustamäe tee 50, 10621 Tallinn, Estonia, gpsr.requests@easproject.com